Henry McKenzie Johnston
6 Pembroke Gardens
London W8 6HS
Tel: (020) 7602 5155

CW00953683

Ottoman and Persian Odysseys

Ottoman and Persian Odysseys
James Morier, Creator of Hajji Baba
of Ispahan, and his Brothers

HENRY McKENZIE JOHNSTON

Author's copy with misprints marked

ERRATA

p 7 lines 29 and 36
for "Annette's" read "Cornelia's"

p 85 footnote
Harford Jones dates should read "1767-1847"

p 90 footnote
John Malcolm's dates should read "1769-1833"

British Academic Press
LONDON • NEW YORK

Published in 1998 by British Academic Press
an imprint of I.B.Tauris & Co Ltd
Victoria House, Bloomsbury Square, London WC1B 4DZ

175 Fifth Avenue, New York, NY 10010

In the United States and in Canada
distributed by St Martin's Press, 175 Fifth Avenue,
New York, NY 10010

A full CIP record for this book is available from the British Library

Library of Congress catalog card number: available
A full CIP record is available from the Library of Congress

ISBN 1 86084 330 2

Set in Monotype Baskerville by Philip Armstrong, Sheffield
Printed and bound in Great Britain by
WBC Ltd, Bridgend, Mid Glamorgan

Contents

Maps

Illustrations

Preface

I first met James Morier, as a person not simply the name of the author of the *Hajji Baba* books, in 1988. I discovered him in Mexico in 1824 taking part in the negotiations for a treaty between that newly independent country and Britain. Seeking more information for the book I was then writing about these negotiations (published as *Missions to Mexico*, 1992), I was put in touch with Alice Cunnack, daughter of Admiral of the Fleet Lord Wemyss and great-granddaughter of David Morier, James's younger brother. She in turn put me in touch with Bernard Bevan, great-grandson of William, an even younger brother. Both were very helpful, and I was privileged to become a close friend of both. In 1991 Alice, to my great surprise, asked me if I would take over from her the task of writing a book about James while she concentrated on one about her great-grandfather and the eldest of the four brothers. She had done a great deal of research, having even visited their birth place in Turkey, and was proposing two books instead of the one she had already begun. I agreed, and she gave me access to her large collection of the (hitherto unpublished) contemporary family letters as well as the results of her research.

Alice then became ill, and it was agreed that I should take over the whole project as one book. She died before I had finished, so I do not know if she would have approved of what I have written. She herself, an academic historian, had had in mind including a lot of the detailed history of lesser known aspects of Britain's dealings with the Ottoman Empire and Persia during the Napoleonic wars, in which her forebears had played their parts; and, naturally, she had hoped to concentrate on her great-grandfather. My first attempt to follow such a plan convinced me that the result would be an uncomfortable, and overly long, hybrid: it should be either a history, with the brothers having only subsidiary 'walk on' parts, or a biographical study with history confined to the minimum to set their lives in context. Moreover, while I recognised that David was the most *simpático* of the brothers, and had the most distinguished diplomatic career of the three eldest, it seemed to me important to concentrate on James, as a well known author whose *The Adventures of Hajji Baba of Ispahan* is still read, but about whom very little is known apart from his entry in the Dictionary of National Biography (which is, in several respects, inaccurate). Fortunately Bernard agreed with me, and was good enough not only to help me enthusiastically with constructive suggestions chapter by chapter, but to give me his general approval of the work as a whole before he died (although I have since re-shaped it). So what we now have is a full life of James, partial lives of Jack and David for the earlier years when all three careers were closely entwined, and sketchy history. And Bernard was quite content that his own great-grandfather, whose naval career was of no great consequence despite his final rank of admiral, should scarcely feature at all.

Alice perhaps would have been disappointed – and I am indeed sorry that I have found it necessary to discard many of the fascinating historical details she had dug up in her own research, and, for that matter, many of the details of life in Smyrna and Constantinople in those days revealed in the letters. I can only hope that any of the other descendants of these Moriers – and of the Waldegrave family with which they were connected by marriage – who read what I have written will be as content as Bernard was, and that others without such a family connection will nevertheless find interest in the Morier story – and find the three brothers as well worth knowing as I have.

In addition to the untiring help of Bernard Bevan, I have received invaluable help from Sir Denis Wright, Professor Edmund Bosworth and Farhad Hakimzadeh in understanding the Persian background. Drs Brian Kelly and Geoffrey Whittaker were kind enough to read contemporary medical reports and give me their professional opinions on the causes of Isaac Morier's death, while the late Hans Van Stuwe translated for me some Dutch papers relevant to the family background. Margaret Morris Cloake lent me the full typescript of her work of translating and editing the journal kept by Mirza Abul Hasan in London, which was severely curtailed for publication, and allowed me to include extracts. The Wimbledon Historical Society enabled me to identify the school Jack and James went to there; and Alan Barrett was good enough to draw my attention to archive references to James's activities – which he came across while researching the life of his wife's forebear, Colonel J D'Arcy, who was in Persia for part of the time James was there. Dr Terry Grabar has allowed me to quote from her PhD dissertation on James; and I have to hope that Dr Ava Inez Weinberger would have agreed to the quotations from her similar dissertation had I been able to find her. To all these I owe much.

A number of people, either individually or as representatives of institutions, have been generous in dealing with my enquiries: my long-time friend, Guy de Bretagne, who devoted much time to enquiries in France in the hope, alas disappointed, of finding Jack Morier's original journal which was captured by the French in Egypt; the Archivists of Harrow School and East Sussex County Council, the Deputy Keeper of Cambridge University Archives, and the Divisional Librarian in Winchester of Hampshire County Council; Hereford and Worcester County Council, who have allowed me to quote extensively from the Harford Jones-Brydges papers in their possession. The Earl of Elgin and Kincardine, and Horatia Diggle (descended from William Waldegrave, 1st Baron Radstock) have both given me access to private family papers and allowed me to quote from them; the publishing house John Murray allowed me access to their archives and to use information gleaned there; the Warden and Fellows of All Souls College, Oxford have allowed me to quote from the Vaughan papers, and the Bodleian Library from Sir Gore Ouseley's diaries. Under Alice Cunnack's Will the family letters I was working with were bequeathed to Balliol College, Oxford. The Master and Fellows kindly allowed me to retain them for several months after her death and to quote from them, while I received valuable help both earlier and thereafter from successive Modern Manuscript Assistants in their library (which already held other Morier papers donated by Alice).

To all these, and to any others I have inadvertently failed to mention, I am deeply grateful, as I am, of course, for the unfailing courtesy and helpfulness of the staff of the British Library (Manuscripts Collection) and of the Public Record Office at Kew. Finally I must record with gratitude the generous practical help provided by Alex MacGregor and his brother William to support me in completing the work which their grandmother had asked me to undertake.

I have been lucky in that nearly all the Morier family letters are readable without great difficulty and, of great importance, were properly dated by the writers. A large number of those from the brothers to their mother are in French, as are her letters to them. The translations of these, and of other French documents, are mine.

Henry McKenzie Johnston
London
March 1997

Foreword

By Sir Denis Wright GCMG
(Ambassador to Iran 1963–1971)

Ottoman and Persian Odysseys is the story, meticulously researched and well told, of three talented young Morier brothers who forsook their father's world of trade for that of diplomacy. This was during the Napoleonic wars when all three, still in their early twenties, became involved in the exciting business of countering French activities and influence in Constantinople and outlying parts of the Ottoman Empire as well as Persia.

The brothers – John (Jack), James and David – were born in Smyrna where their Swiss-born (but naturalised British) father, Isaac Morier,[1] was one of a number of European merchants established in that flourishing Turkish port. Their mother Clara was Dutch, her father David Van Lennep being another prosperous Levant merchant. Although there was only a tiny and distant drop of British blood in their children's veins they were all, thanks to their father's foresight, British subjects. All three brothers served their adopted country well. Jack retired as H M Minister in Dresden and David as Minister to Switzerland, while James, after becoming Minister *ad interim* in Tehran, abandoned diplomacy for writing. In due time all these three brothers were honoured with entries in the *Dictionary of National Biography* alongside those of their father and their youngest brother, William, who had ended as a Royal Navy admiral. Surely a family achievement worthy of the *Guinness Book of Records!*

It is James who is still remembered today, having achieved renown with his best-selling novel *The Adventures of Hajji Baba of Ispahan* and two splendid travel books illustrated with his own drawings. In the first of the latter he all but identified the site of Cyrus's tomb at Pasargadae for which the hunt was then on, and he was the first European to describe and illustrate the Sassanian remains at Shapur,[2] while in *Hajji Baba* he prophetically wrote that the influence of the leading divine in the holy city of Qum was such that 'many believe he could even subvert the authority of the Shah himself'.[3] Having myself spent many happy years in Persia and travelled widely there I hope my Persian friends will not take it amiss if I endorse George Curzon's view, written a century ago, that *Hajji Baba,* for all its levity, is a penetrating study of Persian character and manners.[4]

The originality and importance of *Ottoman and Persian Odysseys* owes much to the excellent use its author, Henry McKenzie Johnston, makes of the mass of almost unknown Morier family papers owned by the late Dr Alice Cunnack, a great-granddaughter of David Morier. Some twenty years ago I had the good fortune to hear Alice read an amusing yet erudite paper on James Morier to a seminar in Edinburgh. A few years later she addressed the Iran Society in London on the same subject. She then told me that she had failed to find a publisher for a book she had written about James and his brothers. I offered to help and she sent me her manuscript. I found it interesting but in need of drastic editing; and this was also the view of the literary agent to whom I submitted it. Faced with this Alice seemed to lose heart and turned to other fields.

In 1984, when researching for a book I was writing on Anglo–Persian relations during the Qajar period, Alice kindly invited my wife and me to stay at her home on the Wemyss estate in Scotland where she let me loose among the Morier papers. They were, I remember, in a large trunk under a bed. I soon realised that here was a rich, untapped archive relating to Anglo–Turkish and Anglo–Persian affairs in the early 19th century crying out for a historically minded author to make use of them. I was, therefore, overjoyed when in 1991 Henry McKenzie Johnston, a stranger despite our both having worked in the Foreign Office, wrote to seek my advice after having been invited by Alice 'to try my hand at a biography of James'. I encouraged him to undertake what was bound to be a difficult task and am delighted with his achievement.

Haddenham
April 1997

1. His business partner in Smyrna, Wilkinson, was the ancestor of R. E. Wilkinson who served in the British consulate there from 1933 until his retirement as consul general in 1970. He was one of the last of the old European families whose world came to an end after the Great War.
2. *A Journey through Persia, Armenia etc* London 1812 pp. 86 and 145
3. *The Adventures of Hajji Baba of Ispahan,* 3 vols, London 1824, ii p. 326
4. Introduction to 1895 edition of *The Adventures of Hajji Baba of Ispahan*

The Morier Family: a simplified genealogical chart

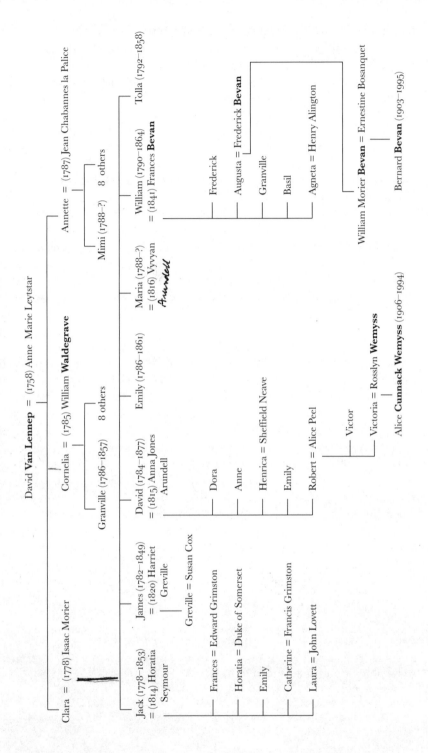

CHAPTER ONE

A Close-knit Family

The only public notice of James Morier's death was a short entry in The Times of Tuesday 20 March 1849: 'At Brighton, on the 19th inst., James Morier Esq., aged 66.' Why no more? Not only was he well known as a novelist, author of the acclaimed *Adventures of Hajji Baba of Ispahan* and several other works of fiction, he had also made his name with two important books on his travels in Persia during the early years of the nineteenth century, and he had filled high diplomatic office in the service of the British crown (as had his older brother Jack and his younger brother David, while a fourth brother, William, was an admiral). However, no portentous obituary was needed for someone whose own published works were – and indeed still are – his own best memorial; and James himself would surely have been more than content with William Thackeray's simple praise, in a letter to a friend four months later, of 'a true loyal Xtian man [with] that precious natural quality of Love wh. is awarded to some lucky minds – such as … Charles Lamb's & one or 2 more in our trade.'[1] But probably not even Thackeray was aware of his modest origins as the son of a Swiss born merchant and his Dutch wife in Smyrna.

Back in the 17th century one Abraham Morier, born at Château d'Oex near Montreux in Switzerland, moved to Vevey to earn his living as a shoemaker. By 1683 he had become sufficiently respected as a master craftsman and good citizen to be awarded the hereditary honour of *bourgeoisie* (citizenship). Two of his grandsons established themselves in business in London, one of them setting up a merchant house in Smyrna (Izmir). Another grandson, François Isaac Augustin, remained in Vevey as a master carpenter; but he, seeing how well his brothers were prospering, sent three of his sons to work with their uncles in London. One later moved to Scotland, while the youngest, Isaac, born at Vevey on 11 August 1750, joined his uncle Samuel in Smyrna. There he became the father of James and his brothers.

The Morier stock was Calvinist – worthy, deeply religious and industrious – but, even taking into account a dubious claim to be connected with the Dukes of Brittany, an unlikely progenitor of future British diplomats. Isaac, it is true, was a lively young man with a sense of fun and humour; but it was his choice of wife which was crucial. Not only did one of her sisters marry into the British aristocracy, she was, on her mother's side, descended from the French de la Fontaines, (Huguenots who had settled in Amsterdam in the 16th century) and the Scottish Colyears. David Colyear had entered military service with the Netherlands States General in the early 17th century and his son by his second marriage, Alexander, had been created first Baronet Colyear in 1677 whilst serving as Adjutant General to William, Prince of Orange, (later King William III of Great Britain). Alexander's son David then served under King William in Ireland, and was made Earl of Portmore in 1703 (an Irish peerage which died out in 1835/). Alexander's half-sister Maria married an Abraham de la Fontaine and their daughter Clara, born in 1682, married a Dutch merchant of Swedish origin, Pietro Leytstar (or Leidstar). Their son, Justinus, born in Constantinople, married a de la Fontaine cousin, Maria, born in 1700 and brought up in an intellectual circle in Amsterdam. Justinus had to move to Angora (Ankara) in 1741 to escape his creditors, and Maria and her young daughter, Anne Marie, had to adapt to living very modestly in a wholly Turkish business community. Deprived of the cosmopolitan society of Constantinople, Maria nevertheless provided Anne Marie with a good knowledge and appreciation of European culture, and was even able to ensure that she grew up with a strong Protestant faith. (The Ottomans allowed their Christian subjects a considerable measure of religious freedom.)

In the Christian community in Smyrna at that time was a successful Dutch merchant, David Van Lennep, descended from a very old Netherlands family which has been traced back with certainty to the 10th century. David had been sent out to Smyrna at the age of 18 to work with a branch of the de la Fontaines. By 1757, when he was 45, he had become a leading merchant there in his own right. He then decided he needed a wife with a God-fearing Protestant Dutch background. Finding no such paragon in Smyrna, David wrote to Justinus Leytstar in Angora to ask for his daughter, Anne Marie, then only 19. To Justinus this request was financially more than acceptable. For Maria it offered an opportunity to move to Smyrna and once again live in a European community. They agreed readily to David's proposal. Anne Marie, of course, had no choice but to obey her parents, but was as keen as her mother to move to a more cultured environment.

Maria died on the journey to Smyrna and young Anne Marie, without her mother's support, had to face the prospect of marriage to someone she had never met who was old enough to be her father. But she was not a product of the de la Fontaines and the Colyears for nothing. On 11 April 1758, only four days after reaching Smyrna, she was married to David in the Dutch chapel. She then enjoyed nearly forty years of complete happiness with the man she used to call 'the old patriarch', surviving as his widow for only five years after his death, at the age of 85, in 1797. Among her grandchildren were James Morier and his siblings, to whom she passed on her genes of intellectual curiosity and ability.

⊕

Anne Marie, although not particularly fond of young children (perhaps because she had been an only child), exercised a profound influence on her thirteen children and many of her grandchildren. Having been brought up with Turkish families in Angora, she had learned to speak their language well and to have great affection and respect for them as a race. She had had no formal education, but this showed only in her unpunctuated and ill-spelt letters written in a sprawling hand. From her mother she had learned classical French (and of course Dutch) and developed an enquiring mind and a love of reading. She was also fluent in Italian and demotic Greek.

Smyrna was then the largest port in the Ottoman empire and one of the principal centres of trade operated by the 'Franks', as non-Muslim Europeans were called. The merchants from England, France and the Netherlands benefited from the capitulations (treaty privileges granted by the Sultans to subjects of non-Muslim states), and lived in their own communities on Frank Street, each with its own consul to represent it in relations with the Turkish authorities and to exercise judicial authority over disputes arising within his national community. Under the capitulations these merchants, collectively known as factories (groupings of factors) enjoyed security of person and property, the right to travel and trade freely in Ottoman lands and to free navigation in Ottoman dominated waters.

Within Frank Street there was intense commercial rivalry between the various national factories, but the two thousand or so people who made up the Frank population lived, on the whole, as one community, united in the ever present fear of action by the Turks against them should the nation to which they belonged offend the Sultan. In this Petit Paris, as Smyrna was sometimes called, Anne Marie quickly established a leading social position, her fame as a hostess spreading far and wide in the Levant. Invitations to her house were eagerly sought, and way of life and degree of culture, rather than wealth and breeding, were the credentials needed to get one. She would invite mixtures of French, English, Dutch, Greek, Armenian and Jewish merchants along with their households, ship's masters and wives. Invitations were also extended to naval officers, travellers on their way to examine archaeological sites, and Turkish dignitaries. Some forty years after visiting Smyrna in 1784 Count Mathieu Dumas could still vividly remember this woman 'celebrated for her beauty, and even more for the rare qualities of her heart and mind ... the sweetness of her disposition ... her graceful movements, her melodious voice and her exquisite taste in both art and literature'.[2]

Young Isaac Morier, not long after his arrival in Smyrna (in about 1767) had found himself a guest in the house run by Anne Marie Van Lennep. His childless uncle had died, but not before he had arranged for Isaac to be put under British protection, from which he subsequently obtained naturalization as a British subject. David Van Lennep saw in him not only a likeable clerk but a prospective son-in-law in a country where young men were plentiful, but suitable husbands scarce. Both he and Anne Marie liked the way his strong Protestant faith kept his natural vivacity and humour from spilling over into the wild behaviour that was the downfall of many a young man exposed to temptation so far from home. He had brought his uncle's customers into the Van Lennep business, but David allowed him to set up on his own after he had proved himself and, in 1774, he was accepted as a member of the London-based Worshipful Levant Company at their Smyrna factory. The Van Lenneps continued, nevertheless, to provide him with lodging and, less than four years later, on 18 February 1778, Isaac, then aged 27, married their favourite (and eldest surviving) child, Elizabeth Clara, then ten days short of her 18th birthday.

This was no arranged marriage, as her parents' had been. It was a true love match between two people who shared a delight in music and society. Isaac, indeed, in a solemn document sworn on 31 January 1778 before the Dutch consul, declared that he was receiving a dowry, 'spontaneously and freely' given, in no way solicited or for his profit. The dowry consisted of 'clothes, gold, silver, jewellery, gems and money amounting to 4040 piastres' (about £400). The document also stated that, 'as a pledge of his pure affection' for Clara, he was contributing to the marriage the sum of 15,000 piastres (about £1,500). Moreover, in this document he signed away any rights he or his heirs might have under law to recover this contribution, leaving it entirely to Clara to do what she thought right in this respect, the occasion arising. Clara had her mother's good looks but, unlike her mother, she loved small children. She had spent a happy childhood helping to look after her younger brothers and sisters, much of it at Sidiköy, a few miles out of Smyrna, where her father had bought a farm. They had a Swiss tutor, Monsieur Dentand (who became a close family friend) and lessons in painting, singing, embroidery and dance. Her only disagreement with her parents, to whom she was devoted, was over her refusal to learn Dutch. She preferred French, which she taught her children with Dentand's help, and, in later years, they nearly always wrote to her in that language. Her parents had provided the couple with their own apartments in their rambling house on Frank Street, and her father built for them a separate small house at Sidiköy. From this union came four sons and three daughters (as well as three boys who died in infancy).

For the next nine years Clara and Isaac were peacefully happy. Isaac's business flourished. The first of the children, John Philip (always known as Jack) was born nine months after the wedding, on 23 November 1778. Another son was born the following summer but lived only 15 months. Then came James Justinius (often called Jem) on 15 August 1782, followed by David Richard on 8 January 1784 and Emily Maria on 6 March 1786. The children were brought up in a loving, extended family of parents, grandparents, and numerous uncles and aunts who were more like brothers and sisters. Indeed one uncle, Peter Van Lennep, was only seven months older than Jack, while Richard (Dick), their mother's youngest brother, was a year younger. Years later James wrote of 'our circle, where brothers, sisters, cousins, aunts & uncles & all the rest of the relationships that exist between us, make one family.'[3] By then the family included an English uncle and cousins, a develop-ment of great significance which began in 1785 when the Van Lenneps sent Clara's next two younger sisters, Cornelia-Jacoba aged 22, and Anna aged 19, to stay with the Swedish envoy in Constantinople, who was married to a relation of the Dutch consul in Smyrna, the Comte de Hochepied. There Cornelia, known in the family as Tonissa, was swept off her feet by a 32-year old English naval captain, the Honourable William Waldegrave, younger son of the 3rd Earl

Waldegrave, who was then on half pay and travelling for pleasure. Although at first not at all sure that they wanted to see their daughter wed to such an impetuous young Englishman (and probably quite unaware of his aristocratic background) her parents soon discovered that he was a man of sound, though undemonstrative religious beliefs, full of kindness and consideration for all, and a connoisseur of art who spoke excellent French. The couple were married in a simple ceremony at Smyrna on 28 December, and left almost immediately for England.

The Van Lenneps certainly never regretted having sent Cornelia to Constantinople. William (who became the first Baron Radstock in 1800) quietly used his influence, in later years, to the great benefit of Clara's sons, and to Clara herself he was a rock-like support when she found herself alone in England with her husband in Smyrna. But it was different in the case of Anna, known as Annette, who on that same trip fell in love with Jean-Frédéric, Comte de Chabannes la Palice, a young French widower who was first cousin to Talleyrand. The Van Lenneps were appalled, having no desire to see their daughter married into the French nobility, of which they were suspicious, and to a Roman Catholic to boot. The comte's family were equally against it, seeing no good in a match with a plebeian Dutch merchant family. The two mothers, allied at least in this common interest, tried to put an end to the romance, but to no avail. Although the couple were separated for some time, they remained true to each other and were eventually married quietly in a catholic chapel in Smyrna on 10 May 1787. But Annette had a rough life. The family suffered in the French revolution and although, thanks to Talleyrand's influence, Jean-Frédéric, who became the Marquis by inheritance in 1789, regained the family home at La Palisse in 1802, he was a maverick character constantly in debt. But to Clara and her children Annette and her husband and children were always a part of that 'one family'.

In 1787 Isaac made a decision which had far reaching consequences. Fond as he was of the family into which he had married, he began to feel the need for more independence and to take his rightful place as the head of his branch of the Morier family. He had bought from a relative a pleasant property with vineyards overlooking Lake Geneva, La Veyre, with the intention of making it his family home and eventually retiring to it. First, however, he wanted to have his sons educated in England and prepared to take over the business in Smyrna, which, meanwhile, he could leave in the hands of his partner Wilkinson. So, waiting only until after the Chabannes marriage, he and Clara, with their own three boys, 15-months old Emily and a Greek nurse, and Clara's little brother Peter (who his parents had now surprisingly decided should also receive an English education) set off for England on 6 June 1787 in one of the Company's ships bound for Marseilles, accompanied by the honeymooning couple. Clara, who was again pregnant, was not happy, having no ambition beyond living quietly in Smyrna and bringing up her family under the loving protection of her mother whom she was heartbroken to be leaving (and never saw again). The relationship between them was particularly close; her mother, in a farewell to all her family written not long before her death, addressed Clara as she 'whom I have always looked upon as a sister more than a daughter.'

The journey was long and uncomfortable, particularly the overland trip through France, and the arrival in London the most dismal moment in Clara's life so far. It was also a searing shock for the two older boys. Isaac had made no advance arrangements for a home, thinking it quite adequate to take rooms in John's Tavern in the Strand (which he had known well in his younger days) while they looked around for one. He packed Jack and James off to live and start their education with a Swiss couple in Greenwich; but he now found that his wife had a will of her own. Clara was not prepared to put up with such a noisy and public place, and she fled, with David and the baby, to her Waldegrave sister in Hertfordshire. Here she found a warm welcome in the heart of the aristocratic Whig establishment. Maria, the illegitimate daughter of Sir Edward Walpole and widow of the second Earl Waldegrave, was now married to the Duke of Gloucester, brother of King George III, and ~~Annette's~~ *nelia's* parents-in-law both had appointments at Court. Probably Clara was then quite unaware of what all that meant in English social terms, especially as her brother-in-law, William, was wholly indifferent to the disparity in 'rank' between himself and Isaac, whom he always treated as an equal. No doubt the sisters would in any case have taken care to see as much of each other as possible; but Isaac's failure to arrange for a home of their own on arrival in England meant that Clara's relationship with ~~Annette's~~ *nelia's* family became particularly close, and William became protective towards her and her children to a much greater degree than might otherwise have been the case. This close link with the English aristocracy was invaluable for the boys, who were as much in need of help as Clara herself.

The experience of arriving in a strange country of which they did not speak the language, and then being banished from their parents to people who did not know them, was traumatic for Jack and James. James, after all, was only just five years old. In a heart-rending letter to his father, Jack, almost nine, wrote from Greenwich (and only reproduction exactly as written in childish French can convey what he was feeling):

> Je me met pour vous ecrire et pour vous dire de venir si vous saviez comme …pauvre Jams pleure quand il pense a vous et moi aussi venez nous voir demain je vous emprie mon cher Papa nous pleurons tant … si vous saviez comme je pleure

At least Isaac was sensitive enough to respond to this tearful cry for rescue and, in January 1788, he installed them in a more suitable establishment in Andover, run by the Reverend Dr Samuel Jay and his wife. Jay had been Anglican chaplain in Smyrna, where he had left a son, and was related to the Lee family there, into which Clara's third younger sister later married.

Isaac now decided, however, that he had made a mistake in coming to England. He did not feel that he was warmly welcomed into the closed Levant Company society in London, which seemed to him more snobbish than society in Smyrna. On William Waldegrave's advice he had eventually rented a house at 25 South Audley Street. Business, however, did not immediately produce the increase in income he was expecting, and life in London was proving more expensive than he had anticipated. Moreover, the political situation in Europe was becoming unstable, and he feared that trade could be badly affected. Isaac became a worried man, and even began to suspect that his partner in Smyrna was cheating him. He felt he must return there; but what was he to do with his family? His decision, after much thought, was to leave Jack and James to complete their education in England, whilst Clara should follow him with the other children as soon as she was fit to travel after her soon to be expected confinement. Clara was delivered of a girl, Ann Mary (always known as Maria) at South Audley Street on 23 January 1788, and Isaac left for Smyrna a few days later.

Although Clara hated the thought of a long separation from her husband, there was some immediate relief in no longer having an anxious, and therefore irritable, man in the house. With the help of the Waldegraves she began now to find London not such a bad place after all. She worried constantly about the expense of having a cook, manservant and maid, as well as a children's nurse; but she had cultivated a number of good friends among the families of the Levant Company merchants, whose imagined coolness towards Isaac had been no more than English reserve. She was taken out in society, and began to enjoy her new life. What was even better, the Waldegraves had come up from the country to spend the winter in their town house at Portland Place (on the site now occupied by the BBC). Through them her social contacts widened still further; and amongst those she met was the artist George Romney, who painted her portrait. William became her 'best friend', which made Isaac furiously jealous when she innocently told him so. His jealously was further inflamed when she informed him that William had advised her against returning to Smyrna. Isaac immediately accused her of improper behaviour and demanded her presence at his side. This in turn upset William, who reacted strongly to the implication that he could in any way be involved in an intimate relationship with Clara; and Clara herself had sharp words for Isaac. But such was their basic love and affection for one another that this storm blew over, and Isaac was not long in realising, after his later return to England, that William's friendship was entirely honourable. It did, however, have an undercurrent of something more. Some years later, Jack conveyed in a letter to his mother from abroad a message from William that his 'love for her is at least equal to that that a brother ever felt for a sister,'[4] surely a hint that there was a trace of more than brotherly love in their feelings for each other, of which they were both conscious, but to which they would never have dreamed of giving way. And who could blame William? The Romney portrait shows a very pretty woman with a generous mouth and deeply appealing blue eyes (wearing a hat which William had bought her for a party given at Hatfield by the Marquess of Salisbury) who must have turned many a man's head; but she was a woman of the highest moral principles who could never have been tempted into marital indiscretion.

Meanwhile the boys, including Peter Van Lennep, were happy in Andover with Mr and Mrs Jay. Teachers came to instruct them in handwriting, arithmetic, geography, English and music. 'Every evening' wrote Jack in February 1788 'we play dominoes and I find things no different from the paternal home.'[5] Young James showed fortitude when he 'had a tooth taken out and uttered not a word because he is so brave and he never says anything when anyone does anything to him.'[6] By April Jack was already able to include a few words of English in his letters to his father. The following month, while on holiday in London with his mother, Jack learnt that Isaac wanted her to return to Smyrna, leaving the children in England. He wrote to his father: 'The idea that mama should go to Smyrna does not upset me much because I think she will be happier with you and Papouli and Yaya [grandfather and grandmother] and all the family, and what a pleasure it will be to join you and mama to help you in three or four years from now if it pleases God.'[7]

Jack was already, at ten, showing maturity. He was going out in society, even being given a ticket to attend a ball in honour of the royal family. After returning to school a month later he wrote to his mother that all three of them hated leaving her, but knew it was for their own good, and that 'they didn't want to feel afflicted for fear it will upset you.'[8] James, according to Jack, was already showing the tendency to greed which in later life caused him to be constantly overweight – 'sometimes he stuffs his mouth so full he can't swallow';[9] but Mrs Jay also reported that he had 'a great interest in dancing and wants to have lessons'.[10] By October Jack was writing to Isaac entirely in English (he had been told he would be given a watch if he did so). By Christmas James was beginning to read French and could 'write so prettily';[11] and it was then that William Waldegrave presented his nephews with a copy of *The Arabian Nights* and, thus, all unknowingly, planting in James one of the seeds of *The Adventures of Hajji Baba*.

Early in 1789 Isaac once again became unsettled, and letters were exchanged between him and Clara over several months while he tried to make up his mind what to do. He had not been long back in Smyrna before he realised he was not needed. He had quickly become satisfied that his partner, Wilkinson, was not cheating him and, in fact, was managing very well. He wanted to be with his wife and family but could not decide whether to join the family in London again, to insist on having at least Clara and the younger children out to Smyrna, or simply to retire to La Veyre and live on the profits from his share of the business. Then came the French revolution, and with it the realisation that business might well become uncertain. After the fall of the Bastille in July 1789, Clara suggested it would be unsafe for her and the children to attempt to travel through France to join him. At the same time, the news reached Isaac that the Chabannes had fled to Switzerland. There seemed, therefore, no choice but to return to England, and he left Smyrna on 8 October 1789, reaching London six weeks later.

Isaac was surprised to find that his wife, who had now moved to 42 Upper Seymour Street, had become a self-assured woman during his absence. She was now perfectly capable of managing without him, and had developed a disturbing tendency of expecting to get her own way. But she was still passionately fond of him, and life again seemed sweet. Isaac was delighted to find that Jack had grown into a clever, hard working and ambitious lad, in many ways older than his 12 years, while fat little James, with his easy going sense of humour and fun, appealed to the boy in him. A naval friend of William Waldegrave, Captain Conway, had suggested that the boys should go to Harrow, an idea which appealed to Clara because, as she put it in a letter to Isaac, 'if the Captain is a typical product of a public school education' then such a move must be good. Isaac, however, would not hear of it. So far as he was concerned, the boys were destined for trade, and education in the aristocratic tradition was not for them. He did, however, want them nearer than Andover, and in any case Jack at least was outgrowing that establishment. In The Times of 6 January 1790 he read a notice inserted by the Reverend Thomas Lancaster of the move of his 'Academy' from Parson's Green 'to a large and commodious House at Wimbledon ... fitted up in a style suitable' for a school 'for young Noblemen and Gentlemen'. The schoolroom was 'at once large and comfortable, Play-ground and Gardens extensive, Apartments spacious and lofty, and nutrition most healthful, with the additional advantage of an excellent Cold Bath'.*

Whether Isaac was able on his own to persuade the Rev Lancaster that his sons were 'young gentlemen', or whether he enlisted the help of William Waldegrave as a suitably snobbish reference, Jack and James were accepted; and, as a result, received an excellent classical education. To this were added important social graces learned at home. Clara had inherited her mother's skills as a hostess, and their house soon became a centre for a small circle of friends and relatives and émigrés from France with Levant connections. During this period, Clara gave birth to two more children, William Robert (who later became a naval officer) on 23 September 1790 and Clara Elizabeth

---

* Thomas Lancaster was the vicar of Merton, where Nelson later made his home with Emma Hamilton. Nelson visited this school, Eagle House, in September 1805 after which it became known as Nelson House, and he took Lancaster's 14-year old son with him as a first-class volunteer in HMS Victory when he sailed on the 15th for what became the great naval victory of Trafalgar. The house, originally built in 1613, is now the home of the Al Farqan Islamic Heritage Foundation, a pleasant irony in light of the many years James later spent in Muslim lands.

(always known as Tolla) on 1 April 1792. (Two further sons born in 1794 and 1796 died in infancy.) Jack and James could now see much more of their parents and siblings, and the family became even more closely knit. The boys also began to benefit from the company of so many older people from a wide variety of backgrounds, and to have the narrowness of their English education broadened by contact with visitors from other lands. Moreover, Isaac became reconciled to the close contact with the Waldegraves, realising that William was quite different from the kind of aristocrat that tended to raise his Swiss hackles. He rented a small cottage in the country near them during the summers, and the children became close friends with their Waldegrave cousins.

In later years Jack and James remembered the time spent in this way with nostalgic pleasure; but for Jack, at least, it was not to last long. Early in 1793 – by which time their home had been moved yet again, to Baker Street in Enfield – he was summoned to work in his father's counting house and start learning the business of a Levant Company merchant. For James there were to be a few more years of carefree happiness and academic education; but the adult world was closing over Jack.

CHAPTER TWO

Jack 1793–1798

'With God's help I will correct my faults.'

Isaac's plans for his family had to be changed when Britain and France went to war in February 1793. He would, otherwise, have taken them all back to Smyrna that year, leaving only James for a few more years at the Wimbledon school. He would also have expected both his sons to make their careers in his business and *Hajji Baba* might never have been created. In the event Isaac decided not only to abandon the plan of returning to Smyrna with his family, but also that it would be too dangerous to send Jack there on his own to begin learning the business with his partner, Wilkinson. Instead he took him, now aged 14, into his London counting house. This was nearly a disaster.

In Smyrna Jack might have found compensations for being deprived of the chance of further academic study, which he pined after; but in London he found the monotonous work of copying entries into ledgers in a dingy office excruciatingly boring. It was too far to go home every evening, so he shared a room in the City with his father during the week. Isaac suffered almost all the time from what the family called the 'blue devils', constantly worrying about business problems. Jack became morose and withdrawn, even rejecting his mother's demonstrative love at the weekends, to her great distress. His siblings could not understand why their adored elder brother had become so distant and forbidding. If this situation had continued for long it might have had a lasting adverse effect on the whole family; but fate (the family tended to attribute everything that happened to them to fate) took a hand after a year. In February 1794 William Waldegrave, who had recently come home from commanding HMS Courageux off Toulon, was preparing to return to the Mediterranean to take over another ship. Appreciating Jack's situation, and the reason for it, he offered to take him to the Mediterranean and either, if his naval duties permitted, get him as far as Smyrna, or at least ensure that he could complete the journey in safety. The offer was accepted, not without trepidation on

Clara's part, but with eager anticipation by Jack who, on 2 March of that year, at the age of fifteen, found himself in Deal. He was now to embark on the life of travel which later took him to destinations as varied as Egypt and the Epirus, Washington, Norway and Dresden.

⊕

Jack crossed to Ostend with his uncle in a naval frigate, and reached Leghorn on 30 March. He may have felt relief at escaping from the dreariness of London, but he became homesick on the journey, despite his delight in the Alps and the picture galeries in Bologna and Florence. Receiving there 'dear and very dear letters' from his parents, had he been alone, he replied, he 'would have allowed the tears that came to my eyes to run freely'; but he 'had the strength to hold them back.'[1]

William Waldegrave now learned that his ship was at Corsica – which had recently been taken from the French – and realised that he might well be engaged in hostilities once he joined her. He could discover no safe passage to Smyrna for Jack (all reports were that even neutral shipping was being attacked by the French), so he arranged to leave him in Leghorn in the care of Isaac's agent. Jack accepted this calmly, assuring his parents that he was going to be fully occupied with Italian and music lessons and would 'always have my head full of good things.'[2] His mother was anxious for his well being, as much moral as physical, and filled her letters with pious maxims which he found 'so pure and so apt for pointing out the good road for his life' that he assured her he had 'the strength (thanks to the religious instruction I have received) to be on my guard against temptation.'[3] For the next few weeks he was content to be pampered by his host and hostess, taking violin and Italian lessons, and making occasional trips to the theatre. His father, when he learned of this, wanted to call him back to London; but Jack, whose professions of home-sickness may have been more to comfort his mother than deeply felt, had no wish to give up his new-found freedom. Showing the determination to shape his own destiny which was to be a noticeable characteristic in later life, he made his way to Corsica in May and persuaded his uncle to secure him a passage in HMS Inconstant, which sailed from Naples on 1 June as part of a squadron escorting a convoy of merchantmen to Smyrna. This provided excitement for Jack.

On 18 June one of the other escorting ships, HMS Romney, found a French man of war, the Sybile, in one of the many sheltered narrows near Smyrna, and managed to close off her escape route. She declined a call to surrender, but after an engagement lasting over an hour struck her colours.[4] Next morning Jack accompanied the prize crew that took her over and described to his father 'decks coverd [sic] with blood and the livers & members of human creatures lying about. The masts, rigging & sides were knocked all to atoms, she was a perfect siv [sic].'[5] Two days later the Inconstant herself cleared for action, only to discover that the suspected enemy ships were Turkish. Jack was disappointed not to see action at first hand; but clearly he had found the whole episode a great adventure and the gory detritus of battle not at all upsetting.

They dropped anchor in the beautiful bay of Smyrna on 22 June, and Jack spent a few days with his grandparents at Sidiköy before moving in with the Wilkinsons. Although he was employed in the counting house, he was also given time for music, Turkish and Greek lessons, and the tutor to the Wilkinson children started to teach him German. He became a member of the Casino, a considerable compliment to a young clerk not yet sixteen, for membership of this club was obtained only by secret election – his Van Lennep connection must have been his passport. Here he could read the newspapers from all the European capitals (and so began to build up his understanding of the political events which were to have so much influence in his later life) play chess and listen to the discussions of his elders, even taking part in them. He was happy in this new life for a while; but, as a result of the education he had received at Lancaster's school, he was academically superior to most of his contempories in Smyrna, and he began to feel a reluctance to be part of their society. He again became moody and prickly, and a worry to the Wilkinsons and Van Lenneps.

There were a number of causes for this reversion to the attitude which had so upset his parents in London. The war was playing havoc with the mails, so that he felt cut off from home. The decision of the new Netherlands republic – in 1795 – to ally itself with France in the Treaty of the Hague made his personal relations with the Dutch community difficult. He was disgusted when 'the Dutch consul and all the merchants went to pay their respects to the [new] French consul on his arrival, so now the little society there is here will be pestered by a set of rascals without education, without manners, the Dutch of course being obliged to receive all the officers etc into their houses … The fact is that the Dutch are worse "sans culottes" than the French themselves.'[6] During the summer there was an outbreak of plague, which meant confinement to the house in the Smyrna heat. This confinement was shared with his fellow but senior clerk, Fontaine (a relative of his mother), whom he disliked intensely. But he was also going through something of a religious crisis (and may well have been affected, without understanding it, by puberty) in an intensive course of instruction from the Dutch chaplain, who had refused to let him take communion until he had purged himself of some earlier teaching (presumably at Wimbledon) that Christ was not God. He became reclusive. Very occasionally he would go to the Casino for some company; and because he was so fond of music his grandmother sometimes managed to persuade him to join the little family orchestra she had organised. But for months over 1795/96 he subjected himself to a punishing programme of self-education. He described to his mother his early morning routine of saying his prayers, reading two chapters of the bible and studying Italian before breakfast, after which he had a music lesson until 10.0 (he was now learning the clarinet), went to the counting house until noon, then a Turkish lesson until 1.0. From 2.0 he worked again in the counting house until the evening. From 7.0 to 8.0 he studied Turkish, and from then until 10.0 he read history and philosophy before spending time on his 'plan of self knowledge', entering in a little book 'impartially' the faults he recognised in himself and 'the good' he had been able to do. He was 'resolved to encourage in no way the inclination that I could have to go out because little by little my present taste for application could break and then adieu to all the effort that I make now.'[7] He was particularly keen on William Paley's *The Principles of Moral and Political Philosophy*, which he thought gave him 'plain and truly philosophical rules wherewith to improve the turn of mind I have taken to seek solid pleasures and advantages instead of the vain & arrogant footsteps into which so many young people betray themselves. I really often think with pity of those unhappy beings styled killers of time of which there are not a few here.'[8]

Jack was in danger of becoming a prig, and it is not surprising that the Van Lenneps and others should have become worried about him and reproved him for boorishness. It is evident that misunderstandings had already arisen between him and Wilkinson, whom he found difficult to talk to, and that he felt he must have given offence, for he told his parents that if this were so he wished Wilkinson would 'candidly call me aside & tell me, for I receive reproof with as great pleasure as praise when I know I deserve it. Tho' I don't like the cause of it, when I am conscious that I deserve it I receive advice with a thankful heart.'[9] Unfortunately he was not often ready to accept that he deserved reproof. His parents had to write to him about a letter they had received from Dentand, which drew from Jack the revealing comment:

> I am persuaded of Monsieur Dentand's friendship & good intentions towards me in writing to you as he has done. I hope it will some time or other be in my power to show him my gratitude. It may, I don't deny it, be in my

character to receive reproof sometimes, as he says, with little *docility*, but in the open manner he has spoken to you I shall be for ever thankful.

But he wished that Dentand

> ... would reproach me directly in person, which has never been the case. I will be annoyed if he had such a bad opinion of my amour propre in thinking that in reproaching my faults at the time he sees me guilty I showed lack of respect by a bad lack of *docility*. I have an impatient character, I know, but at the same time I find myself less *blameworthy* in this respect than when I was with you, or so to say I had too much liberty from your goodness, which made me sharp when I was in the least degree deprived of it. At present when I am with people of hard character compared with yours I have to conform to their wishes which, happily for me, keep my tendency to anger much in check. I don't say that I am not from time to time ... *sullen*, but less than before ... Great as my defects may be, I will correct them, it is to be hoped with God's help which, if it is not only to reward my dear and estimable parents, will preserve me so that I can show my gratitude and love in their old age.[10]

Jack was already showing a characteristic which dogged him through life, a quickness to believe himself unfairly criticized and a tendency to think others, not himself, in the wrong. Along with this, however, went the saving grace of an instinctive generosity of spirit and compassion for anyone in difficulties.

Jack's religious crisis seems to have resolved itself by the summer of 1796, although not to the extent of turning him at once into a sociable person. Indeed, he never did become much of a 'party' man, remaining always someone who took life rather seriously. But to his father he described walking in his room one Sunday when 'my sensation of love to God Almighty (heightened by solitude) broke out so strongly that tears came to my eyes & my thanks were so fervent and sincere to my Maker for having given me the means of improving myself, and such worthy parents, that I felt myself very comfortable when calm ... [I had] brought my reason to such a state of subjection as to be happy nowhere but when I am *vis-à-vis* myself.'[11] He had already ceased to torture himself with dreams of scholarship, believing he had no 'precision of thought', and that he was 'not intended for a politician or any of those professions where arrangements of ideas are so necessary.' He had accepted that as 'the eldest of the family it is much better to adopt a substantial way of getting bread than one that depends upon interest'[12] and had become:

> fully persuaded that a merchant forms one of the principal and one of the most useful members in a community. The power of the state depends on the general body of merchants as well as the maintenance of many poor

individuals. The duties of a merchant are upon as large a scale as those to
be performed by any statesman. In my opinion no man can show his real
sentiments of honesty or fraud as he to whom the interests of so many are
trusted.[13]

This, however, was whistling in the dark, although he did not then
realise it.

⊕

Jack may have thought he had come to terms with his destiny, but he
had certainly not come to terms with his position in commerce. During
1797 he had several disagreements with his father, who was thinking of
taking on another Smyrna partner prepared to put £5000 into the
business in exchange for a guaranteed return of 8 per cent. True, the
business needed more capital, but Jack considered the person in
question 'an unworthy fellow, ignorant, who has been guilty here of
many tricks.' He wrote angrily to his father about any proposal to
bring in anyone 'over my head' when he felt that it was time he
himself became a recognised 'name' in the business, even if not yet a
full partner, and that he should now receive £100 for each year of his
apprenticeship, which he could use to start trading in his own name to
gain further experience: 'I shall my dear Sir feel myself so ill used as
to say I must come and stay in England where at least I may be quiet
under the authority of proper superiors, my parents.'[14]

Isaac must have found such an attitude difficult to deal with at long
range, and there followed much correspondence discussing whether
Jack should return to London or Isaac should go out to Smyrna, so
that they could come to some agreement about the future. Eventually
Jack could stand his father's prevarications no longer and, in February
1798, he made up his mind to go home. He sailed from Smyrna on 9
March in company with a Mr Tomlinson and the Wilkinson tutor, who
was escorting two of the boys to school in England. Their ship was
bound for Trieste, flying the flag of the Austro-Hungarian empire,
with which France had made peace at Campo Formio in October of
the preceding year. It was assumed that this would make them safe
from French attack, and Jack loaded 65 bales of cotton to sell in
Trieste. Three weeks later, however, they were stopped by a squadron
of Tripolitanian warships (a country nominally part of the Ottoman
empire but enjoying effective independence) bent on taking any prizes
available. By good fortune their commander, now calling himself Murat
Bey, turned out to be a renegade former British mate of a merchant
ship captained by a friend of the Morier family, and he immediately

realised who Jack was. Behaving, as Jack later put it, in a way 'worthy of an Englishman,' he promised the party his protection and, after they had been driven eastward by a violent storm, saw them safely ashore on the coast of the Morea (Peloponnese). He even took charge of Jack's bales of cotton, and carried out his promise to see that they were despatched from Tripoli to the agent in Trieste.

Two days later, a French naval ship on patrol from the Ionian Islands (which had come under French dominion on the fall of Venice the year before) called there. Jack, not yet 20 and showing already the diplomatic skill which he developed so successfully in later years, talked the French commander into giving them his protection rather than taking them into custody as enemy subjects, and they were transported by him to the island of Zante (Zakinthos) where they managed to secure passage in a ship bound for Trieste. Before they could embark, however, the local French commandant arrested them and sent them in custody to Corfu. Here Jack was once again successful in persuading the French to behave honourably, and they were eventually issued with passports for travel to Venice, where they arrived on 17 May.

Jack, who considered that 'never such a set of companions would be found as my fellow travellers [who] in all the dangers we have run … never lost courage,' was surely justified in writing to his parents 'I have the pride to say that, thank God, I have passed the most giddy part of life … with credit to myself … My very odd journey & adventures as far as here have made me 10 years older in experience & prudence.'[15] They had indeed, and being determined to get some commercial advantage out of his journey, he parted from his friends to make business contacts in Trieste and Vienna. He got back to London in the middle of August, tired and suffering from almost continuous diarrhoea. It is clear that he had now accepted that his future lay in commerce in Smyrna, and that he had quite genuinely turned his mind to making a success of it. He might well have done so. But deep down he must have realised, however dimly, that it would never really satisfy him. It was loyalty to his father and concern for the financial well being of his mother and the family that kept him at it – along with the belief, so deep seated in all the family, that God was directing his life. While his recent adventures had served to complete the process of growing up and given him extra confidence in his own abilities, and while he had obviously found pleasure in the stimulus of face-to-face dealings with potential business clients, there was still something lacking in his life. Dramatic events, however, were soon to fill this void. Meanwhile his brother James took his place in Smyrna.

CHAPTER THREE

James 1799–1803

*'One's whole happiness may be made to
depend totally upon oneself'*

While Jack was in Smyrna, James had continued for a while at the Wimbledon school before, in his turn, taking his place in his father's office in London. Unlike his elder brother, he had accepted this happily, and he gave his parents none of the concern they had suffered from Jack's moodiness. He put up cheerfully with his father's 'blue devils' and adapted easily to routine in the counting house. He was just as studious as Jack, delighting particularly in classical and biblical history; but from his earliest days he had displayed a sense of humour which was markedly lacking in his brother. At this stage in his life, at least, he had no particular ambition to shine as an academic or, indeed, in any walk of life. For him life was something to be enjoyed, the quirks of those around him to be observed with almost detached amusement (he later developed a wickedly satirical ability with the pen and the paint brush and as an artist was to excell at portraying scenes both accurately and pleasingly). He made friends easily, and people enjoyed his company. James felt no qualms when Isaac decided, six month's after Jack's arrival in London, that he should replace his brother in Smyrna.

In the event, James found the next seven years little to his taste, but he set off in March 1799 full of confidence and happy anticipation. Aged sixteen, he was older than Jack had been when he first went out, which was a help, and he had the advantage of being armed with advice from his brother, and with a longer apprenticeship in London behind him. Like Jack he had been inculcated with strong religious principles; but with his naturally happy and fun loving nature he wore these principles lightly, untroubled by self doubts. He enjoyed the good things of life, but was seldom disturbed by any crisis of conscience between these and his duty towards God, which was for him part and parcel of life, just as breathing and eating were two inseparable parts of existence. Later in life he could, on occasion, be priggish and a little self satisfied, but he never displayed the dry, even forbidding seriousness that Jack developed. All this made his life in Smyrna a much easier experience than Jack's.

⊕

James travelled as civilian supercargo on board HMS Ranger (28-gun class 6 frigate under command of Captain Gooch) – part of a naval escort for a merchant fleet of some 120 ships – with some of the firm's merchandise as cargo. He left Falmouth on 5 March 1797, reached Gibraltar on the 17th and Palermo on 5 April. He had with him a letter of introduction from his uncle to Nelson, which he hoped to use here, but they sailed too soon with another convoy for Smyrna. He merely remarked in his letter home 'there is a Sir Wm Hamilton who is here with the King of Naples & his lady who lives with Lord Nelson', and that 'beautiful as Palermo may be I prefer London ... the houses are ... so dirty they are disgusting, all the Italians have such a slutty appearance that the "roast beef" face of an Englishman is immediately recognisable.'[1] James's attitude to foreigners was ever superior and insular.

James reached Smyrna in June. With the French fleet under Napoleon now at large in the Mediterranean, Smyrna was overflowing with merchantmen of many nations, all afraid to venture to sea. In his first letter home after his arrival, dated the 15th, James wrote that he was:

> now compleatly [sic] established a Smirniote & make up my mind to look forward to a long stay here ... It is at first rather an unpleasant prospect, but as it is always the wisest method to make the best & put the liveliest face on everything ... I thus reason within myself 'Why should I have the least prejudice against staying here? The virtuous man, the man who can look up to his Creator and say "I am ready whenever You command me to resign my life" in whatever situation he may find himself, good or bad, is always happy. An inward consciousness tells him that it is in his own conduct and in the sweets of religion that he finds a true satisfaction.' I reflect in myself, is it not possible for me to say the same thing, cannot I be truly good? It certainly requires a continual watchfulness, strong resolutions and great efforts to resist every alluring temptation, but when once virtue is made a habit, like everything else it takes deep root difficult to be eradicated. I do not say that a man can ever be a true model of perfection, that can only be in the Almighty, nor do I say that a man can be so completely firm and resolute as to withstand the greatest temptations; but certainly he may be truly virtuous.[2]

There may have been an element of 'image building' in James's frequent inclusion in his letters home of such pious platitudes, but they were not insincere, that was his upbringing, and there was no insincerity in the enthusiasm with which he pursued religious studies in Smyrna under the guidance of the Wilkinson tutor, the Rev John Frederick Usko.* To his father he wrote:

> You cannot conceive what a great pleasure I receive in the instructions of so good & intelligent a man. The farther one *searches* into matters of divinity & to the things appertaining thereto the more one likes to proceed. It is certainly a science so interesting, so sublime, so instructing & so proper to rivet into a man's heart the virtuous resolutions he may have formed that I think it is a duty incumbent on all those *who have it in their power* to make themselves perfect in every thing that regards God, to do so not only on account of the happiness which such instructions insure us in the life to come, but on account of the regard, respect & confidence paid to those who are known to have Godly principles in the common transactions of life.[3]

He may nevertheless have found it difficult, because of his natural gregariousness and sense of fun, to avoid all occasions when behaviour may have strayed from such high standards. He evidently discovered quickly that small expatriate communities can be treacherous. 'The esteem of my friends is my greatest aim', he wrote, but 'in such a country as this … I think one cannot be too much upon one's guard in maintaining an irreproachable conduct, particularly as there are so many malicious pens that cannot refrain from looking into others' concerns and speaking always of the bad side of the question.'[4] He had in fact had to deal with rumours which had reached, and disturbed, his parents. Such occasions, however, must have been rare, for he found many aspects of life in Turkey 'detestable'. But at Sidiköy he found the antidote. 'The joys we have here outweigh the evils' he wrote. 'What purer, more innocent joy than a walk on a fresh autumn morning with a book in the hand. One can give oneself up to such agreeable thoughts while walking alone, & the quiet & the serenity of the countryside produces such pure feelings, almost divine, that all the joys that the world can provide are not to be compared with them.'[5]

There was indeed a stratum of romanticism in James's make-up, and during this time in Smyrna he began to display a characteristic which was evident throughout his life. To use modern slang, he was 'laid back', and this applied particularly to money. He was not lazy

---

* John Frederick Usko, 1761–1841, was English of Prussian origin, educated in Germany, went to Smyrna as evangelical pastor in 1782. He returned to England in 1807 and was given a parish in Dorset

when once embarked on a course of action in which he was interested, and he was not entirely devoid of ambition; but personal happiness was for him more important than wealth, and when he discovered from the firm's books that his father was in the habit of risking great losses in his efforts to make big profits, he remonstrated with him:

> What are riches to a man who to acquire them must make the greatest sacrifices & undergo the greatest calamities? ... In my opinion I think a small competence & contentment so preferable to riches to be got with pains & torment that nothing in the world should make one leave the first plain path to walk in the other difficult ones.[6]

And although he did occasionally aspire to positions of distinction, his attitude to personal ambition was similar, as evidenced in a letter written from Smyrna in April 1800, in which he expressed the view that:

> life passes in continual hope ... and useless wishes. Everyone aspires to obtain something he does not possess & when he gets it his hopes rise to something greater. The ambitious man, not content with his lot, hopes for some honour, for some position of distinction, and he says to himself: ah! when I reach that height I shall wish for nothing more. But as soon as he gets there something else attracts him, he has a new wish and the same words escape him. The business man, the sailor, the soldier, in fact all those in all states of this life are all the same. What good fortune then for him who knows how to enjoy the present as it is.[7]

He was, nevertheless, pleased when his father suggested making him a partner. He confessed then that he was not entirely without 'the ambition of young men to rise quickly in the line of life in which they are placed. I assure you I burn with impatience for the moment when I shall be *revêtu* with some confidence in the management of your concern.' And he hoped his father 'would advance me as much as possible in the house, not in the lucrative way, because as to that I am totally indifferent, but by making my name appear so that I take an active part in the business, as it is my ambition to make our establishment as flourishing as possible as much as that depends on activity, application and attention.'[8] Isaac did in fact make him a partner in 1801, but business was not good and Wilkinson, with a large family to support, became unwilling to agree to a part of his share in already diminishing profits being passed to a third partner. It was typical of James's concern for others that, on discovering this, he immediately told his father that:

> for my part I perfectly coincide with him; for in considering a man who has the support of so many on his hands, to give up a part of his bread to one

who is single, who can find his way in the world by twenty different ways, it is very natural to suppose he would not do that without great repugnance.[9]

This attitude of James's was generous, but he may also have hoped that it would make it easier for his father to agree to release him altogether from a life he was by now sure was not for him. Although he had become fond of Wilkinson who 'treats me really like his best friend & son ... I should be ungrateful were I not to be sensible of his goodness & I as well put a full trust in him',[10] he found being lodged with him uncomfortable because he 'keeps so little order in his house, has got such a numerous family of children, ill bred, spoilt by a weak mother, that it is quite an annoyance to me ... to be among them'[11] (unaware then that he would later fall in love with one of the 'ill bred, spoilt' daughters). It was unsatisfactory to be a partner in name only, with no certain share in the business, especially as his father neither seemed willing to listen to his ideas on how to improve trade, nor able to decide whether he wanted James to remain where he was. At the beginning of 1802, in desperation, James took the bull by the horns. With filial duty he told his father: 'I would with pleasure sacrifice my own pleasure to yours. If you really wish me to stay here, say so at once.' But he went on:

> To stay here ... in the hopes of making a fortune seems to me to be an idea truly absurd. Twenty or thirty years hard labour might perhaps do it. Fortunes are not acquired here so easily & when once a person has remained here twenty years he hardly cares if he ever quits the country afterwards. He becomes as it were naturalized. Such a prospect to a young man entering into life is ... truly distressing. I should look upon myself as miserable & my existence here would be such were I to imagine that, instead of passing my days in the place where Christians reside, my whole life was to be confined to one Smyrna street ... to live in a society never formed for a man of liberal sentiments and enlarged principles. To stay here three or four years more so far so well. I might perhaps manage with economy & prudence to gain a small independence. But to sacrifice the best part of my life in this hole to provide a sustenance for the remaining part in another country seems to me a lookout rather unpleasant.[12]

Fortunately, James believed with 'Aristotle that one's *whole* happiness may be made to depend totally on oneself'[13], and having fired off this broadside he settled down to make the best of things while his father made up his mind. He decided to give up his Turkish lessons in favour of the classical languages, to take up the 'cello and to spend as much time as possible with the Van Lenneps and their friends at Sidiköy, where he made music with his aunts and found that 'the society, altho' consisting but of the inhabitants of 2 or 3 houses, makes as it were one

family, & as every one brings a dish to the feast, I mean some talent
... the little circle is never wanting for amusement. The greatest
concern is who will laugh the most.'[14] In July Wilkinson generously
gave him a bonus of 3,000 piastres (about £300) from the profits of
the previous trading year, and allowed him to go off for three weeks
on board a naval frigate visiting the Aegean islands and Athens. During
this trip he made drawings of the ruins and local costumes. He was
much affected, however, by his Van Lennep grandmother's death in
December 1802, being deeply impressed at the way 'she met [death's]
approach with all the calmness in the world' and feeling that 'her
example must teach us how necessary it is to be prepared for the awful
moment.'[15]

Isaac finally agreed that James could at least return to England for
consultations about his future, and he set off from Smyrna in April
1803, announcing to his parents that he would travel through Italy in
order to see as many as possible of the classical sites, because it would
be good for his education and help to consolidate his character. 'Youth'
he wrote 'is ever eager after novelty & what can more satiate its
curiosity than travelling? Its eagerness when properly directed may be
productive of the highest good' – an interesting foreshadowing of his
later travel books – and once again, as when he first set out from
England, he assured his parents of his 'firmest resolution' to resist all
'the temptations held out to youth in this debauched age' and 'to stem
the current, to push against such a sea of infamy, with all the energy
that religion & the love of virtue inspires, & if I make myself singular,
such singularity is the only blameless one, and such as every man
ought to make himself conspicuous in.'[16]

Here, approaching his 21st birthday, was a very different young man
from the eager youth who had set out from London four years earlier.
He had become disillusioned with the world of commerce and life in
Smyrna. But in his heart he knew that he would have to return, to do
his filial duty without complaining; and indeed, after only four months
at home, this was his fate. Little did he know that this apparent
misfortune would turn out to his long term benefit.

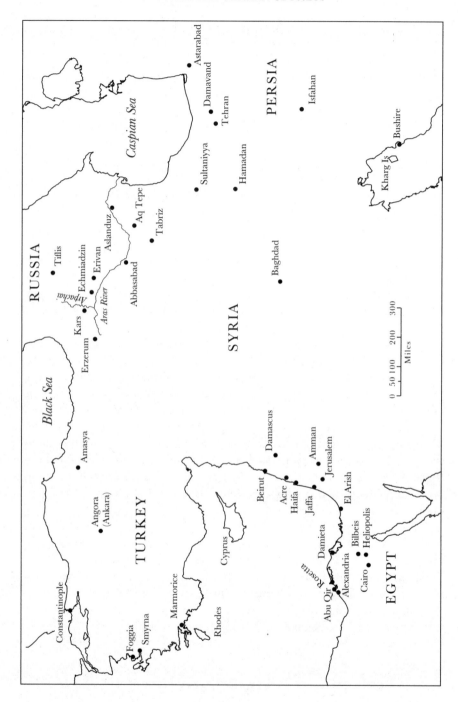

Map 1 Turkey, Syria and part of Persia

CHAPTER FOUR

Jack 1798–1803
'A very deserving young man.'

Although Isaac did not grasp the fact, when Jack arrived back in London, in August 1798, he was determined to find something more intellectually challenging than the life of a Smyrna merchant. His uncle, William Waldegrave, who understood and sympathised with him, once again came to the rescue. Thomas Bruce – 7th Earl of Elgin and 11th of Kincardine – appointed ambassador at Constantinople, was looking for a Turkish speaker to join his suite. On William's recommendation he offered the job to Jack, of whom he certainly would not otherwise have heard.

In those days it was rare for anyone outside the ranks of high society to make a career in diplomacy. Appointments as personal secretary to an envoy could be obtained, through influence, by lesser men, but they rarely led to a salaried post on the official diplomatic establishment. They were usually the personal gift of the envoy concerned, and the recipient became in effect part of his personal household. The job usually amounted to little more than making fair copies of the envoy's correspondence. In agreeing to Jack's accepting Elgin's offer, Isaac saw it as no more than an opportunity for his son to fill in some time before the business would be big enough to afford him a partnership. He could also make useful contacts with the influential Levant Company officers in Constantinople, and find new openings for trade. But it turned out, improbably, to be the first step for Jack in a new career in diplomacy.

Up to that time the status of His Majesty's representative at the Sublime Porte, as the court of the Ottoman Sultan was called, had been anomalous. The Levant Company had long had the statutory right to appoint consuls and ambassadors and, although they would usually accept the choice of ambassador made by the government, they paid his salary and considered that his job was to protect their interests, even if these should not always coincide with those of the government. In Elgin's case, however, although the Company had been formally consulted about his appointment, they had had no chance to object, if they had wanted to, and were not asked to pay or even contribute to his salary. The government had decided that the political relationship with the Ottoman empire should be separate from the commercial. As a result of these developments, Jack found himself immersed in political work and unable to do much to advance his father's business interests. And when, a year after his arrival in Constantinople, he decided to take his chance in staying in the diplomatic line instead of returning to the life of a merchant, he tried to justify his decision to his father:

> I have often reflected … on your feelings at my quitting the line in which I could have been most useful to you – perhaps to myself – but I considered at the same time that I was giving a fairer chance to my younger brothers for their own rapid advancement in life by withdrawing myself between you and them. You will I trust put that construction upon my resolution rather than attribute it either to a disgust for the profession of merchant or to an ambition to move to a higher circle … My brother James is I firmly believe quiet [sic] able to supply my place … Still … should I fail I am ready to resume my former situation without taking away from my brothers any advantages which they shall have deserved by their perseverance.[1]

High sounding sentiments to cover ambition! But Isaac was too gentle a man to try to force his son back into commercial harness. As it turned out, the move was, eventually, to save Isaac himself from disaster.

Elgin, now remembered mainly for his collection of the Parthenon marbles in the British Museum, was in fact not all that interested in the political dimensions of his job. He saw it as an opportunity to make a notable contribution to the arts and scholarship by being able to penetrate the classical world of Greece – which had for so long been closed to scholars because of the Ottoman occupation. His first concern in assembling a suite to accompany him and his newly married wife, Mary Nisbet, was to find people who would help him in these non-political endeavours. Fortunately for the future of English painting, he failed to persuade young J Wm Turner to come as his official artist, finding instead, in Italy, Giovanni Batista Lusieri. He also recruited the Reverend Joseph Dacre Carlyle, a 40-year old celibate professor of Arabic anxious to discover lost works by the great Greek classical authors, and the scholarly Dr Hector McLean to investigate the causes of the epidemics of the plague and smallpox which were so frequent in the area. He employed the Reverend Philip Hunt as Chaplain, who, although only 28, was not only a good preacher but also fluent in French and Greek. William Richard Hamilton,* just down from Cambridge, was chosen as private secretary, with Jack as his assistant.

The party sailed from Portsmouth on 4 September 1799. Jack was at first somewhat over-awed to find himself in the company of such scholars; but he soon discovered Hamilton and Hunt, particularly the latter, to be good company who put him at his ease, as did the Elgins themselves, who were 'very pleasant and affable'.[2] HMS Phaeton, a one-deck frigate of only 38 guns under command of Captain Morris, was an unimpressive vessel for an imposing ambassadorial arrival at Constantinople, and certainly could not be made as comfortable as Elgin's status deserved. In addition to the personal suite of five, accommodation had to be found for a courier, three personal maids for Lady Elgin (by now two months pregnant), some other female servants and Lady Elgin's dogs. The solution was to divide the state room into six compartments by green baize curtains. The Elgins had one each, the female servants two between them, one was used as a mess and the five 'gentlemen' had to share the sixth (the courier being relegated to a corner of the sailors' mess deck). Jack was thus sharing, with four others, 'a little cabin twelve feet long, six broad and 6 high [containing] five beds, 13 large trunks, 8 small do, 6 basons [sic] etc, 6 hats, 5 dressing gowns, 5 great coats and boat cloaks, 3 servants getting ready our shaving apparatus and a cabin boy brushing shoes; 5 foul cloathes [sic] bags, 4 portmanteaux, 2 pewter bottles, 2 lanterns, 2 umbrellas, a travelling library, brooms, supernumerary blankets, quilts, brushes, carpets etc in most glorious confusion, and an eighteen pounder with its tremendous apparatus of carriage tackles, iron crow, balls and grape shot'.[3]

Why there should have been an extra basin and hat is not explained, but despite this chaotic crush Jack wrote to his parents after the first few days at sea that 'every thing promises the most perfect harmony and contentment' – which speaks volumes for the personalities of the group. He found that life on board encouraged laziness: 'one reads,

---

* William Richard Hamilton, 1777–1859, managed to rescue the Rosetta Stone from the French who tried to smuggle it out of Egypt in 1801, and he played a major part in getting the Parthenon marbles to England. He was under-secretary in the Foreign Office 1809–22, minister at the Court of Naples 1822–25, a founder member of the Royal Geographical Society and trustee of the British Museum 1828–58.

but not with profit, for one is disposed to gossip all the time for distraction', but he did settle down to some serious reading of modern and ancient Greek, finding that 'in the company of savants such as I am with one can make good progress.'[4] And he gave his companions Turkish lessons.

Elgin was received at the entrance to the Dardanelles on 2 November with great ceremony by the Capitan Pasha (the senior admiral and commander of the Turkish navy) in his flagship, the 132-gun Sultan Selim (which must have made the Phaeton look very insignificant). It was a slow business – with almost no wind and a contrary current – reaching Constantinople itself.[5] On finally reaching Constantinople (9 November) the Elgins were transported in golden chairs to their home in Pera, the district on high ground to the north of the Golden Horn above Galata, where the diplomatic corps lived. Their 'home' should have been the English Palace, but this imposing residence had been totally destroyed by fire a few months earlier. The Turks, in a gesture of great significance, had decided to hand over to them instead the French Palace, which they had taken into their possession on declaring war against France the previous year. It was a shock to the Elgins, however, to discover that this was in shambles, having still been occupied until a few days before by French prisoners. They 'found nothing but bare walls', not even a bed, and Jack told his parents that his first few days 'were of the most fagging nature' as he worked with his bare hands to try to make some rooms habitable immediately. He was rewarded by Elgin's 'giving me the best appartment next to himself' which had 'a charming view over the Seraglio Point'.[6]

Elgin now found that he had been thrust into a tricky situation. His predecessor, Robert Liston,* had been recalled in 1796 and since then the embassy had been in the charge of Charles Spencer Smith, Liston's personal secretary and an employee of the Levant Company. Possibly because he was first cousin to the Foreign Secretary, Lord Grenville,† he had been allowed by the Foreign Office to style himself envoy plenipotentiary (rather than simply chargé d'affaires) although he had

---

*   Robert Liston, 1742–1836, Minister in Madrid 1783–88, in Stockholm 1788–93, ambassador at Constantinople 1793–96 and again 1811–21. He was also head of mission in Washington 1796–1801 and at the Hague 1801–04.
†   William Wyndham Grenville, 1742–1834, Baron, brother of 1st Marquess of Buckingham, Foreign Secretary 1791–1801.

no credentials as such from His Majesty's Government, which at that time regarded the Ottoman Empire as rather a marginal concern. Turkey had avoided taking sides in the war which had erupted between Britain and France in 1793, and although her neutrality leaned towards France this was thought to be of little practical significance so long as she did nothing to affect adversely the trade of the Levant Company. This situation changed, however, when Napoleon Bonaparte invaded Egypt in 1798. The Sultan had at first been disinclined to react strongly to this invasion of what, although nominally part of the Ottoman Empire, was in effect an independent Mameluke domain. Napoleon and the French foreign minister, Talleyrand – who were principally concerned with Egypt's strategic importance for threatening Britain's position in India – assured him that no permanent occupation was intended. The sultan saw advantage in having the Mameluke power reduced. Domestic political pressure, however, forced him to take some action. He had already made overtures for getting British help to expel the French when the news was received on 20 August of the destruction of the French fleet by Nelson at the Battle of the Nile (which in fact took place off Abukir) on 2 August. This persuaded the Sultan to declare war on France on 9 September. The French chargé d'affaires, Pierre-Jean-Marie Ruffin, as was the Turkish custom with the diplomatic representative of a country which displeased them, was incarcerated in the Seven Towers, and all Frenchmen sympathetic to the revolutionary regime in France were arrested.

Surprising as it may seem now, these events had not immediately persuaded His Majesty's government to give Turkey an early indication of support by the despatch of a full ranking ambassador: Elgin was not appointed until November 1798, and even then it was another year before he actually reached Constantinople. Before this, however, there had been a practical response to the Turkish overtures to Spencer Smith. A military mission under command of a German in British military service, Brigadier George Frederic Köhler, was sent out to replace the French military advisers the Turks had been relying upon, along with a small naval squadron under command of Sir Sidney Smith* (who, most unusually, was also appointed joint envoy plenipotentiary with his brother Spencer). It was January 1799 before Sir

---

* William Sidney Smith, 1764–1840. His knighthood at that time was Swedish (although officially gazetted in England), awarded in 1792 in recognition of unofficial service with the Swedish navy against Russia in 1790. Promoted rear-admiral 1805, vice-admiral 1810 and admiral 1821, he got a British knighthood with KCB in 1815.

Sidney, in HMS Tigre, reached Constantinople, but he was able to mount his famous defence of Acre and force Bonaparte back to Cairo in May, becoming as a result a hero in Turkish eyes.

When it was first decided that Elgin should be sent to Constantinople it was intended that he should conclude a formal treaty of alliance with the sultan as a prelude to military action. When it was learned that Spencer Smith had already done this (without express authorisation) Elgin was told to formally ratify it on arrival, and to negotiate a further treaty to allow British ships and trade access to the Black Sea. But on his arrival he found that Spencer Smith had also pre-empted him in this. It was not surprising that the Smith brothers felt Elgin's presence was now hardly necessary, or that, having lost their status as joint envoys plenipotentiary, they should be reluctant to cooperate with him. Spencer was instructed to remain as secretary of embassy under Elgin, although allowed, as a sop to his pride, to retain the honorary rank of minister. Sir Sidney, at least, still had his naval command; but for Spencer it was a bitter pill to swallow.

⊕

Elgin was too preoccupied, on first arrival, to be immediately aware of Spencer Smith's animosity, which was carefully concealed; but he soon found himself at loggerheads with both the Smiths and the Levant Company. Spencer Smith he found to be conducting business of interest to the Levant Company/ direct with the Turks, without consulting him. Spencer was even instructing the officers of the Company not to correspond with the ambassador. Elgin fell out with the Company itself over the appointment of his chief dragoman. It was the rule in Turkey that no foreigner could conduct business with officialdom without using a dragoman – someone recognised by and acceptable to the Turkish authorities as interpreter and go-between. Elgin declined to accept the services of the Company's chief dragoman, Dané, a Frenchman by birth, choosing instead Pisani, who had for many years been their *chancelier*, the official in charge of the books. The Company responded by dismissing him from this post and complaining to London.

Sir Sidney gave Elgin trouble in a different way. When Bonaparte had returned to France in the summer of 1799 he had left his army under the command of General Jean-Baptiste Kléber (1754–1800), who had decided in September to open peace negotiations with the grand vizier, then at Jaffa at the head of the Turkish army. Sir Sidney had intervened, insisting that Britain, as ally of the Turks, must be

associated with these talks. By the time Elgin reached Constantinople
Sir Sidney had, to the annoyance of the Turks, effectively taken over
the negotiations and was proposing that the French, in exchange for
evacuating Egypt, should be allowed to return to France with all their
arms and equipment. The Turks did not approve, but both they and
the French had assumed, wrongly, that Sir Sidney was acting with the
full authority of the British government. When Elgin discovered what
was going on, he decided that he must send a representative to Jaffa
to make clear to Sir Sidney that he could not act without his approval.
In the circumstances he could hardly send Spencer Smith on such an
errand, so he chose Jack, as the only other available Turkish speaker
on his staff.

A young man (Jack was just 21) sent out with the authority of his
ambassador behind him could be sure of being listened to; but unless
he used that authority with tact and sensitivity he could end by doing
more harm than good. Elgin had noticed with approval Jack's way
with the Turks when he had gone with him to call on the Capitan
Pasha on board the Sultan Selim. Since then there had been other
opportunities for Jack to show not only that his Turkish was quite
adequate, but that his manner of doing business with Turkish officials
was acceptable to them. As for his initiative, he had shown plenty
when coping with all the practical problems of getting the French
palace made habitable. Jack told his father that Elgin, when offering
him this post, had given him time to reflect:

> … but there were so many evidently weighty motives for my accepting his
> offer and he himself gave me so much encouragement that I did not hesitate
> a moment. He said he parted from me with very great regret because I had
> been of greater use to him than he could have expected from any person
> whatever, and he assured me that my absence would in no way detach me
> from his person, that I should always have his protection and that I might
> remain in Syria* just as short or as long a while as I pleased … If I render
> any service in Syria I shall not only have a claim upon L^d E but upon
> Government. My going there with formal instructions as a minister will alone
> entitle me to some consideration at least much sooner than were I to return
> to England with Lord Elgin as little known as when I left it.[7]

Jack was somewhat exaggerating his position in calling himself 'a
Minister' for he was given no such rank; but he was ambitious, and if
youthful enthusiasm led him to paint his appointment in glowing
colours, it was only that he saw it as the start of a career and a reward

---

* That part of the Ottoman Empire known as Syria comprised what is now Syria,
  Lebanon, Israel and Jordan.

for his patience. In his private journal* Jack wrote that 'he did not doubt the sincerity of [Elgin's] intentions to help my advancement, all the more because that had come unsolicited: I had never let him guess my aspirations and the hopes I was building on his protection, hoping by such disinterested conduct to gain his complete confidence.' But perhaps Elgin had been a more astute judge of Jack's intentions than Jack realised, for he did what he could to get him 'noticed' at home, and urged on him the importance of getting as much influence as possible exerted on his behalf by his friends in England.

The Turks were delighted when Elgin told them of his intention, and that he could 'answer for' Jack's 'prudence, ability & discretion.'[8] Jack was called in to join a discussion with the *Reis Effendi* (foreign minister), who briefed him personally, assuring him that he would 'be treated by the Vizier as his son', and arranging that he should have a personal servant, a personal *janissary* (guard) and a dragoman, as well as giving him an outfit allowance of 2000 piastres (about £200).[9] Elgin gave him written instructions in which he was formally appointed as one 'accredited on the part of His Majesty' to reside at the grand vizier's camp, with the 'immediate object' of establishing 'a regular and authentic system of communication with me ... You will use every endeavour to acquire ... the fullest details of the military proceedings ... of the circumstances of the countries which are the seat of the war ... [and] of the plans of the French.' If he found 'the apathy of the Turks such as to afford no authentic intelligence' he was authorised to employ secret agents to obtain it. He was to send reports not only to Elgin, but also to the governor-general of India, and 'an object of the most constant attention' was 'to show every degree of respect and afford every assistance which your position may enable you to render to Sir Sidney Smith.' He was told that his 'situation does not authorise you to exercise any authority', nevertheless he was 'to employ your utmost carefulness to maintain the harmony ... and to encourage the hearty cooperation of the Turks' against the common enemy.[10]

Elgin was, in fact, expecting Jack to help him out of an awkward position. He realised that getting the French out of Egypt was of first importance and, therefore, that Sir Sidney's proposals – for letting them leave with honour, rather than as prisoners of war – although not authorised by London, might be appropriate. The Turks, however, expected Elgin to prevent this, proposing a *ruse de guerre* under which the

---

* This journal later fell into French hands and the quoted extracts are taken and retranslated from the parts which were pubished in French in the bulletin put out by the French occupying forces in Egypt, *Courier de l'Egypte*.

French would be persuaded to board Turkish ships to take them back to France, but would then be made prisoners. Elgin declined to 'give His Majesty's authority to any proposal derogatory to the character of British integrity,'[11] but felt unable either to prevent the Turks going ahead with it, or to give Sir Sidney a direct order to drop his negotiations with the French until further instructions could be received from London. He merely instructed Jack to see Sir Sidney as soon as possible and convey his views in terms more direct than he chose to use in his formal communication. In the event Jack was unable to meet Sir Sidney before he had concluded a formal agreement with Kléber.

James was on a visit from Smyrna at this time, and Elgin not only offered to let Jack take his brother on his mission as personal secretary, he suggested he might also like to travel via Smyrna to see his friends and relations there. Jack declined both offers, thinking the former 'would have done him [James] more harm than good ... it would have been to snatch the bread [of Smyrna] from his mouth.'[12] But he hated leaving James behind: 'I almost wish he had not come', he wrote home in one of his rare displays of sentiment, 'our parting will be so sudden that the pain of separation will exceed the pleasure of our meeting.'[13] However he did get to Smyrna, unexpectedly. Instead of going overland to join the Turkish army, he went by sea, leaving on 22 December in a small gun boat, the Mary Anne, which he found very uncomfortable, 'an old tub of a thing' which was incapable of sailing at all to windward.[14] Because of this they had to seek shelter at Foggia (Foca) and, as this was within riding distance of Smyrna, he was able to pay a surprise visit on the Van Lenneps at Sidiköy for New Year. The wind then took them to Rhodes (where he had thought he might find Sir Sidney) and then into the Bay of Marmorice. From here they had to be towed out to sea by a rowing boat, only to be blown back to Rhodes (where at least they could replenish their fast dwindling provisions). He did not enjoy the trip: 'My captain and his No 1, although good lads, are only midshipmen with no other education than one receives on board a man o' war.' As he could have only a few books with him he was 'very bored'. Their diet was mainly 'pilaf and water, from time to time a chicken' and he suffered 'some moments of spleen which gave me bad wind.'[15] Eventually, on 31 January 1800, he was able to join the grand vizier at El Arish.

After a few days ashore Jack was 'in the best of health possible & quite a soldier, sleeping upon sand & living on air.'[16] But he found that negotiations with the French had been concluded before his arrival: Sir Sidney and the grand vizier had signed a 'convention' under which Kléber agreed to evacuate Katia, El Saliya and Bilbeis within ten days, and Cairo within a month, the French troops assembled at Alexandria to await shipping (to be provided by the Turks) to transport them, with their arms, to France. Kleber undertook that none of the troops would again fight against the Turks or the British, in return for which they would receive passports guaranteeing their safe passage to France. The Turks promised to keep them supplied with food until they left. Jack, although pleased that the French would be leaving Egypt, would have preferred it had they been forced to surrender as prisoners of war. He noted in his journal that he had hoped to see Sir Sidney at Rhodes in order, before joining the grand vizier, to 'concert steps for the *ruse de guerre* which we should adopt for the evacuation of Egypt by the French.' On coming up with the Tigre off El Arish, however, he had found Sir Sidney much concerned with:

> ... the idea that the safety of the Ottoman empire depended upon the strict observation of the convention [and that] in putting into execution the proposed *ruse de guerre* one would be putting matters back into their original state ... I observed that this had been proposed in case the French had not been sincere in their first overtures and that the safety of the Ottoman empire required some vigorous measures of this kind in order to deliver Egypt from its invaders. Sir Sidney, however, thought that my advice to the Turks should be to insist upon the religious observation of the treaty and simply protest should it be broken.

It was, of course, too late to convey Elgin's request that Sir Sidney should do nothing without further orders, so Jack could only join the grand vizier's army encamped at El Arish and do his best to carry out his formal instructions. He took steps to establish his status as Elgin's personal representative quite clearly. 'His Excellency' he recorded in his journal 'consented to let me sit beside him on the same divan, but this was only because I had made clear that I would not visit him unless he accorded me this respect.' When it came to gathering information, however, he found that Turkish ministers were:

> ... so little persuaded that questions are made for the sake of mere information, that they suspect the views of those who make them to be combined with a more remote object: this creates jealousy and renders them very reserved in whatever regards their internal institutions and regulations. Their secretaries might perhaps be bribed; but they are men of so little curiosity that the intelligence to be derived from them would be but vague.

He was shocked at the lack of discipline in the Turkish army, which he thought could 'well be compared to an armed rabble.' At one stage on the march towards Cairo the grand vizier tried unsuccessfully to stop a large contingent from Albania firing off their muskets for fun, and Jack's tent 'was pierced in many places' while he discovered 'a fellow deliberately levelling his musket at my hat, just time enough to get out of his way.'[17] Jack did not interpret this as animosity towards him owing to his status as a non-Muslim foreigner, for he had 'never been insulted, on the contrary, as soon as they see the English uniform they begin to curse the French.'[18] Jack was astonished at the casualness with which they pitched their tents 'where they please' so that the whole camp 'resembled a large fair' with 'tradesmen of all descriptions' plying their trades. 'Some keep coffee houses ... others are horse dealers; and a number of public cryers are constantly employed in describing to the multitude things lost, or in selling divers articles at auction.' Security seemed non-existent. When he arrived at the camp late at night he 'walked through the midst ... without being once challenged ... I might have been a spy or an incendiary and should have escaped with impunity.' And hygiene was totally ignored. The camp had been there some time and the air was noisome 'from the putrid carcases of horses, camels etc', while there was no medical service whatsoever.[19]

It seemed at first a relief to Jack when, on 5 February 1800, this multitude of some 80,000 (of which he reckoned at least half were but civilian hangers on) began to move towards Cairo in the wake of the withdrawing French. But, despite being provided with four horses by Sir Sidney, and having seven camels to carry his luggage and provisions, he did not enjoy the experience of marching 'through a most unhospitable sandy desert yielding nothing but brackish water' with troops who were 'unprovided with the most urgent necessities such as bread for the men & oats for their horses' and were 'totally without discipline, always mutinous when in want of anything.'[20] At Bilbeis, however – which they reached on 19 February – they were only twelve hours march from Cairo and Jack, full of optimism and foreught, sent his janissary into the city to secure him a good house from which he hoped to establish a branch of the family business once the French had left. This turned out to be premature.

Unknown to Sir Sidney, or even to Elgin (who, when he learned of the signature of the convention, gave it his approval and started to prepare passports for the French) the government in London – having been told of Kléber's overtures and the possibility that the French might be allowed by the Turks to leave Egypt with honour – had issued an order to Lord Keith* (the naval commander-in-chief in the Mediterranean) that the British must insist upon full surrender as prisoners of war. This news was conveyed on 16 March to Kléber, who had already begun to try to wriggle out of what he had agreed at El Arish. He was complaining that the Turks were not adhering to their undertaking to keep the French troops supplied, and insisting that a British representative should come to Cairo with a full guarantee of safe passage before he would evacuate the city. These complaints caused Jack to suggest to the grand vizier that 'all this was simply playing for time perhaps in the hope of reinforcements coming from France, and that there was every reason to doubt their good faith.'[21] Kléber, who did not appreciate the complete lack of communication between the various British parties, accused them of breaking their word, and tried once again to open separate negotiations with the grand vizier. The latter was unwilling to accept Kléber's first proposals and refused to listen when Jack suggested he should temporise while he (Jack) sought further orders from Sir Sidney. Kléber then lost patience and, on the 19th, sent a message to the grand vizier that he was going to attack. At dawn the next day, Kleber opened fire with his artillery on the Turkish advanced post at the site of ancient Heliopolis, some five miles from Cairo. The response by the Turks was so incompetent that they were completely routed within a few hours. At first they sent small groups of cavalry and infantry against a line of some 15,000 French troops, but they did little more than engage in what Jack described as ineffectual skirmishes. Moreover they soon ran out of ammunition, the French then advanced in line and the entire Turkish army turned tail and fled 'in all directions'. Jack reported that the grand vizier tried to rally 'this dastardly rabble', but without success – no doubt partly because he did so from his own comfortable quarters where he continued to recline on his sofa smoking his pipe. He was only roused from this when told that two lines of approaching troops, which had been mistaken for his own, were in fact French. Only then could he be persuaded that he was in danger, when he too fled.[22]

In all this confusion Jack became separated from the grand vizier's suite during the night of the 20th and got completely lost, spending

---

* George Keith Elphinstone, Viscount Keith, 1746–1823. Career naval officer, rear-admiral 1794, vice-admiral 1795, admiral 1801. Created Baron Keith of Stonehaven Marischal (Irish peerage) 1797, and Viscount (British peerage) 1814.

most of the next day hiding in a cornfield from patrolling French detachments. He managed to rejoin the grand vizier on the 22nd, and immediately urged him to make a stand and counter-attack. The grand vizier, however, had completely lost his nerve, and he sent word to Kléber proposing a resumption of negotiations. Jack considered it vital to inform Sir Sidney of this development, and was allowed to go himself to find him. He set off for Damietta, where he persuaded the Egyptian crew of a small boat to take him to the Tigre (which he believed to be off Alexandria). A storm forced them to seek shelter in a small bay where, too late, they discovered a French party. There was no time to throw his papers overboard, and in any case they were in only three feet of water, so Jack hid them in the sand ballast at the bottom of the boat, hoping that it might be possible to recover them later. He was sent under escort as a prisoner to Rosetta, and thence to Alexandria. Fortunately for him, Kléber's ADC, who had brought the message to the grand vizier on the 19th that hostilities were about to recommence, had been held as a hostage, and had provided Jack with a *laissez passer* for his mission to Sir Sidney. On the strength of this the French authorities at Alexandria allowed him to board the Tigre, which was lying off the coast.

When Jack reached the Tigre he discovered that Sir Sidney had known for some time about the British government's orders to make the French prisoners of war and, convinced that there had been some misunderstanding, had tried, unsuccessfully, to communicate with both Kléber and the grand vizier in the hope of preventing precipitate action while he sought clarification. Now, although shaken by his first experience of the battlefield, Jack rejoined the grand vizier and set about trying to convince him that the debacle at Heliopolis had not been the fault of the British, but his own in refusing to continue the further discussions proposed by Kléber. At the same time, however, he tried, as he put it to Elgin, to 'irritate him against the common enemy by accusing them of firing the first shot without waiting for the last proposal' and arguing that the Turks now had 'an opportunity of punishing these atrocious invaders which should not be lost and that their total destruction should be left to posterity as a monument of just vengeance against such perfidy.' He believed he had thus persuaded the grand vizier 'that England was as faithfully as ever their ally.'[23] But, although the vizier's son had managed, despite the rout at Heliopolis, to reach Cairo with a body of troops and inspire the local population to rise against the French garrison, the grand vizier refused to renew hostilities, and shortly after this the Turks in Cairo surrendered.

Jack now found the atmosphere at Jaffa distinctly hostile and, after being three times threatened with assassination by Turkish soldiers, he withdrew to the ship which had brought him. But the grand vizier continued to seek his advice. Kléber had been magnanimous, allowing the Turkish troops in Cairo to rejoin their compatriots and sending further proposals for renewed negotiations. Perhaps as a means of regaining credit with the Turks, but perhaps also from conviction, Jack advised the grand vizier not to fall into what he felt was a trap. He repeated his belligerent advice, giving it as his opinion 'that the frequent proofs the French had given of their insincerity and perfidy made it evident that such vigorous measures should be pursued against the common enemy as to make the severity of the punishment equal so unparalleled an infamy as their invasion of Egypt'.[24] He even wrote direct to the one Mameluke bey who had remained on the side-lines during the brief Turkish occupation of Cairo to try to persuade him to oppose the French, whom he described as treacherous enough to pretend 'to respect your religion ... when they do not even acknowledge the existence of a Supreme Being.'[25] He nevertheless had absolutely no desire to be personally involved in military action again. He told his parents that he despaired 'of being able to hold out the fatigue if we are yet again obliged to march into Egypt'[26], although he also said he was ready 'to remain with the army were it resolved that every Frenchman in Egypt should perish and expiate for their numerous crimes.'[27] He had already asked Elgin to recall him, appealing also to Hunt to plead his cause. Having had no reply he wrote to Hunt again on 5 May:

> You know very well how willingly I volunteered in this service ... Five months have elapsed, and only twice have I heard from L[d] E, not a word yet of any thing from Government. With so little encouragement how can I go thro' the life I lead with courage? If my services are thought too inconsiderable for a reward ... I wish to know it, because it is not from choice that I am daily running the risk of my life by the plague [from which his dragoman had died] or by the hands of assassins ... With the smallest encouragement there is no one that will sacrifice more than I will for the public service. A hope of advancement would suffice. Had I set out with a previous considera-tion from Government it would have been a compact, an obligation to put up with all the inconvenience of the situation for the advantage it afforded.[28]

Jack, in fact, was now thoroughly rattled by his experiences, and was losing his nerve. He was also worried about the consequences of having lost his papers when captured by the French. He had to assume that these had fallen into French hands (for they had not been found when Sir Sidney had sent a party to try to recover them from the boat in which Jack claimed he had hidden them), and he understood the damage which his private journal might cause. He had good reason to be worried on this score.

⊕

The British government, having at last heard about the convention of El Arish, had decided that it should be honoured. News of this reached Jack from Elgin on 1 June. The grand vizier, obviously relieved that he would not after all have to rouse his army into action, was nevertheless reluctant to lose face by conveying this news himself to Kléber, and asked Jack, as the British representative, to do so. Jack therefore wrote directly to Kléber, and his letter arrived more or less simultaneously with one from Sir Sidney proposing that they should negotiate a new convention on the basis of the El Arish agreement. All seemed set fair for what Sir Sidney had all along wanted – a peaceful withdrawal of French forces from Egypt – when fate intervened. Kléber was assassinated on 14 June, and his place taken by Jacques Menou, who had never approved of Kléber's readiness to surrender Egypt. The French had also come into possession of Jack's papers, including his journal with the compromising entries about the *ruse de guerre*. Just what had happened to these is not clear. One version is that Jack had not hidden them in the bottom of the boat from which he had been captured but had handed them to an Arab with the promise of a 'modest' reward if he conveyed them to the Turkish camp, and this Arab, 'preferring a more certain and easier benefit' had taken them to the French commandant at Damiette, who sent them immediately to Kléber.[29] What the truth is does not really matter, nor at what stage Kléber became aware of the papers – although it is clear that he had them before he was assassinated, because extracts from Jack's journal began to be published in the French occupation newspaper *Courier de l'Egypt* dated 20 Prairial (9 June). It is unlikely, however, that Kléber would have wished to make mischief with them as did Menou, who immediately found in them an excuse to reject all the proposals for the revival of the El Arish arrangements. In rejecting Sir Sidney's overtures he wrote: 'The French Republicans do not know what is meant by *ruses de guerre* which are mentioned in Mr Morier's papers; they have no other rule of conduct than courage in battle, generosity after victory and good faith in their treaties'.[30] Menou declined to have any truck with the grand vizier, still less with Jack, giving orders that 'any one who in future contacts the army of the Republic in Egypt on his behalf will be considered and treated as a spy. In accordance with

international practice he will be hanged, and the same fate awaits him
if he dares to make contact himself.' He declared that what Jack had
written in his journal showed 'unequivocally that this Morier is a
knave' who must be disowned by Elgin, at the same time threatening
reprisals against some British prisoners in his hands should the Turks
try any tricks.[31]

Jack, not surprisingly, now became even more rattled. After reporting
these new developments formally to Elgin, he wrote privately to him
on 27 June:

> I feel perfectly unequal to perform the task any longer ... the impediment
> which the discovery of my papers will put to my holding any communication
> with the French commander-in-chief renders my stay still less urgent. Be
> assured, my Lord, that my zeal for the Service can only be heightened by
> the confidence you have placed in me, but I can go so far as to say that no
> consideration would tempt me to prolong my stay with this army any longer.[32]

And, hearing that Köhler was at last on his way to join the grand
vizier's forces, he waited only till his arrival (on 4 July) before setting
off for Constantinople. The grand vizier, after making an unsuccessful
attempt to persuade him to stay, gave him a snuff box encrusted in
diamonds, 5,000 piastres and an Arab horse. In his formal letter to
Elgin resigning his appointment Jack trusted to his 'goodness' not to
refuse it, saying 'I would go thru' more than I have, but I assure you,
my Lord, I am not now able to do it.'[33] He was comforted, however,
by the letter he carried from Köhler, who could:

> ... not enough acknowledge the obligations we lay under to the polite and
> friendly attentions of Mr Morier and this is doubly enhanced by the influence
> and high consideration in which he stands with His Highness the grand
> vizier: he extolled his prudence and wisdom in the management of business,
> and in short spoke in the most unbounded approbation of the whole of his
> conduct during the expedition into Egypt and on most trying occasions.[34]

Elgin, in forwarding a claim for Jack's expenses (amounting to 12,245
piastres), assured the Foreign Office that 'Mr Morier unites great
application, knowledge and habits of business, and I venture to
recommend him to your notice as a young man who has turned his
attention with much effect to those studies which are likely to make
him useful in the foreign line particularly in this country.'[35] He also
told the Foreign Office that, in his opinion, Jack's decision to leave
Jaffa had been quite correct because 'his appointment to the Turkish
camp was solely occasioned by there being no Englishman on the
spot', and now that the operation had become 'purely military every
encouragement to political negotiation ought to be removed.'[36]

Moreover, Elgin now, in light of Menou's attitude, was all in favour of evicting the French from Egypt by force, making clear to the Foreign Office that his opinion on this was in accord with Jack's, not with Sir Sidney's: 'It is a conviction which I neither conceal nor can abandon ... that every body of Frenchmen acting against us are revolutionists ... all united ... in the great principle of doing as much harm, particularly to Great Britain, as they possibly can.'[37]

⊕

It was generous of Elgin to support Jack's action: perhaps he felt some obligation from having urged acceptance of the appointment – and he himself was not in the easiest of positions in all the muddle there had been over the El Arish convention. But Jack in fact deserved support. He had proved resourceful and determined, and capable of making shrewd analysis of what was going on around him. He may have allowed his prejudices against foreigners in general, and the Turks and French in particular, to show, but, for instance, before finally leaving Jaffa he wrote a masterly report on the various factions in Egypt – as guidance for any British troops that might now be involved in hostilities there and, he hoped, in dealing with the Egyptians once the French had been defeated.[38] It would not be fair to suggest that even indirectly his carelessness in having his private journal with him and losing it in action led to the continuation of hostilities. Menou had obviously been determined on this, and only used Jack's journal as a propaganda excuse for his own action. After all, Jack's journal had not revealed any details of the *ruse de guerre*. The furthest he had gone was in saying that it was something 'proposed in case the French had not been sincere in their first overtures.' Some time later Sir Sidney wrote that he 'rejoiced to see by the publication of Mr Morier's harmless journal that [the French] have found nothing of consequence, and that they have cried out fire only from seeing a little smoke.'[39] Apart from the threat that now hung over him should he have the misfortune to fall into French hands (which affected his later journey back to England), the loss of his journal did not adversely affect Jack's future career. Lord Grenville, in replying to Elgin's reports, wrote: 'The conduct of Mr Morier ... appears to have been dictated by the most zealous and disinterested regard for the promotion of His Majesty's Service and has been received here with the highest approbation.'[40] But the episode haunted Jack for a while yet.

Back in Constantinople Jack received a copy of the *Courier de Londres* (a French emigré newspaper published in London) containing an article outlining the events in Egypt leading to Menou's refusal to negotiate and his outburst against Jack. The writer suggested that this 'animosity' arose 'from circumstances which seem to indicate that Mr Morier was still a bit of a novice in his profession', and described the circumstances of his capture and the loss of his papers into French hands. A crucial passage was: 'If one can believe an eye witness one should also lay the blame on this same Mr Morier ... for the rout of the vizier [at Heliopolis] whose military dispositions were made according to [his] advice.'[41] Jack thought this actionable, and asked his father to consult a lawyer. Later, however, he thought better of this, writing: 'It is hardly worth while to take any notice of [it] – a person in a public situation is exposed daily to the raillery of a set of enemies ... I know the author whom I despise as much as I pity the pains he has given himself to tell a lye [sic]. He is a Frenchman. I shall always glory in having that nation for enemy.'[42]

Jack was still, however, not free from military duty. In October 1800 the British government decided to mount an all-out attempt to liberate Egypt, and despatched to the Mediterranean a force under Sir Ralph Abercromby.* This force was to form the northern arm of a pincer with a force from India approaching from the south. Elgin decided that Jack should join Sir Ralph at Rhodes, explaining in a personal letter that he was sending his secretary because he was:

> ... accurately informed of the business under my management, the nature of our interests in this country and the state of our relations here with foreign powers. On these points I considered it be of the highest importance to Your Excellency to be put in possession of positive intelligence. He carries with him every paper which I have thought might be interesting ... Mr Morier, tho' not in the habit of interpreting in Turkish, will be of peculiar advantage to Your Excellency from being able to correct inaccuracies of the dragoman's upon whom he will be found to be a most efficacious check ... I recommend him to you as a very deserving young man whose object is to bring himself forward in the foreign line, and I am confident Your Excellency will consider his views where there may be an opportunity of distinguishing himself and where his merit entitles him to your protection.[43]

---

* Ralph Abercromby, 1734–1801, professional soldier, made KB 1795 after distinguishing himself in the Duke of York's disastrous campaign in Flanders. Responsible for the capture of Trinidad from the French in 1796. Refused peerage. Made commander of British troops in the Mediterranean 1800. Died of wounds in Egypt.

Jack was not pleased at this new assignment, but he told his parents that 'as I am with my countrymen any hardships which I shall have with them will give me much more satisfaction than those thrown away upon rascally Turks'[44] and that he was leaving 'in the highest spirits imaginable', seeing in it another opportunity of coming to the notice of ministers.[45] He left Constantinople on 11 December 1800 and reached Rhodes six days later, arriving before Abercromby. The Quartermaster-General, Colonel Anstruther*, had already arrived to set up facilities for the force, and Jack was billetted with him in a 'room 24ft by 12 lighted by 18 windows without a glass in them'. As it was blowing a gale, they were like 'two unhappy sinners sitting at a table wrapped up in an old sea cloak and looking more like the witches in Macbeth than the followers of an Emb: Extr.'[46]. Sir Ralph arrived on 30 December with a fleet commanded personally by Lord Keith, and Jack was taken aboard HMS Northumberland which sailed for Marmorice Bay – where Sir Ralph intended training his force in what would be an opposed landing on the coast of Egypt. Jack was well received by both Commanders-in-Chief and dined with Lord Keith before transferring to Sir Ralph's ship, HMS Kent. He was attached to Sir Ralph's personal staff as civil secretary, his main responsibility being liason with the Turks, who were 'showing as much cordiality as their supine apathy will permit them to do' and were expected by Jack to be of little military help. Although, he wrote, 'their resources are many did they know how to apply them, and their troops good', they lacked 'a head to guide them.'[47] He volunteered to accompany General Moore† on a visit to the grand vizier at Jaffa, and told his father he 'had sufficient time to become very intimate with him; and from his excellent qualities both as an officer and as a private man I shall endeavour to cultivate his friendship.'[48] Alas for Jack's hopes of useful backers, both Moore and Abercromby were the victims of war, the former at Corunna in 1809, the latter in Egypt within a few months.

There was a brief and happy reunion with his brother James, who came over to Marmorice on a visit from Smyrna, before to his surprise, and indeed to his relief, he was sent back to Constantinople at the end of January 1801 with despatches from Sir Ralph, although also with a request that he should be allowed to return to the army.[49]

---

* Robert Anstruther, 1768–1809, professional soldier, died as a general at Corunna the day before the battle.
† (Sir) John Moore, 1761–1809, professional soldier, major–general 1798, KB 1804, the subject of Charles Wolfe's (1791–1823) poem *The Burial of Sir John Moore* (1817).

Jack's hope on returning to Constantinople – on 5 February 1801 – was that Elgin would not be able to spare him to go back to Abercromby. 'I do not regret' he wrote to his father 'that my situation with the army was not made a permanent one. I would willingly put up with the inconvenience of living with military men, whose habits and views are so different from my own, could I at the same time be employed in a department which required a close application.' His ambition had now become urgent and he saw no hope of being able to use his abilities with the military in a way which would be noticed where it mattered. Although he realised that 'the knowledge of men and things' which he had gained would be useful, what he felt he now needed, if he was to shine in diplomacy, was 'much application to be well informed on the principal points in history as well as the duties of the foreign line.'[50] Elgin, however, could spare him, and although Jack gained a short respite by falling ill, he was sent off again on 4 March. He reached Rhodes on 25 March, but with a high fever which kept him there in bed until he was well enough to set off on 2 April for Egypt, where Abukir and Rosetta had already fallen to Abercromby. On his arrival in Egypt on 12 April he learned that Abercromby had died of wounds. He felt that this entitled him to return to Constantinople, on the ground that his appointment had been to Abercromby personally, but decided instead to offer his services to General Hutchinson,* who had taken over the command. Hutchinson, however, declined the offer, and Jack wrote to Elgin on 19 April that he would be taking the first available vessel back to Constantinople, regretting that:

> ... circumstances have prevented my conforming to His Majesty's desire and to my most ardent wish of sharing the toils of this army in the service of my country. Still, I feel the satisfaction of not having abandoned my object before I had done what was in my power to accomplish it.[51]

This insincere expression of disappointment that he could not continue to serve with the army was no doubt intended to look good on his record, and fortunately Elgin, who had at last managed to get Spencer Smith removed, had not forgotten his promise to recommend him as successor in the post of Secretary of Embassy.† He now sent Jack off to London with despatches and instructions to make a full

---

* John Hely-Hutchinson, 1757–1832, Baron Hutchinson (later 2nd Earl of Donoughmore). Professional soldier. Major-general 1796, created Baron after capturing Alexandria in 1801, succeeded to earldom in 1825.

† Secretary of Embassy (or of Legation) was a full appointment in the diplomatic service, and the holder of the post was the second-in-command of the mission.

personal report at the Foreign Office, with the commendation that 'Mr Morier ... knows more about Egypt than any individual I have yet met with here. I have a further inducement to take this step from the accuracy of Mr Morier's acquaintance with the Turkish empire. No communication by writing can convey an adequate view ...'[52]

Jack reached London in early July 1801 and spent the next three months once again in an unhappy relationship with his mother while he anxiously hoped for a decision in his favour over the post at Constantinople. While in Turkey he had been accused by his mother of extravagance which caused financial problems for his father, on whose account he had been drawing to meet his personal expenses (which had not yet been repaid by the Foreign Office). In reply he had tried to justify this debt: 'it was only necessity that obliged me to contract it: the situation which I was going to occupy demanded a respectable appearance' and protested that he had been repaying it as best he could. And he went on:

> I shall always regret having caused [my father] inconvenience by this delay after all the goodness he has shown to me ... My father's numerous family makes me realise the necessity of lightening his burden ... I have yielded place to my brothers and [James] is now capable of taking my place. This will make one less mouth to feed. Whether I succeed or not I shall always rejoice to see my brothers prosper ... I have nothing to reproach myself for since entering my new career. I have sacrificed my ease, I have risked my life, I have weakened my health to show my zeal. I don't care if I am not recompensed for this, I shall not die of hunger. Pardon me, my good mama, but you have obliged me to justify myself. I no longer expect anyone to interest themselves in me, enough has been done in setting me on my road. Let us see what my own efforts will do for me.[53]

This petulant declaration of independence must have hurt his mother, but he made no amends once back in England. He did reluctantly spend a few days with her in Brighton, where she had gone while workmen were in their house in Welbeck Street, but he then made official business in London an excuse for not joining her again, unkindly writing: 'You know what it was like the first three days I was with you: well, I realised that my humour affected you too, but it didn't depend solely on me to be more cheerful – I made an effort from time to time without success.' And he continued to sulk at Welbeck Street on his own 'from morning to night with no other company than the builders and their hammering', wondering whether, on his mother's return from Brighton 'I must look for lodgings or will you give me a hole.'[54] He could be most insensitive and ungracious.

⊕

While in London Jack wrote a detailed paper on Egypt for the Foreign Office[55], but failed to get appointed to the vacant post of secretary of embassy at Constantinople, which went to Alexander Straton. So he had to return to Turkey in his old capacity. He travelled overland, reaching Pera on 8 November. He now discovered that Elgin was expecting to be recalled, and the mission reduced to the rank of legation. Once again his hopes of promotion were raised, because Straton would probably be regarded as too senior to be downgraded to secretary of legation, and he might therefore get that post. He settled back into the old routine while awaiting developments. He was on good terms with Straton. They worked well – and hard – together. Elgin fell ill at the end of 1801, and Jack was briefly left in sole charge in March 1802 while Elgin went off to Scio and Athens on convalescence and Straton visited Egypt. In August the Elgins decided to return to Constantinople via Smyrna, and Jack went there to meet them. Although invited, Lady Elgin was unable to go to Sidiköy to see old Mrs Van Lennep, but Jack was, and thus saw his grandmother for the last time before she died. He only hinted at the pleasure this reunion gave him when he wrote to his mother, explaining: 'You know that I do not shine in sentimentality – my grandmother will have to supplement what I lack in this.'[56] Perhaps his mother was able to forgive him some of his earlier boorishness on receiving this indirect self criticism.

By Christmas 1802 Jack was again in the dumps, because his hopes of the appointment in Constantinople seemed finally dashed. His uncle, by now Baron Radstock, had been doing his best for him in London, recommending him as 'a tolerable good classick' with a knowledge of Turkish, Persian and modern Greek, and fluent French and Italian, and 'uncommon natural abilities, many acquirements & an ambition & application which enables him to make himself master of any object that he undertakes. To these he adds the most correct principles & a degree of steadiness & direction that I never yet met with in any person of his years';[57] but he had written pessimistically to Jack, who had heard nothing from the Foreign Office. To his father Jack now wrote:

> I look upon my expectations of obtaining the place of Secretary as quite vanished and fallen to the ground. My consciousness of having done my duty must serve as my reward for my labours ... I am almost distracted to

think I must come upon you again, dear father, instead of bearing the burden which you have so long born. I question whether Lord E will ever do anything for me ... and ... I fear ... that to return to my former profession would be signing my sentence of complete & everlasting misery ... [I] beg of you to think of some plan for me. In the numberless situations in London could nothing be found for me?[58]

At the end of 1802 Elgin at last received his letter of recall and, leaving Straton in charge,* he and his family, accompanied by Jack, sailed on 17 January 1803 in HMS Diana for Athens, where they spent a week while Elgin tried to sort out some problems over his collection of the marbles. They all had to undergo quarantine at Malta in February. Here the Elgin parents took the fateful decision to go to Marseilles via Naples and then overland through France. While they were doing so the peace which had been signed with France in October 1801 broke down. Elgin, as a diplomat, should have been able to count on safe passage, but Bonaparte ignored this and he was interned, along with all other British citizens between the ages of nine and sixty. Jack, however, with Menou's threats still hanging over him, had been allowed to continue by sea with the Elgin children, and reached England safely. He was called for interview to the Foreign Office in August, where he was told he was being considered for a consular post in Egypt. He did not relish this, and tried to put them off by submitting a memorandum laying down a long list of conditions that would have to be met if he were to accept:

> The decided approbation which the services of Mr Morier have met with from His Majesty's Government had led him to hope that the reward he aspired at, namely to obtain rank in the Diplomatic Service, would have been granted to him. Still, as proof of his readiness to come forward wherever he may be deemed most useful to his country, he chearfully [sic] accepts the situation that His Majesty's Ministers have now been pleased to offer him at Alexandria, and as by doing so he on his part sacrifices for the time being all the blessings and comforts of social life, so he humbly presumes that in consideration of these sacrifices and of his past services, His Majesty's Government will on their part readily come to an arrangement with him on the following lines.

There followed a list of ten points, including an expected undertaking that the appointment would be of short duration at a place 'where the climate impairs the constitution'; that 'in consideration of the dangers of that residence both from the turbulence of the inhabitants as well

---

* A replacement for Elgin, William (later Sir William) Drummond, was appointed in May 1803 but he stayed only a few months, leaving Straton again in charge.

as the calamities of the plague, the salary be liberal' and a decent allowance given to cover all his expenses, including entertaining 'all naval officers and travellers ... [who] would expect to be well received'; and that there should be a clear understanding with the Levant Company to prevent 'the confusion that arose in Constantinople between Lord Elgin and Mr Sp Smith'.[59] Whether as result of this, or for some other reason, his posting to Alexandria was cancelled and instead, in December 1803, he was offered and accepted a consular appointment in the Greek part of the Ottoman empire, a development which eventually led to entry into the diplomatic service proper.

CHAPTER FIVE

James 1803–1806

'An excellent young man but who lacks perseverance.'

While Jack had been serving under Elgin in Constantinople and being given a taste of military life, James had been getting a taste of life as a merchant in Smyrna (chapter 3), which he had accepted with better grace than Jack had before him. On his return to London in 1803 the whole family was together again for a few months. James must have felt some envy on hearing of Jack's adventures, and on learning in December that he was now apparently free from the merchant shackles, and about to go off again on government service. For his part James simply had to accept that his father wanted him back in Smyrna; but, being the person he was, he took it all philosophically and, with good grace, set off across the North Sea to begin an overland journey to Turkey.

The first stage was in a packet boat to Heligoland where, after a night's stay, he boarded a small Danish vessel bound for Husum. They should have arrived there in a few hours, but they ran into fog and had to spend an uncomfortable night on board 'in all the luxury of vermin and foul stenches'. When they managed to get going again at the end of the second day they were forced by ice to anchor well off the coast and transfer to a small rowing boat. After a while the boatmen gave up the struggle against the tide, and James and his fellow travellers were 'obliged to get out and wade for a mile & more through mud & half broken up ice ... with a deluge of rain, a hurricane of wind and a dark night.' They nearly lost an 'unfortunate little Frankfurt Jew' who 'fell into a bog & what with fright & weakness he would have been expunged from the list of Israelites' had others not come to his aid. (How they got their luggage ashore is not explained.) James, however, was already a hardened traveller, and he simply ended this letter with a laconic 'so much for my passage' and the statement that he had continued on 'very bad roads'.[1] He reached Vienna on 10 January 1804 and Bucharest on the 25th, having lost his luggage –

which he suspected had been cut loose from the roof of the coach somewhere along the way. Because of the severe wintry conditions the journey from Vienna had taken twice the normal time and, very apologetically, he had to tell his father that he had been forced to give a promissory note on him when he ran out of funds.

James reached Smyrna early in March, arriving in the dark after having 'trotted for the distance of almost thirty miles [from Magnesia] & my horses & mules were nearly knocked up.' The first house he came to in Frank Street was that of Consul Hochepied at whose door he knocked. It opened directly into the living room where a crowd of family and friends were gathered. Great was their surprise to see James at the door, travel stained and weary; but this was nothing compared to the consternation which immediately followed. 'A poor mule who could scarcely walk from extreme fatigue, thinking to have completed his journey & taking the parlour door for the stable, dashes in to the great astonishment of the company. The fright became general. Screams issued from every mouth … .' With some difficulty the beast was persuaded to leave and James went on to the Wilkinsons.

His simple room with the Wilkinsons seemed like a haven to him after he had got 'a table made six feet by four [covered] with a green cloth [and planted] in the centre of my chamber [so that] both it & myself are complete fixtures in the room, so that I can say my apartment is not entirely furnished without myself being in it.' He was not, however, a recluse like Jack. He was soon off on an excursion with a 'party composed of eight [which] was very merry & as we had bachelor fare so had we the agreeable liberty to do as we pleased.' And he frequented the Casino in the evenings where he played billiards, 'a pretty & gentlemanly amusement [which] accustoms the eye to be precise, steadies the hand & exerts the body very essentially.'[2] But he was only making the best of what he could not avoid, a life and society to be endured rather than enjoyed. 'It is but the hopes' he wrote to David 'of making myself a competency to set me above want that at least enlivens the prospect [of years in Smyrna] … The conviction of doing what duty requires from me, of being useful to my family & of advancing the broken interests of my father, greatly compensate me for the many truly disagreeable evils of living in a place where there is continually some thing occurring to destroy one's quiet, & where one continued round of sameness & inspired dullness carries on from year's end to year's end.' And he was glad when, after Easter, most people left for the country and he found some peace, for 'I am very fond of being left undisturbed, not that I don't like company, but it is better to have none' than to have to put up with the noise of the large

Wilkinson family. In this quiet, he turned to 'books [particularly Virgil], pen and pencil' for recreation, and derived what comfort he could from his contemplation and sketching of local scenery and rural sights. Urged on by David, he took to composing rather bad poetry. He was sorry that Wilkinson's sons had not spent longer in England to shake off

> the certain sort of manner peculiar to the people of this country, difficult to be described, which those who have made any stay in it are apt to adopt. 'Tis a greekish, unmeaning sort of way, both of talking & acting ... There is a great affinity I think between the manners of a people & the idea of their language. The Frenchman laughs, grins, shrugs his shoulders, talks & jabbers a great deal, but analize what he has been saying, you will find that he might have said in three words what he has been saying in a hundred ... An Englishman is in general a man of few words & his language is so energetic as to express much with little talk or fuss. The Turkish is exactly the same. The Greek is all the contrary; 'tis the counterpart of the French.[3]

When James left England his father was in serious financial trouble, having lost heavily in several dealings to his own account.* He tended to blame his trading misfortunes on Wilkinson, and he had once again been thinking of returning to Smyrna himself in order to sort things out and even, perhaps, break up the partnership. His sons had been aghast at this idea, and had tried to dissuade him. And when James reached Smyrna he found that the business was in fact in better shape than it had seemed to Isaac and was 'now thank Heaven on the best of footings & superior to any other in town.' He found that his 'most intimate friends such as the Van Lenneps were ... of the opinion that [Isaac] would instead of being of utility be the only barrier or impediment to the prosperity of the house,'[4] which merely confirmed him in his own conviction that it was his father who was making all the wrong decisions and that, although Wilkinson was perhaps not as good a businessman as he ought to be, if he, James, could be left to carry on the trade with him without interference from Isaac, there was a chance that he might at last get a partnership and perhaps even make for himself an income of £5-6,000. Both James and David urged their father to recognise Wilkinson's honesty, integrity and desire

---

* There is an unsubstantiated family story that Isaac was actually incarcerated briefly in Fleet prison for debt, from which he was rescued by his brother-in-law, William Waldegrave; but there is no reference to this in surviving letters.

to help. Wilkinson was, indeed, taking a very generous attitude, leaving it entirely up to Isaac to decide whether the partnership should be dissolved. James told his father that 'if by remaining with him you think that the house will flourish more than if we separate, he will continue in the same amical footing with you, if otherwise he professes himself as strongly attached to you as ever, will be happy to see me get on in life, & will assist me in every thing that lays in his power'; and he would be ready to let Isaac remove his share of the capital to meet his commitments in England but still receive his share of any profits the house might make. James urged his father not to break up the partnership or remove his capital, but rather to sell his Swiss property to meet his debts, even though this might postpone the day when he, James, might aspire to replacing his father as partner. 'As for me, my dear father' he wrote, 'my utmost ambition is to render your life comfortable & to acquire an easy subsistence to my best of mothers and sisters. I am young, without any particular attachments in life to render a fortune yet so necessary to me as to you, & can wait contenting myself with what it has pleased God to let me enjoy.'[5]

James may have thought then that he had no 'particular attachments', but it is quite possible that Wilkinson had already detected that he and his daughter Maria might be be feeling an attraction to each other, and that, like old Van Lennep before him in relation to Isaac, he would be happy to have James as a son-in-law. Certainly, by July 1804, he was responding with cautious encouragement to hints that James would be interested in a partnership, but there was no sign, when James was able to join his brothers Jack and David in Athens for a few weeks in that month (see chapter 6), that James himself was aware that he was about to fall in love with one of the family he found so annoyingly noisy.

While the brothers were together in Athens they received the splendid news that their father was expecting to be appointed consul general at Constantinople, a post in the gift of the Levant Company. Not only would this solve most of the family's financial problems, it would mean that James need no longer consider his father in discussing the future of the business in Smyrna with Wilkinson. Although sad to be leaving his brothers again – as he took the boat from Cape Sounion he looked back longingly at them silhouetted against the blue sky 'seated among the white columns of the temple of Minerva'[6] – he returned to Smyrna in a more cheerful mood. He began to build a whole series of 'castles in Spain' as various possibilities for his future presented themselves. An old friend of his father's, St Barbe, who had played a leading part in rescuing Isaac from his creditors, was suggesting that James might come into business with him in London. By the end of the year Wilkinson had collected several consulships in Smyrna and might, therefore, decide to pull out of commerce altogether, leaving open the possibility that James could join with his sons to carry on the business. Mrs Wilkinson was in line to inherit a considerable sum from her recently deceased brother – the captain of a Dutch East Indies trader who had prospered – which would provide useful capital. But James was still, nearly a year later, unable to decide what would be best. To his sisters he declared that 'to plan & say I will do this & that becomes merely a pastime of a moment, or is like the children's amusement of building houses with cards which the first breath of wind overthrows ... I have at last found that it becomes a burthen to one to carry through life the restlessness for future events.'[7] But he had now discovered that he was in love, which was affecting his ability to think of anything else. His father realised this when, in February 1805, he reached Smyrna on his way to Constantinople. He was delighted to find his son 'big, fat and well ... loved by all, praised by everyone, in fact his conduct in all respects is perfect.' But he also found that 'although in all respects an excellent young man, [he] lacks persever-ence'[8] and needed to be forced into a decision about his future (and preferably out of his infatuation for Maria Wilkinson). Isaac thought her a pleasant and well brought up young girl, but too young, and with no prospects of a good dowry. So he decided to take James with him to Constantinople.

Perhaps James himself was wise enough to see that a separation from Maria would be best, for he seems to have gone off with his father in April 1805 quite happily, looking forward to helping him settle in to his new duties. He was kept busy as a clerk making copies of Isaac's letters; but he soon decided that he had no desire to live in Constantinople. 'Society [here] has a detestable tone' he wrote to his mother; 'the young ladies receive a miserable education. Their conversation is only of wicked little tales which are never lacking in small societies & they occupy themselves only with the business of others. Ah, my dear mother, how I pity those who have to spend their lives in this town.' With his father he attended formal receptions which he thought detestable:

There is such a mixture of farmyard courtiers upholding etiquette in the lowest possible style. The ambassadors ape their different sovereigns and talk of their local communities, consisting perhaps of a few hundred individuals, with as much disdain as their kings and emperors talk of their subjects. The dragomans, introduced into all the social gatherings, grovel before their ambassadors, and the members of the communities suck up to the dragomans. In any gathering in one of the national 'palaces' one sees all sorts, from gilded and braided lords to the most insignificant merchant. Just imagine what kind of manners that introduces, they are all execrable. All the time there are examples of immorality which should shock any well born person but which have become so common in Pera that they are spoken of lightly. The system of intrigue which the Turks invented, and the infamous practices of the seraglio, have been introduced into all the ambassadors' palaces. I tell you, in this country honest folk are the rarest and knaves have the most standing.[9]

By June, James had given up the idea of joining St Barbe in London. Whether because of difficulties with St Barbe, or from a reluctance to go, is not clear. In the same month the new ambassador, Charles Arbuthnot[*], arrived. James may have had some idea that he might find employment with him. He accompanied his father on board the ship to welcome him, and reported to his mother that they were received:

> ... ambassadorially ... It was worth seeing all that. Servants, personal maids, children, nursemaids, all on top of each other and expecting great things at Constantinople & in the middle of it all Mrs Arbuthnot, pretty little woman in the latest fashion seeming happy with the view of the town & Bosporous & hoping to find herself in an agreeable country. My God! What disillusionment awaited her on land where an immense crowd of Turks and all sorts of people awaited while she was stuffed into a chair to be carried to a house without furniture & without the smallest arrangement for such a large family. As for the men, they take everything in their stride, but a woman like the ambassadress who comes from the great fashionable circles of St James Street into these of Pera, just imagine what she thinks.[10]

But no employment with Arbuthnot was offered, and James returned to Smyrna in August, with his father's permission to marry Maria in four or five years' time (she was then only 15) provided Wilkinson was then in a position to provide a decent dowry.

---

[*] Charles Arbuthnot, 1767–1850, under-secretary in the Foreign Office November 1802 to June 1804, ambassador at Constantinople 1805–07, joint secretary Treasury 1809–1823. A close friend of Wellington, he died in Apsley House, a widower.

CHAPTER SIX

Jack and David 1804–1806

'We felt we were two exiles without friends.'

While James had been trying to come to terms with merchant life in Smyrna, and Jack had been enduring hardships with the Turkish and British armies in Syria and Egypt, David had been growing up quietly in England. He had not even been away from home since they had all arrived in 1787, except for two years at Harrow School, which he had entered in January 1796 at the age of 12 (and was fag to Viscount Althorp, later third Earl Spencer). He had left Harrow at the end of 1797 and then spent six years in private study and in his father's counting house, reluctantly because he would much rather have gone to Cambridge, the expense of which was beyond the family means. But they had not been unhappy years, for he was a naturally cheerful and loveable boy, adored by his mother and sisters. He had had a sudden spurt of growth and had become a lanky young man with spindly legs, quite unlike his two heavily built elder brothers; but he cheerfully accepted the teasing he got about his shanks – when, in those days of breeches, a nicely rounded calf to show off was what every man wanted. His mother was very protective, believing he was not very robust, and it was probably at her insistence that he was not sent off to Smyrna at 16 or so. There had been some talk of his going into the church, but nothing had come of this. When he was 17 there had been an attempt to get him a secretaryship at the admiralty or employment in India. Lord Radstock wrote, in October 1801, to Lord Hobart:[*]

Mr David Morier is not yet eighteen years of age. However notwithstanding his youth, such, my Lord, are his natural talents, such has been his education,

---

[*] Robert Hobart, 1760–1816 (after whom Hobart in Tasmania was named), son of 3rd Earl of Buckinghamshire. After controversial political service in India as governor of Madras he was made Baron Hobart of Blickling in 1798 and, in March 1801, secretary of state for the Colonial and War department.

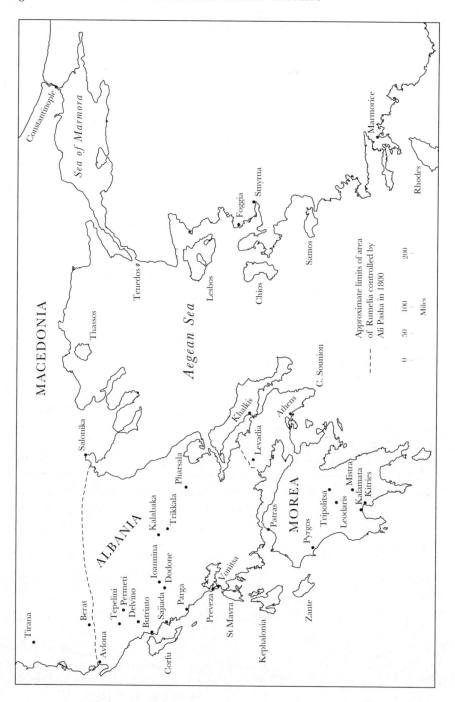

Map 2 Ottoman Greece 1800

& such is his love of study, that I will venture to say, that he will thoroughly qualify himself for any situation whatsoever as a man of business, into which he should have the good fortune to be placed. The more complex, the more arduous the task, the better.[1]

Nothing had come of this either, and there must have been much anxious discussion in the summer and autumn of 1803 about how David could begin a life of his own and cease to be a burden on the family's tight finances. The solution had been found when Jack, in December of that year, now aged 25, was appointed 'His Majesty's Consul General for the Morea, Albania and the adjacent territories of the Ottoman Empire' with an allowance for a secretary which could be used to employ David.

At that time, the frontiers of the Ottoman empire in Europe lay well to the north of what is now Greece. Bosnia and Serbia were included, and further east, beyond the Danube, the principalities of Wallachia and Moldavia (now parts of Romania) were tributary lands governed by princes chosen by the sultan from the Phanariot community of Greeks in Constantinople. To the west Montenegro lay outside the Ottoman dominions, as did Dalmatia and the old Ragusan (Dubrovnik) republic. The Morea was the name given to the classical (and modern) Peloponnese. Albania then included the Epirus of modern Greece, ruled from his seat at Ioannina by the notorious Ali Pasha, who was also by then a vizier (ministerial rank) and governor of a large part of the rest of northern Greece. This gave him great authority over many other pashas, although from time to time he had to exert this by force over those unwilling to accept it. Administratively all the Ottoman territories were divided into *pashaliks* and subdivided into *vilayets* ruled over by *agas* with the title of *bey*. Ali Pasha, like all pashas, paid tribute to the sultan to retain his position; but so long as the sultan received what he considered was his due, and the pashas did not openly defy his ultimate authority, they were left in virtual independence. They used this independence to build up their own wealth through heavy taxation of the populations over which they ruled. Pashas at the extremities of the empire were assumed to have sufficient interest in this virtual independence to wish to resist any attempted foreign incursion.

Dalmatia and the Ionian Islands had for long belonged to Venice; but by the Treaty of Campo Formio in 1797 Austria had acquired Dalmatia, and France the Ionian Islands. After Turkey went to war with France over Bonaparte's invasion of Egypt in 1798, the islands were taken by a joint Russo–Turkish force and were then formed into the Septinsular Republic under the joint protection of the Turks and Russians, the latter keeping military garrisons in the main islands and a sizeable naval force at Corfu to deal with any French attempt to return. The Venetians had always also controlled the four principal coastal towns on the mainland, Butrinto (Buthroton opposite Corfu in modern Albania), Parga, Preveza guarding the entrance to the Gulf of Arta (Amvrakikos) and Vonitsa on the southern shore of this gulf. It was feared that Ali Pasha might support the French if they attempted an invasion. There was also a question mark over the Morea, particularly in the south-east where the fiercely independent Maniot Greeks had not long before welcomed with enthusiasm a Corsican officer of Maniot origin from Bonaparte's staff and a French ship bringing munitions. There seemed to be a serious risk of a French invasion, and it seemed very likely that such a move would be supported by the local population.

That, in outline, was the geo-political scene into which Jack and David were thrown at the beginning of 1804. 'The first and most essential object' which Jack was instructed to pursue was 'the necessity of impressing upon the Governments of the Morea and Albania the indispensable expediency of employing every exertion in their power to be prepared for resisting with effect the designs which the French Government entertain with respect to those provinces. You will ... urge them ... never to ... suffer themselves to be deceived by any assurances of the French Government denying the existence of any such projects as are imputed to them.' Although they were also to be assured that every effort would be made to warn them of any preparations for invasion, nevertheless they 'must rely upon their own exertions to repel the French army if it should effect a landing.'[2] Jack was given presents to the value of £500 to distribute to people of influence in pursuance of this objective, and authorised to incur additional expenditure up to a maximum of £5000 in actual cash bribery, a very considerable sum in those days. He was allowed to spend up to £450 a year on payments for dragomans, janissaries and a clerk (David), and to draw as required for his extraordinary expenses. With such a formidable brief, but apparently with very little to offer in the way of practical help in resisting the French, it was perhaps not surprising that David, as they prepared to set off, told his parents that Jack was 'very nervy'.[3]

Jack, now 25, and David, who had celebrated his 20th birthday just a month earlier, sailed in a convoy from Portsmouth on 6 February

1804 on board the Hindoostan – a 1200-ton 3-masted armed merchantman belonging to the East India Company (not long back from playing a part in Lord Macartney's abortive mission to China) – which was taking supplies to the fleet off Toulon. David, although a little nervous at setting forth on such a journey when he had scarcely even been out of London before, and wondering how he would get on with his older and rather serious brother, whom he scarcely knew, assured his parents that he was 'quite at my ease with the protection of my dear brother and with the idea of not being a burthen [sic] to you, my dear father, and perhaps of being of use now & to all the family hereafter.'[4] And, like his brothers before him, when setting out into the world for the first time, he thought it necessary to reassure them as to his moral behaviour: 'Being fully aware of the many temptations and allurements to which I in particular am exposed, both from my youth and inexperience, I take every method of keeping alive in my heart those principles of virtue & religion which you have been at such pains to inculcate ... The methods I mean are constant employment in something usefull [sic] & interesting, and an effort to gain a habit of reflection.'[5]

At Gibraltar, 'after much hunting about the town [they were] lucky enough to find a room in what is said to be the best inn in the place.' They dined with the Governor, Sir Thomas Grigg, who received them 'very graciously.'[6] They then transferred to another merchantman, the Pelican, on 12 March, sailing again in convoy and reaching Malta on 1 April. The Governor there, Sir Alexander Ball*, who had served in the navy with Lord Radstock, was also attentive and became a useful friend. They enjoyed a round of parties, but David found that the Maltese nobility consisted 'of people with the lowest and vilest appearance' who gave themselves 'ridiculous airs and graces,[6] while the women were 'mostly so ugly as to make one afraid.' Jack was never a very enthusiastic correspondent with his family, except on business matters with his father, and David begged his mother 'not to impute to Jack any other cause for his not having written long letters than what he alleges to be his incapability of filling pages with nothings'[7] – something which David himself was all too good at – while he explained to his sisters: 'as Jack, you know is not famous for tormenting people however dear to him ... with sentimental nonsense like mine, you must take my word for it that he does not love you a bit the less,

---

* Alexander John Ball, Bt, 1757–1809, after a distinguished naval career was largely responsible for the capture of Malta from the French in 1798 and was made governor in 1801, dying there in 1809.

though he does not trouble you with letters.'[8] They were indeed a contrast, these two brothers, Jack serious and unemotional, David bubbling always with warmth and the free expression of affection – which was perhaps why they got on so well together most of the time.

⊕

From Malta HMS Thisbe brought them, on 22 April, to Patras. It was a difficult and discouraging start to their mission. The town was full of Turkish troops and they were forced to beg accommodation with the Levant Company's consul, Nicolas Strane, who was not particularly welcoming. He had been appointed back in 1782, succeeding his uncle in the post, and had been happily living in Patras since then enjoying the income received from his right to charge 2 per cent on the value of every cargo shipped in or out by merchants of the Company. He did not want anyone else with consular authority in his bailiewick. However, he let four rooms in his house to Jack and David and their two servants – one English (William) and one Italian – for 250 piastres (about £25) a year and agreed to feed them for 65 piastres a month. In this rather chilly atmosphere David wrote to his mother that he had 'never felt our separation so acutely as when our frigate, the last sign of England, sailed away. We felt we were two exiles without friends, with no one to care for us ... in a country where everything seems strange and barbarous. We have both felt regrets for dear England, with a poignancy of which I did not think we were capable.'[9]

It was not only Strane who was reluctant to see Jack in the area. The Turks themselves did not like any representative of another government residing anywhere in the empire outside Constantinople, and it was only their need to keep Britain's friendship that persuaded them to agree to issue Jack with the necessary authority (*berat*) to exercise consular functions (which they insisted on restricting to Albania and the Morea) and permits (*firmans*) to travel throughout the area and, reluctantly, in the 'adjacent territories'. Jack, however, was determined to waste no time in getting on with what he was convinced was an urgent and vital task. During his few days in Corfu he had learned that French agents were believed to be active in the Morea, since instructions to them had been discovered in the possession of a Frenchman in London some time before. He believed that the Greeks, unwilling subjects of the Turks, would be likely to 'rise to a man' in rebellion should the French land. He feared that 'no arguments drawn from the misery of other nations who have been deluded by the perfidious caresses of the French' would be likely to persuade the

Greeks 'to abandon for the present all hopes of emancipation and stand firm' unless he could also convince them that the British and Russians were fully committed to supporting the Turks.[10] So he and David set off from Patras on 24 April to call on Mohammad Pasha, the ruler of the Morea, at Tripolitsa (Tripolis) and assess the situation for themselves.

Travelling down the west coast to Pyrgos, before striking inland through the mountains, took them five days on horse back. Jack thought that this coast was wide open to a French invasion, with its extensive beaches and the lack of any defences, whether natural or man made. Such forts as there were had become virtual ruins, with only a few ancient and useless cannons on the crumbling walls. His experiences in Egypt had left him with no great opinion of Turkish soldiery, and he was sure that the 6000 or so troops in the Morea would be no match for a determined French attack. There were in addition some 1000 militia; but these were more of a menace to the local population than to an external enemy, recovering from them by force the money and food which the government failed to provide regularly. Jack became convinced that it was necessary to double the size of the Russian forces in the islands, and to station a British naval squadron at the mouth of the Adriatic, if there were to be any hope of beating off a French attack on this part of the Ottoman empire. He was happy to discover, however, that local support for such an attack was not after all very likely. He found the Greeks so cowed by the brutality of the occupying military that they were reluctant to talk freely to him; but at least it seemed that they were not simply waiting for the French in order to rebel. They were far more interested in being allowed to live in peace, unmolested by the Turkish soldiery, and it became clear that if French agents had been active they certainly had not succeeded in rousing a spirit of rebellion. Jack found it 'impossible to witness [the Greeks'] abject situation without pitying them', but he thought it highly unlikely that they would dare to support the French unless they could see the Turks defeated first. He was at pains to try to convince them that they should support Turkish resistance to an invasion, otherwise they would be worse off than they were now.

A party such as Jack's travelling anywhere in the empire with *firmans* from Constantinople was treated with great respect. Messengers would go ahead to warn the headmen of villages, agas and pashas of their approach, and they would normally be received with as much pomp and parade as local facilities allowed, with lodging already prepared and probably a feast laid on. As Jack and David were to discover later, this was by no means guaranteed in the more remote areas of Greece;

and Jack was actually rather pleased that they arrived at Tripolitsa earlier than expected, and so were spared the formal reception the pasha claimed he had been preparing. But they were received in friendly fashion, and provided with decent quarters. Jack's interview with the pasha, on 7 May, went well. The pasha, and all the leading Turks he met, seemed thoroughly pro-British, grateful for the help given in Egypt, and confident they would not be let down this time. Jack was more concerned, however, over what might be the attitude of the Maniots in the south. They had always resisted Turkish rule, and it was only under the threat of punishment by force of arms – after their support for the Russian attempted invasion in 1770 – that they had reluctantly agreed to pay tribute to the Porte in exchange for being allowed to have an aga from their own people. The present one, Andon Bey, had made considerable progress in persuading them to live peaceably, but he still had the problem of the deposed Zanet Bey, whose properties had been destroyed as punishment when it had been discovered that his son had organised the landing of the French munitions. Zanet Bey was in rebellion in the mountains with a considerable following, which had become larger when the Turks had been unwise enough to try to force the Maniots to supply a regular number of men for the navy. Jack saw all this as representing a serious risk of local support for the French. Against the advice of Mohammad Pasha, who thought it was too dangerous (and who would have been in trouble had such an important Englishman come to harm), he and David went off to meet Andon Bey.

On the way to Andon's headquarters near Kalamata, they called on the Greek Metropolitan whose seat was at Mistra. Built on the slopes of a steep hill overlooking Sparta, crowned by the great mediaeval castle of the Villehardouins, even today, although now mostly in ruins, it gives an idea of the magnificence it once had under the Palaeologi, in the days before the Byzantine empire fell to the Turks. It still had a certain grandeur when Jack saw it. The Turks had not found it comfortable to remain there for long, in the face of the hostility of the particularly proud Greeks whose home it was, and had handed it over to the Orthodox church (on which they relied to keep their conquered subjects quiet). But there had been support for the Russians when they had tried to invade in 1770, and the Turks had then destroyed a large part of the town in punishment. The Greeks, however, had a devout respect for their church, and the present bishop had enjoyed considerable success in keeping order since then. Jack found him to be much more interested in preserving his lucrative position, which he owed entirely to the sultan, than in encouraging ideas of Greek rebellion.

Indeed, he had been 'zealous in administering oaths of fidelity and pronouncing anathemas against any who would favour the French'[11] and Jack came to the conclusion that there was no longer much danger of trouble there.

The bishop was uncomfortable when Jack announced his intention of going on to see Andon Bey, but he gave him letters of recommendation, while urging him not to attempt the most direct route over the high mountains because they were infested by robbers. So they took a northerly route through Leondaris (Megalopolis) reaching Kalamata on 13 May, and meeting Andon Bey at his palace at Kitries a few miles to the east next day. Jack came to the conclusion that here too there was not much danger now of support for the French, whose landing of munitions seemed to have been little more than an opportunist diversion to sow uncertainty by supporting the rebel Zanet Bey. Jack also agreed with Andon Bey that, since there was little chance of defeating Zanet Bey by force, the sensible course would be to persuade the Porte to pardon him, which Jack promised to try to do. Jack's opinion of the Greek attitude was that they were at heart anti-French because they had heard of 'their gallantries, their atheism and their sacrileges, and as the Greeks are jealous of their women and bigoted in the extreme, they must possess a natural aversion and dread of French principles in those respects.' Nevertheless, he could not bring himself to trust them for, as he put it, 'the Greek character resembles the French. They are both equally false, vain and ambitious for power, which they ever abuse'[12] Discovering the identities of French agents working in the Morea – in the guise of physicians who were 'controlled' by the French commercial agent in Zante (Zakynthos), the southern-most of the Ionian islands where Zanet Bey's son was living – he sent the names to Constantinople, and on his way back to Patras he called again on Muhammad Pasha, to urge him to have them thrown out.

Both Jack and David were in the best of spirits on their return to Patras on 23 May. It had been a tiring month, but they had enjoyed the activity and the experience of being treated with deference. Even the normally restrained Jack was taking a romantic pleasure in 'going native': 'We have permitted our moustachios to grow, we smoke and eat with our bare fingers' he wrote, 'I am afraid we are in a school that will sooner fit us for Arcadian swains than sharpen our wits for the diplomatic career.' Patras itself, however, took the shine off their pleasure. Although most of the Turkish garrison had by now withdrawn, before doing so they had indulged in an orgy of rapine and pillage, the consequences of which appalled even Jack, hardened as he was to the behaviour of the soldiery. He now found Patras to be 'the most disagreeable in point of society I ever was at' and life in it 'detestable', while David considered it might be 'good enough for Turks who are accustomed to the sight of mud walls, wretched faces and to one another, but for Christians, to inhabit the Shades below must be preferable.'[13] To make matters worse, a bad earthquake early in June severely damaged Strane's house (nearly killing Jack) and they had to move into tents. So, after finishing his lengthy reports for London, Jack decided to respond to the invitation he had received at Tripolitsa to visit Ali Pasha in Ioannina.

At Ioannina – which they reached on 19 June, escorted from Preveza by a military guard – they were very well received. Ali Pasha, at this stage in his career, was in some respects more powerful than the sultan himself. Born approximately 60 years earlier at Tepelini in northern Albania, son of a pasha of two tails (the second highest rank), he had been brought up by an ambitious and ruthless mother to be a particularly successful brigand in a part of the Ottoman empire in which the sultan was content to let traditional feuding between local and virtually independent chieftans continue, so long as it did not interfere with the regular payment of tributes. At the age of about 20, Ali and his gang had been captured by Kurd Pasha of Berat who was also head of all the police in southern Albania, Thessaly and the Morea. Kurd Pasha had taken a liking to this handsome and intelligent young man of great charm, and spared his life. After a few years living peaceably at Berat under the protection of Kurd Pasha, Ali had had the temerity to ask for the hand of his daughter in marriage. This was refused, and instead she was married to Ibraham Pasha of Valona, who thus became Ali's lifelong enemy. Ali, furious at his rejection, had again taken to a life of banditry and, by trickery, had been able to get his companions to convince Kurd Pasha that they had killed him, and so claim the reward of 5000 piastres which had been offered for his capture. With this useful capital, Ali went from strength to strength, eventually (in 1768) marrying the daughter of Caplan Pasha of Delvino, a bitter enemy of Kurd Pasha. By more treachery, Ali had then succeeded in having his father-in-law (whom he hoped to succeed) executed, by persuading the Porte that he had been disloyal. He failed in his bid for this pashalik, but it only took him a few more years of intrigue and treachery to get himself appointed pasha of Trikkala in Thessaly, together with the post of chief inspector of roads. This post required him to rid the countryside of robbers, a duty which he tackled with such enthusiasm and success that, when Turkey went to war with Russia and Austria in 1787, he was given an important military command. Even this, however, had not diverted him from his chief aim, which was to gather further pashaliks; and the following year, again by out-and-out deceit, he had managed to seize control of Ioannina and get the Porte to confirm him as pasha there as well as at Trikkala.

Once in position in Ioannina, Ali Pasha's next aim was to gain control of the four coastal towns which belonged to Venice. He thought he saw his chance when the French took over these islands in 1797, but the French were not prepared to go further in responding to his overtures of friendship than to give him some help, in the form of arms, in his struggle to suppress the unruly Suliots in the mountains to the south-west of Ioannina. When Bonaparte invaded Egypt, Ali Pasha, far from regarding this as reason to become the enemy of the enemy of the sultan, his nominal ruler, had made a further attempt to ingratiate himself with the French, offering a military alliance if they would let him have the island of St Mavra (Lefkas) – in a strategically important position off the mouth of the Gulf of Arta – and the four coastal towns. The French had turned him down, whereupon Ali Pasha had informed the Porte that he was going to attack the French, not, of course, revealing that his only aim was to capture these towns for himself. He was successful in seizing Butrinto and the particularly important Preveza – a feat for which he received the thanks of Nelson, conveyed personally by one of his officers, and the reward of being raised to the rank of pasha of three tails by the sultan. After Corfu was taken by the combined Russian–Turkish force and put under Russian protection, however, the Russians, who did not trust Ali Pasha to be a loyal ally against the French, persuaded the Porte to make him surrender Preveza. In exchange he was appointed concurrently governor of Rumelia with the rank of vizier, which made him, in effect, independent ruler of most of Greece north of the Morea, from Levadia in the east northwards to Pella in Macedonia, and south of a line roughly from the present junction of Greece, Albania and former Yugoslavia to the coast at Avlona (Vlor).* But the Russian commander in Corfu, Count Mocenigo – himself of Greek origin from Zante but brought up in Russia, whither his father had fled after the unsuccessful Greek rebellion stirred up by the Russians in 1770 – was determined to reduce Ali Pasha's power, and decided to give active help to the

---

* The exact limits of the administrative area of Rumelia (or Rumeli) at that time are difficult to determine.

Suliots. So Ali Pasha then had to concentrate on a final suppression of these troublesome people, which he did in 1803, massacring those who did not succeed in taking refuge in Corfu and the other islands. It was not surprising that he was disinclined to cooperate with the Russians in any plans to resist the French, even more so when he found that Mocenigo was supporting some of the agas to the north, who were also trying to break free from his control.

When, therefore, Jack and David made their first visit to Ali Pasha in 1804, they were meeting a man who had shown himself both politically treacherous and very powerful, but one who (for the present at least) was anxious to be friends with Britain. He lived in great splendour at Ioannina, with several hundred women in his harem, as well as a coterie of good looking youths, his appetites being voracious and varied. He combined a total ruthlessness with a genuine taste for learning and civilized culture, and Ioannina – which today is the home of one of Greece's largest universities – was already known as a centre of academic excellence. He could exert a magnetic charm and persuasiveness, which caused a Frenchman to write that 'to resist him it is necessary to be possessed of a perfect knowledge of his character, and always to hold the picture before one's eyes; and still his dissimulation is so disguised and so profound that one almost feels self-reproachful for being on one's guard and acting with a salutary distrust.'[14]

Ali Pasha was disappointed, as he made very clear, to find that Jack had brought no reply to the requests he had already made for arms through Nelson and others. What he wanted was 'powder, cannon, mortars, shot and shell', an engineer officer, three bombardiers and three artillerymen to train his troops, who could ask what payment they wanted, and some British ships to be stationed off Albania to be 'guided by the information' he would supply. In exchange he would provide a safe port for use of the British navy, as much timber as they wanted for repairs, and three or four thousand men should there be a French attack. He made clear to Jack that he distrusted the Russian influence on the Porte, and would actively oppose any attempt by them to occupy the old Venetian coastal towns, even if the sultan agreed to it. He was disarmingly frank in saying that he no longer had any faith in the French because they had never paid him for supplies he had sent them during their occupation of Corfu; and he made no attempt to hide his belief that the Porte was out to reduce his power. The help he wanted from Britain, he made clear, was in order to be able to resist this. He was convinced the Ottoman Empire was near collapse and that Britain would soon find herself in disagreement with the Turks (a shrewd forecast). If he got the help he wanted now – and he emphasised that his request must be treated with great secrecy – Britain could count on his assistance in the future.[15]

Jack could do no more than listen and promise to convey these views to London. His assessment was that, in this area too, a Greek uprising to support a French invasion was unlikely. They appeared to him to bear Ali Pasha's rule with little sign of discontent 'owing perhaps', as he put it somewhat ironically, 'to the indulgence of Ali Pasha, who knows the levity and vanity of their character, freely allows them of gratifying both in the building of spacious houses and the wearing of fine apparel, advantages which in the estimation of modern Greeks are a very liberal return for their contributions in money.' As for Ali Pasha himself, he thought 'his mind, though wholly untutored, possesses an uncommon degree of natural sagacity which shows itself especially in his management of the Porte, upon whose authority he has never yet encroached by open violence for, knowing the venality of that government, he gains his ends equally by means of gold, at the same time that he keeps up every appearance of loyalty.'[16] In other words, Jack, who was not an enthusiastic supporter of the Turks, was beginning to feel that Ali Pasha had his points. Nevertheless, he was conscious of 'the jealousy with which at Corfu and Constantinople they look upon every thing that goes on at Ioannina'[17] and decided it would be unwise to stay longer than a week to gather what intelligence he could. However, as David explained to Lord Radstock later, they could not 'vouch for the truth of one jot of the information derived solely from the Greeks who never speak truth but by mistake. The worst that can be said of it is *si non é vero, é ben trovato*'.[18] They were even misled in their wish to visit the site of the ancient oracle of Dodone, being directed to Dramisios to the north-west of Ioannina although it is in fact to the south-west (but not confirmed as such until 1875).

Jack now decided to spend a few months relaxing in Athens, and they left Ioannina on 1 July. Rather than return by way of Patras, he chose to add to their knowledge of the country by going east over the great Pindus mountain range and across the plains of Thessaly, even though it was almost the hottest time of the year there. The route over the Pindus mountains was an arduous climb, and when they descended into the desert-like area of the Meteora, passing the extraordinary cylinders of rock towering several hundred feet into the air with their monasteries on top accessible then only by baskets let down on ropes, they found the heat almost unbearably oppressive. They spent an uncomfortable night at Kalabaka, leaving very early next morning for Trikkala where they rested for the whole of the next day, setting off only as dusk fell in order to avoid further travel in the heat. Crossing the plain where Caesar defeated Pompey in 48 BC, they stopped briefly at midnight for refreshment at a *khan* (a sort of caravanserai) where they found 'half a dozen people stretched out fast asleep under the stars ... [and] a little apothecary's shop full of old broken bottles, pills and a dozen huge plasters' the uses of which they never discovered. On leaving after their meal they realised that David's pistol was missing from his saddle pocket. With cries of 'thief, thief' they insisted on having all the gates barred while a search was made, much to the annoyance of the sleepers. Prime suspects were the Turk and the Greek in whose care the horses had been left. The brothers' *tatar* (messenger), furious at not finding the pistol, 'flung himself on the unfortunate Greek, kicking and punching him.' The Turk then drew his pistol, which fortunately misfired; but by this time the whole place was in such an uproar, all in the dark, that Jack decided they should leave. A few hours after their arrival at Pharsala the apothecary turned up with the missing pistol, which had been found in a dung heap near where the Turk had been eating. Fortunately for this Turk, he had already left by then, else, as David wrote to his mother, 'our Tatar would assuredly have returned and killed him on the spot'.[19]

They reached Athens on 11 July, and spent three months there, two of them with James for company. Returning to Patras on 18 October, and having heard in Athens of their father's appointment to Constantinople as consul general, Jack began to feel that he need no longer concern himself so much with earning the best possible income for the sake of the family. He felt he was doing himself no long term good at Patras, and he told his mother: 'If I have no opportunity to distinguish myself here I simply must return to look for other employment, for rather than resolve to spend my life in this miserable country I would renounce all consular honours, which I daily consign to a hundred thousand devils, to be able to live on a quarter of what I have now in a peaceful country where at least the air is healthy.'[20] And he applied to the Foreign Office for permission to take home leave, on the grounds that there was nothing for him to do at Patras and that his health was suffering.[21] But while waiting for a reply he decided, in the middle of November, to visit the southernmost Ionian island, Zante. There he and David got the free use of a splendid house from the steward of the owner, who had gone to Venice. They had only to pay for the food prepared for them by the owner's chief cook, and they had 'absolutely nothing to do but eat, drink and sleep' while they gave moral support to the young English consul, Wright, 'a perfect gentleman', whose beautiful young wife was mortally ill with consumption. Society, however, 'neither Turk nor French, but an unfortunate mixture of both' was dull because the women were confined to their houses 'more strictly than in a Muslim harem. They are not allowed to sing, dance or even play an instrument, and they only go out masked.' They found the men living in the past century, full of useless ceremonies. The day after their arrival 'all the foreign consuls came to pay formal visits in court dress', and Jack was delighted to find not a single one of them at home when he tried to return their calls next day.[22] They hoped for better things from the Russian commandant, but he turned out to be a soldier to his finger tips, who spoke only Russian and German and whose weekly 'at home' was so ghastly that, after trying it once, Jack and David determined never to attend again, preferring to stay at home playing cribbage. But there were one or two more cultured Russian officers who organised enjoyable evenings, with Russian soldiers performing national songs and dances.

Isaac turned up on 12 December, on his way to Constantinople, accompanied by a king's messenger with orders for Jack to go to Corfu to await the arrival there of Charles Arbuthnot, who had been appointed ambassador at the Porte. At Corfu they were delighted to find Captain William Leake of the Royal Artillery – who was related through his aunt's marriage to the Lee family in Smyrna and, therefore, indirectly to them, through their aunt's marriage into the same family. Leake had been sent out, with the agreement of the Turks, to make maps and gather military intelligence, and was on his way to deliver a letter from Nelson to Ali Pasha in Ioannina. David – who had got to know him in London – had heard with joy of this appointment, revealing, albeit indirectly, that he had been finding his brother's company a bit of a strain. 'A third person,' he had written to his uncle, 'is indeed absolutely wanting in a country like this, for there is always a chance that one out of the three will be able to keep the others in good humour which, between the two best disposed persons in the world, cannot always be preserved in a spot so destitute of recreation.'[23] David found plenty to interest him in Corfu, and told his mother that he had no desire to return home yet.[24] The parades for the annual festival of the island's patron Saint Spyridion, and the celebration by

the occupying forces of the Tsar's birthday on the same day, provided
an exciting spectacle; but his calvinism was outraged by the former,
with its veneration of a corpse in its ceremonial coffin, 'its horrible
face visible, black and disfigured, the mouth all crooked in a frightful
grimace' and the people with 'more faith in this miserable mummy
than in our Saviour.' He thought the local opera 'truly very respectable'
with an orchestra 'as good as that of Sadler's Wells', but its limited
repertoire rather boring.[25] The rub was in the local society. There was
'company enough and parties enough to fill up an evening with the
bustle of a rout, but when one cannot in the whole list of them
address oneself to an honest man or woman, what pleasure can a
person of the most common feeling of propriety find in their society?'[26]
He found their 'morals so depraved and so blatant that however small
a spark of good principles a foreigner might himself have, the disgust
he must feel will protect him from temptation. The women only wait
to be married before they give themselves up to all possible excesses,
and there are such large numbers of them leading wicked lives that a
good woman, if one is to be found, is a rarity of no worth in their
eyes.'[27] When Carnival came round David and Jack could not 'degrade'
themselves to take part, for even 'the leading people of the place are
seen to mingle with their valets and hairdressers unmasked.'[28] Even the
Russian army, it seems, could not be counted on to behave properly,
and Jack's only apparent diplomatic task, to uphold the dignity of
Britain without giving them offence, could be difficult. There was a
serious incident when a visiting British officer received from a Russian
general 'an insult of the grossest nature'. Failing to get an apology he
demanded the usual satisfaction, and Jack and David were both present
next morning at dawn. Fortunately, the Russian could not face a duel
with pistols and 'made a most contrite and humble apology'. David
considered his 'conduct through the whole affair was pusillanimous to
the last degree and it has made on the people here an impression very
much to [Russian] discredit & to the advantage of the English.'[29]

Early in January 1805 Jack at last received a reaction to his reports
to the Foreign Office. He was gratified to be told that 'His Majesty has
been pleased to approve of the diligence and zeal you have exerted in
procuring information, and of the manner in which you appear to
have conducted your intercourse with the Turkish governors in Albania
and the Morea.' The Foreign Office, however, had been warned by the
ambassador at Petersburg that the Russians were becoming suspicious
of Jack's activities, and they therefore cautioned Jack not to overdo his
generosity to pashas: 'It is certainly by no means the intention of His
Majesty's Government that you should risk, by any misjudged

parsimony, a diminution of the influence which it is so desirable for you to acquire ... but it is extremely important that you should use the utmost circumspection in the distribution of your presents, as any thing which bore the appearance of profusion or prodigality might excite unfavourable suspicions' both in the Russians and in the Turks. Nevertheless, they instructed Jack to take 'every favourable opportunity to impress upon the Turkish governors the propriety of treating the Greeks with greater lenity', but also to 'use your utmost exertions to confirm the Greeks in their allegiance to their lawful government.' He was also to assure the Greeks 'that if their conduct is open and loyal it will be the endeavour of [both Britain and Russia] to protect them from oppression.' Furthermore, Jack was to 'abstain most carefully from' interfering in Ali Pasha's quarrels with agas and other pashas, and hint to him that his attitude towards the Porte and the Russians may have been the cause of the delay in responding to his requests for material military help.[30]

Jack was by no means averse to trying to get better treatment for the Greeks; but he was not at all keen on saying anything which might suggest that they would get official support against Turkish oppression. He did not trust them. 'The Greeks are vile enough to promise anything and to perform nothing' he wrote in reply to the Foreign Office:

> It is not natural to suppose that those who by supporting the Turks prolong their misery can be popular amongst them. The only way, therefore, of establishing real and solid influence with the people would be to promise them the effective relief which they expect the French to give them, and that, they will conceive, can only be effected by taking the country from the Turks. As long as that strong measure is not to be resorted to, and the safety of the country is entrusted to the efforts of the Turks and the loyalty of the Greeks, it appears to me that any appearance of courting the latter would only tend to increase their anger as it would excite in them a magnified idea of their consequence.[31]

But he was equally cynical in his opinion of the Turkish pashas, who, he knew, were interested only in making money. This meant that he could hope to gain influence with them only by buying it, although he admitted that even then there was no guarantee that they would keep their side of any bargain indefinitely. So far as persuading them to show more leniency to the Greeks, he thought it best to apply pressure in Constantinople.

⊕

When Leake returned to Corfu, on 16 January 1805, he reported to Jack that Ali Pasha had seemed to understand that it might not be politic for Britain to respond favourably to his requests for material help just then, and had assured Leake that this would not affect his friendly feelings towards Britain. He had promised, for what that was worth, if given proper material support 'to engage with all the forces he could spare in any expedition against the enemies of England, as far as Naples and Malta to the southward and to the north as far as the frontiers of Russia.' But he had stressed that he thought the help he had given in expelling the French should be recognised by granting him the governership of the former Venetian coastal towns.[32] News had just reached Corfu of another break out by the French fleet from Toulon, and it was assumed that it would be heading for the Adriatic. Although unable to persuade Count Mocenigo of the need, in such circumstances, to drop his opposition to Ali Pasha and do everything possible to secure his support, Jack decided to go back to Ioannina to try to get this. He and David, first destroying their papers in case there was a French invasion in their absence, left Corfu on 10 February and reached Ioannina on the 13th after four days of difficult travelling accompanied by Ross, the king's messenger and their servant William. Landing on the coast at Sajiada, a place where Ali Pasha's writ did not run, they found themselves at the mercy of people 'entirely lawless and devoid of any sense of order or civilization.' They had to wait there overnight while horses were fetched from a village some 14 miles away and could find shelter only in a kind of shop filled with packages of figs and raisins, brought by a Turk who was optimistically hoping to sell them 'in this miserable place'. Their night was disturbed by rats gnawing at the produce and jackals howling in the hills. They reached Filiatis next night, 'half dead with hunger', where they passed another miserable night in a hovel. The following day a mule fell off a bridge into the river 10 feet below, fortunately without harm to itself, but soaking their bedding it was carrying. Some ten hours later they were overtaken by nightfall near a village where they asked an old woman for shelter. At first she thought they were 'bad men', but eventually she relented and lit a fire. Jack gave her a gold piece next morning, which called down blessings on their heads.

Their fourth day was a struggle through storms and floods before they could reach Ioannina and comfortable quarters in which to recover. Ali Pasha was at Tepelini but, declining Jack's offer to meet him there, returned specially to Ioannina, arriving on the 19th and bringing with him a considerable force of Albanian soldiers which, he made clear, were for opposing any French landing. He also made clear, however, that this was out of respect for the British and that he was still bitter over Russian behaviour towards him. He told Jack that if the Russians wanted his cooperation they must stop interfering in his domestic quarrels, and he must be allowed to organise the defence of the coastal towns. He was prepared to give one of his sons as a hostage to prove that he had no intention of annexing them. Jack had some sympathy with Ali Pasha, but could offer him nothing.[33] Although it was obvious that the atmosphere was not suitable, he carried out his instructions by raising with him the matter of the oppressive treatment of the Greeks, which not surprisingly was badly received. Jack in fact, although having no particular love for the Turks, took the view that 'the Greeks, considered as a nation, in their present state cannot be kept in order but by a government like the Turkish'[34], and went so far as to tell the Foreign Office that it was 'the fierce nature of the people [Ali Pasha] is endeavouring to reduce to order rather than his own disposition that obliges him sometimes to be cruel.'[35]

Jack learnt, after three weeks at Ioannina, that the French fleet had again put back into Toulon. This meant that the immediate alarm was over and Jack and David returned to Corfu, undertaking a journey almost as hard as the outward trek. Snow was now the problem, and they were held up for a whole day in one of Ali Pasha's blockhouses kept by a small garrison, during which they experienced a severe earthquake. Jack was determined, however, to see for himself the country the Suliots had for so long defended against Ali Pasha, and to assess its military significance in the event of a French invasion. They spent another day struggling through ankle deep snow to do this. At Parga they had to wait a few hours for a boat, which they passed in a house where the owner used their presence for personal gain by charging the locals two *paras* (roughly one penny) a time to come in to view these strange foreigners. David thought this was valuing them *le* rather cheaply since 'they pay more at the Exeter Change* to see the monkeys and considering all the circumstances one may fairly set down at least 10 paras for the sight of 5 persons with hats and boots on.'[36]

On their return to Corfu they were required to spend some days in quarantine, because an outbreak of the plague in parts of the mainland had alarmed the island authorities. There they met a Greek doctor

---

* Exeter Change was a menagerie owned by a Mr Pidcock on the site in London now occupied by the Strand Palace Hotel.

who told them a great deal about the Suliots and their treatment by
Ali Pasha, which David used years later in a published novel, *Photo the
Suliot*. Once free from quarantine, Jack again tried, unsuccessfully, to
persuade Count Mocenigo to adopt a more reasonable line with Ali
Pasha. He complained to the Foreign Office that Mocenigo's attitude
was a reprehensible departure from the broad basis of disinterested
policy on which Britain and Russia should be acting. The truth was,
he explained, that Ali Pasha was afraid that Russia wanted to gain
control of Albania, and it was therefore only the British who had any
hope of influencing him, because 'we may govern him by opinion,
they can do it only by force of arms.' In Jack's view, successful
opposition to a French attack on this part of the Ottoman empire,
which would probably come from the north, could be assured only if
the pashas felt they were in effect defending their own territories.
While they might have their own domestic quarrels one with another,
an external threat would unite them. They would have no interest in
working with the French; they would prefer to be members of a state
whose authority they could sometimes resist than under a foreign
power which might remove them. Proof of Ali Pasha's attitude could
be seen in his readiness to provide such large numbers of troops. It
was true he had only discharged his duty to the sultan; but, like other
pashas, this was at the risk of losing his men and, therefore, his ability
to defend his independence. Jack also pointed out that, despite his
suspicion of the Russo-Turkish alliance, Ali Pasha had zealously shown
his willingness to be friends with Britain. Jack thought this should be
rewarded, perhaps by letting him have as a gift the arms and
ammunition he had asked for at his own expense.[37] Moreover, Jack had
been offered facilities for raising a corps of Albanian troops, which he
thought could be used to release some of the British garrison in Malta
for active service against the French, and he suggested he should be
authorised to take this up. He thought they could become very
serviceable men under the direction of British officers, that he himself
should be given the rank of colonel in the British army for the purpose,
with the privilege of choosing the officers, and that he should return
to England to discuss the details.[38] Nothing ever came of this.

Arbuthnot turned up at last on 2 June. He too saw Mocenigo and
at least got him to agree to his sending Jack back to Ioannina with a
personal letter, which he showed to Mocenigo, tactfully inviting Ali
Pasha to be less distrustful of the Russians and to stop fighting the
agas with whom they were in friendly contact. With this Jack was able
to gain considerable influence over Ali Pasha, who had obviously made
up his mind – at least for the present – that friendship with Britain was

in his best interests. He was full of protestations that his quarrels with some agas were purely domestic and of no concern to the Russians; and he blamed unruly Albanian officers, whom he promised to discipline, for the complaints about him from the former Venetian towns. Reporting this to Arbuthnot, Jack repeated his belief that it was Greeks, acting as Russian agents, who were deliberately stirring up trouble; and he suggested that even if one accepted that Ali Pasha was not really loyal, 'it will be found that the Porte derives from him much greater security in this quarter than they would from one in a less independent situation.'[39]

Jack might have done well, a few decades later, in the 'Great Game' – he had a grasp of the realities of power politics in the context of tribal warfare. He may perhaps have been influenced by Ali Pasha's gesture in presenting David with a magnificent horse complete with harness in Turkish style, while himself getting the same from the bishop of Ioannina; but he was nevertheless quite prepared to stand up to Ali Pasha when he thought humanitarianism demanded it. On a visit to the island in the lake, he and David found marooned there '60 poor Suliot women and their children', captured in the last phase of the war against them two years earlier, and that they had neither land nor money. In the monastery they found the wife and children of one of the Suliot chiefs actually held as prisoners, and the twelve year old son, who had seen his father put to death, flung himself at their feet thinking they had come to kill him now. 'It was I assure you' David wrote 'the most touching scene to see the misery of these innocent people whose only crime had been to love their homeland.' Jack gave them some money and later got Ali Pasha to 'as good as promise to give these poor people some ground to cultivate like the other peasants of this province.' It is doubtful that Ali Pasha actually did so; but David felt better believing they had 'lifted from their misery people one could only admire for their fortitude.'[40] Jack also persuaded Ali Pasha to free from their chains a gang of Suliot prisoners undergoing hard labour near Ioannina, and send them with their wives and children to villages near Tepelini instead, while keeping one of their chiefs as hostage for good behaviour. But even here Ali proved less than sincere. Although these unfortunate Suliots were unchained and sent north, Jack discovered later that they were then put back in chains, which so annoyed him that he wrote to Ali Pasha 'as a friend to Your Excellency' to warn him 'that if it is your sincere desire to secure to yourself the good wishes of the British Government you will only succeed by keeping your word with them.'[41]

David based part of his novel (loosely) on these experiences, and his meetings with Ali Pasha. He was very impressed by the pasha's palace on its rocky promontory jutting out into the lake, particularly a large room with crimson sofas 'magnificently and elegantly embroidered in gold' ranged round three sides and a huge Gobelin tapestry from one of the French royal palaces on the floor. 'The ceiling and wainscotting are profusely gilded and variously painted, but without being at all heavy ... on the fourth side is a sort of closet where Ali Pasha's turban, a sort of skull cap, is exposed to view, & in a little nasty cupboard close to the fine embroidered sofa we saw a dirty fellow shut up a greasy comb he had just been using.' On a jetty over the water there was a 'kiosk or pleasure house ... very elegantly furnished and divided into several compartments all paved with marble, in the centre of which a fountain continually playing keeps the whole place quite cool.' When they went to call on the pasha in his palace they 'were conveyed to & from it in a fine gilded boat brought from Constantinople.' He thought it a pity that the women made up their faces with thick layers of paint and blackened their eyebrows to meet in a ferocious frown 'in such a manner as to disfigure the prettiest features'; but he admired their headdresses which he thought 'the milliners of Bond Street would be very happy to imitate.'[42] Leake rejoined them on 28 June and, on one of the day-long excursions they made together from Ioannina, they came across (without realising it) what was obviously the site now known to be that of ancient Dodone, situated 'in a valley at the foot of a high mountain and surrounded by lower hills' with ruins of 'a square citadel flanked by towers, and a theatre and remains of walls of dressed stones [which] could hold four thousand people.'[43]

While at Ioannina, Jack was advised by Straton – who was expecting soon to go to England and not return to Constantinople – to apply for the post of secretary of embassy. He did so, also asking Lord Radstock to support his candidature. But he made it a condition that a post should be found for David first because 'although I wish from the bottom of my soul for a change, I should rather remain here all my life than abandon David, to whom I owe so much of the credit if I should retain any here.'[44] This compliment was not solely a demonstration of brotherly love, for it was David who had been keeping the meticulously detailed notes of their travels on which Jack based his official reports, and compiling all the factual information they could gather about the economies and demographies of the regions they visited. David, however, would have none of this self sacrifice from his brother. Having read what Jack wrote to his uncle, and being allowed to add his own message, he said that he could 'never consent that any consideration touching myself should induce Jack to sacrifice any personal advantage accruing to him ... I trust he will not risk an enviable situation by persisting in conditions for me, who will always in time get something somewhere.'

⊕

After a short break in August in the village of Kalaritis, Jack and Leake decided to go to Salonika via the north of Albania to complete their knowledge of terrain with potential military importance. Leake set off alone first, Jack and David following on 19 September, stopping first at Permeti – where they were put up by Ali Pasha's son and enjoyed a day's hare hunting. After this they left the area controlled by Ali Pasha, and found that his letter recommending them to the protection of neighbouring pashas had only limited value. At their first overnight stop the village headman's first reaction to their arrival was to order Jack to unbuckle his sword, an order which Jack thought it advisable to obey. He was in fact unable to read the letter, but a present of a good luck charm and a half sugar loaf finally 'softened his haughtiness'. Next day they hurried through a village where many were sick with the plague and laid out in straw shelters along the road; but at Berat, the seat of Ibrahim Pasha, their reception made them feel very uneasy. Jack gave the pasha the obligatory present, on this occasion a handsome snuff box, but received in exchange only a dozen lemons tied up in a dirty handkerchief. The pasha then made them hang around like beggars for more than an hour before reluctantly allocating them a bare granary for the night. This had a leaky roof, windows without glass and a rotten floor through which the wind whistled. They had suffered from malaria in Ioannina and next morning they all felt feverish and looked yellow, so, fearing a recurrence, they fled back to Permeti. There, on the advice of Ali Pasha's son, who told them that there was serious unrest in north Albania, and also anxious to get out of a region in which the plague was present, they decided to give up their idea of exploring the north, especially as they now had word that Leake was ill with fever on the coast. So they set off towards Salonika by mountain tracks already under snow. But Jack had other reasons for abandoning the plan to explore northern Albania. He was running out of money, having been unable to get any in either Ioannina or Berat (where obviously the locals had no faith in English promissory notes at that time); and, while 'as a private traveller' he might have been prepared to put up with his treatment, he thought it wrong to expose himself to it 'as an accredited agent of Great Britain'.[45]

Even now, however, they were not out of trouble. Before reaching
the plain of Macedonia they had a particularly unpleasant experience
in a primitive village where they had to find shelter for the night. It
was inhabited only by women, 'furies' David called them, and on
approaching what looked like the most important house they were
greeted with curses and threats by the group spinning wool outside.
Desperate for shelter and food, they made offers of generous payment;
but it was only the language of Ali Pasha's *firman*, with its threats of
punishment to anyone not responding to it, that finally convinced the
women to give them shelter. It was perhaps understandable that,
without their menfolk – and one of them expecting to give birth any
minute – they did not want a group of strange foreign men in their
midst. Even when Jack and his party were finally installed in the
house, they were subjected to shouts of abuse from those outside. They
passed a miserable night, fully clothed, in the same room as the women
and children, two of whom were suffering from whooping cough; but
they left next morning under a shower of blessings after giving their
'hostess' a present of gold.[46] They finally reached Salonika on 9
October where, after a week of plan and counter-plan, Jack decided
to send David off to Constantinople for a rest while he stayed to await
an answer to his request to take home leave.

David was able, from Constantinople, to visit James in Smyrna.
Although he had been too young when taken to England in 1787 to
have clear memories of it, he was invaded by 'a crowd of feelings both
happy and sad' when shown the old family house at Sidiköy: 'I would
have been insensitive,' he wrote to his mother '... not to have felt, in
a place which has always been the home of virtue, strengthened in
resolution to copy the example.' He was delighted to be told that he
reminded everyone of his mother.[47] James awakened in him 'the love
of study and sedentary occupations which I confess all this travelling
had weakened';[48] and meeting Robert Walpole,* 'a young man with the
most perfect manners' he 'blushed to my ears' to realise his own
ignorance beside one so well educated.[49]

On David's return to Salonika (29 January 1806) Jack set out
immediately for Constantinople, leaving David to look after the few
consular affairs needing attention. But David had received a big
disappointment. A letter from Hamilton, now in the Foreign Office,
had reached Jack, and David had to tell James, 'my aspiring hopes as
to the Office are completely b...d'. Hamilton had advised Jack 'to give

---

* Robert Walpole, 1781–1856, grandson of Horace Walpole, Earl of Orford, Greek
  scholar, later author of two important travel books.

up all thoughts of placing [David] in Downing Street – so very seldom is it that those who enter in the situation of clerk can ever rise to places of trust & responsibility – at least not without much greater interest than could not fail to ensure a much more rapid rise in any other profession.'[50] David confessed to his mother that he was worried about his future. While he was all right so long as Jack held his present post, should that come to an end he did not know what he could do: 'The idea of being subordinate to just anyone is unpleasant.'[51] And he was apprehensive on other grounds. He was expecting that he and Jack would be heading north into Bosnia soon to encourage resistance to any invasion which might come from Dalmatia, now under French control. To James he wrote:

> It is natural to anticipate the fatigues and probable dangers of the occupations which may fall in our way, but don't you agree with me that the soul is much more at home in even dangerous activity than in inglorious ease and indolence? ... I confess with shame my distrust of my fortitude and resolutions in moments of peril. That is no reason, however, for wishing to avoid the trial of it, because nobody knows what he is capable of before he is put to the test; and, besides that, the virtues of fortitude and perseverance are only to be acquired by practice.[52]

Meanwhile, however, the Turks had decided to renew diplomatic relations with France, and Arbuthnot ordered Jack to return to Ioannina to try to keep Ali Pasha from succumbing again to French blandishments. Jack thought that, in the continued absence of the practical military help which Ali Pasha had been requesting, he had little chance of success; but he did as he was told, collected David in Salonika and reached Ioannina in May 1806. There he found Ali Pasha entertaining two Frenchmen, François Pouqueville and Julien Bessières. They were an interesting pair, but Jack's correspondence does not reveal whether he was aware of their background. Both had been captured by Barbary pirates on the way back to France from Egypt after the battle of the Nile. Bessières had been sold into slavery to Ali Pasha but had escaped after three years to Corfu and been handed over to the Turks, from whom he had obtained his release by the intervention of the Russians. Pouqueville was a doctor who had been given considerable freedom of movement, although a Turkish prisoner, in exchange for his medical services, and was eventually released and allowed to return to France. Jack immediately assumed they were there at Ali Pasha's invitation, but in fact Bessières had turned up as an official emissary bearing gifts from Bonaparte and a request for the pasha's support in re-establishing relations between France and Turkey. Pouqueville had been appointed French consul general at Ioannina with a *berat* from the Porte, which gave him a rank above all other foreign consuls in Albania. Ali Pasha assured Jack that he did not welcome their presence, and he appeared to be annoyed that Pouqueville was busy distributing French propaganda, and currying favour amongst the Greeks by providing medical treatment without charge. Jack was suspicious, with justification, for Ali Pasha, as usual, was keeping all his options open; but he could only accept the pasha's warm assurances of continuing friendship for Britain and his need of British advice. Ali Pasha, however, was still having trouble with the Russians in Corfu. Jack sent David over to remonstrate with Mocenigo, but this had no effect. He realized that his own relations with Ali Pasha were in jeopardy unless he could prove British friendship with practical aid and, in particular, by bringing Mocenigo round to a better attitude. Therefore, in early June, he decided to send David home to England with despatches, and to withdraw himself to Patras. Jack's motives were mixed. He had heard of the formation, following William Pitt's death on 23 January 1806, of the 'Minstry of all the Talents' under Lord Grenville, in which Charles James Fox became foreign secretary. 'Unknown as we are to all the new Ministers' wrote Jack to Lord Radstock, 'I thought it as well to profit of the necessity to make them acquainted with the state of things here to send [David], by which means he may be known and get something decided about my situation.' Naturally he hoped that his uncle would approve and would do what he could to use his own influence. But he declared himself 'less anxious for myself than for David who I wish to see reap the same benefits I do, having shared all the difficulties & dangers of my mission', which, he added, 'have hitherto been nothing in comparison to what they will be if the French, as is likely, make some attempt on Turkey.'[53] Jack, it seems, was also anxious to get his young brother out of the dangers he saw ahead.

CHAPTER SEVEN

James and Harford Jones 1806–1807
'This very clever man.'

Constantinople in 1806 and 1807 was the seat of political turbulence in which the lives of Jack, David and Isaac were dramatically changed. At the same time, James's life took a completely new and unexpected turn.

When Isaac in 1804, virtually bankrupt, received the appointment from the Levant Company of consul general at Constantinople it seemed that the family's troubles were at an end. His friends rallied round to help pay off his debts and, although distressed to be leaving his wife and daughters behind for possibly several years, he had set off from London in a more cheerful and optimistic frame of mind than he had displayed for some time. When he turned up in Zante in December of that year while Jack and David were there, the latter had reported to his mother: 'Never have I seen him looking so well and so cheerful ... His journey has given him new strength and the bearing of a young man.'[1] (He was then in his 55th year.) He had then made his way to Smyrna from where James had reported him performing 'all the duties of a young man during Carnival: he has danced, he has set everyone going ... everyone says ... that he looks more like my brother than my father.'[2] But once he had reached Constantinople he was again beset by problems.

It was Arbuthnot, whom he had met in Vienna on his way out, who had suggested his going to Smyrna to see his relations, and had advised him to wait there until he reached Constantinople and could sort out some difficulties the Turks were making over the appointment of a consul general as well as an ambassador. Isaac, however, had become impatient, and he and James had moved there in April 1805, arriving before Arbuthnot (chapter 5). Isaac was treated by the Turks with friendly civility, but he was not allowed to exercise his official functions. Moreover, he was caught up in jealousies within the Company, and on Arbuthnot's arrival he found himself in an anomalous position. His appointment had been clumsily handled in London. Ministers had agreed with the Company that Isaac should be their servant, independent of the ambassador, taking orders only from them and dealing direct with the Turks on commercial matters unless the backing of the ambassador was required over a particular issue. However, there had been no prior consultation over these arrangements with either the Turks or Arbuthnot, and the latter, when he discovered what had been arranged, was unwilling to have a consul general not under his control. The Turks, for their part, wanted to deal with only one British representative. Fortunately, Arbuthnot was a kindly man, who did not want to see Isaac deprived of an income he so obviously needed. He therefore proposed to the Foreign Office, with Isaac's full agreement, that the appointment should be a joint one as both the Company's representative and the king's consul general, with the corollary that in the latter capacity he must take his orders from the ambassador. When David reached Constantinople from Salonika in November he was able to tell his mother that there was 'no gayer gallant in the whole quarter [of Pera]. He flirts with all the women, who prefer him to all the beaux, and I can tell you that there are very few young men who can make themselves as agreeable as him.' Perhaps suddenly aware of the effect this might have on a deserted wife he added: 'I don't think you need be jealous, for it is only his amusement to play the gallant.'[3] And as Isaac had also obtained the East India Company's representation at Constantinople, with its additional income, he had every reason to feel pleased with himself.

As it turned out, Isaac had little more than a year in which to enjoy this new prosperity and begin making plans to bring his wife and daughters out to join him; but during that year he had the additional pleasure of again seeing his two eldest sons. Jack's visit was brief, but James stayed longer. He had been unable to settle down in Smyrna on returning there in August 1805 after his previous visit (chapter 5). David, on his visit to Smyrna at the end of the year had tried, unsuccessfully, to tease James out of his infatuation with Maria, but had ended by deciding that his brother's 'affections could not be better directed, for she is loveable from every point of view and has received an education from Mr Usko which makes her even more estimable.'[4] They both, however, had realised that the only sensible course would be for James to get right away. It had taken several more months of restless indecision before finally, in June 1806, he fled back to Constantinople to put himself in his father's hands. He had no idea then of what he would do next. He knew that he did not want to spend the rest of his life as a merchant in Smyrna, but he did want to marry Maria. He was going to have to wait several years before either his or her father would agree to this and, in the meantime, he would have to find a way of earning a decent living. His immediate motive had simply been to escape from the torture of being in such close physical proximity to the girl he could not yet make his wife. But at Constantinople he met Harford Jones* and his life was changed completely.

Harford Jones had been the East India Company's representative in Baghdad for some years, until removed because of a dispute with the pasha. He was now on his way back to England and an uncertain future. He was ambitious, and believed he would be able to get a position in Persia once he could persuade the government at home to listen to him. He had considerable charisma, and James was obviously captivated by this man who had lived for the last twenty or so years in the Levant in close relations with people whose history and way of life he wanted to know more about. Harford Jones would have been flattered by such admiring interest, and probably saw in James – eighteen years his junior, with a lively mind and outgoing nature – a sort of substitute for the son he did not have. (He had a natural son, born of a local woman with whom he had lived in Basra, of whom he was fond, but this was not quite the same thing as having a true heir.) He certainly saw in him a very acceptable aide should he succeed in being sent to Persia as a diplomatic envoy of the British government, and he obviously made this clear to James when he offered to take him back with him to England in October. James, even with no certain employment in view, eagerly accepted, writing to his mother about 'this very clever man who has many connections and good friends, and who has given me clear proofs that his friendship for me and his promises are sincere.' He hoped there would be 'some little hole [in her house] into which I can burrow: I shall be happy with a corner of the pantry or the coal cellar so long as I don't disturb you.' But Harford Jones had invited him to Herefordshire for Christmas 'where he has promised to introduce me to a crowd of respectable people and families. So much the better since that will advance us in the world.'[3]

Meanwhile, however, Isaac and Jack were about to be caught up in the political developments which Arbuthnot had seen coming some months earlier.

Convinced that the sultan was planning to take advantage of Bonaparte's military successes to ally himself again with the French,

---

* Harford Jones, 1767–1847, made a baronet in 1807, became Sir Harford Jones-Brydges in 1826 when he added the extra name in memory of his descent through his maternal grandmother from the Brydges of Old Caldwell, Herefordshire.

and renew war with his old enemy Russia, Arbuthnot had appealed to London for a naval force to be sent out to demonstrate to the Turks that they were playing with fire. A force of five ships of the line arrived off the Dardanelles at the end of November. This fleet was under the command of Admiral Sir Thomas Louis,* who took one of them, HMS Canopus, up to Constantinople to join HMS Endymion. But war between Russia and Turkey had already erupted, with a Russian invasion of Moldavia. This did not mean that Britain was automatically at war with Turkey; but Arbuthnot, whose wife had recently died, leaving him with four small children to look after, and in such distress that he was almost incapable of making diplomatic decisions, lost his nerve. After sending the Russian Ambassador to safety in Canopus he himself boarded Endymion with his family and personal staff. He then summoned Isaac and all the men of the Company on board for a meeting and, without warning or giving them a chance to collect their wives and families, he got the captain to cut his cable after dark and slip away to join the rest of the fleet off the Dardanelles. There they were joined in February 1807 by another five ships of the line under command of Admiral Sir John Duckworth[†] who, with Arbuthnot and Isaac on board his flagship, sailed up to Constantinople to try to frighten or bombard the Turks – who by then were in formal alliance with the enemy France – into submission. This venture was a disastrous failure and Duckworth, suffering considerable damage to ships and men on the way back to the Dardanelles, withdrew to Malta. Here Isaac and the Levant Company men were landed (and remained for two years). Arbuthnot sailed off to England and Duckworth went off to support a British military expedition mounting an attack on Egypt. Diplomatic relations between Britain and Turkey were naturally now suspended.

While all this had been going on, Jack was in Zante. After sending David home from Ioannina in June 1806 he himself had returned to Patras. There he had fallen seriously ill and had taken himself off to Zante to recuperate. When he learned of the outbreak of hostilities

---

* Thomas Louis, 1759–1807, entered the navy in 1770 and was present at the Battle of the Nile in 1798. Promoted rear-admiral in 1804, he was created baronet in 1806 for his part in the Battle of San Domingo in that year. He died off the coast of Egypt not long after this expedition to the Dardanelles.

† John Thomas Duckworth, 1748–1817, took part in the Battle of Quiberon Bay in 1795, was promoted rear-admiral in 1799 and made KB in 1801. He was commander-in-chief at Jamaica 1803–05 and commanded in the Battle of San Domingo in 1806. Governor and commander-in-chief Newfoundland 1810–13, created baronet 1813.

between Turkey and Russia he returned to Patras, and was readying himself to go off again to Ioannina to see Ali Pasha – who had taken control of Preveza – when he heard of the Duckworth fiasco. Jack realised now that he could be of no further use in Greece, and indeed was at risk of being made a prisoner, so he sent a message to Sir Alexander Ball in Malta for a ship to rescue him. Unfortunately Jack discovered only much later that Leake, who had gone to Salonika, had not heard of the events in Constantinople in time to escape being interned.

By the spring of 1807, therefore, the course of the Morier fortunes had changed fundamentally. Isaac and Jack were together in Malta, with no idea of what would now happen to them. David was back in England, also facing an uncertain future. Only James, having hitched himself to Harford Jones's wagon, seemed to have a chance of making some sort of career for himself.

CHAPTER EIGHT

James 1807–1809

'A life such as I never dreamed of.'

Back in England at the end of 1806, Harford Jones set about trying to persuade the British government to take Persia seriously. In 1804 the Russians had invaded the Persian Caucasian provinces. At that time there was no permanent British diplomatic mission in Persia and it had been through Harford Jones, then in Baghdad, that the shah had vainly appealed for British help under a treaty concluded in 1801. Rebuffed by the British, the shah had made overtures to the French, and Harford Jones was now intent on persuading the government in London of the serious threat this posed for India. This took time and, during the first couple of months after their arrival in England, James's mind, according to his brother David, was 'in such a state of suspense as to unfit him for serious application to any particular object.'[1] But by February 1807 Harford Jones had not only succeeded in his self appointed mission, he had also managed to secure for himself the post of special envoy from King George to the shah. James, now aged 24, was to go with him as his private secretary.

There were hitches, however. The government changed in March, William Cavendish Bentinck, 3rd Duke of Portland, becoming prime minister and George Canning foreign secretary. The appointment of Harford Jones was not confirmed until May. Then the East India Company, who would be paying for the accompanying staff, insisted on appointing their own choices as secretaries. Harford Jones reluctantly agreed to accept a Major Smith as his Public Secretary* instead of Charles Vaughan† (who himself had no objection); but he

---

* Public secretary was the equivalent of secretary of embassy or legation, ie the holder would take charge in the absence of the head of mission.

† Charles Richard Vaughan, 1774–1849, a fellow of All Souls College, Oxford, had met Harford Jones on his Asian travels 1801–03. He subsequently entered the diplomatic service and was ambassador in Switzerland 1823–24 and the USA 1825–35. He was knighted in 1833.

threatened to resign if James was not made his private secretary – and won. Then Russia – by the Treaty of Tilsit in July – became an ally of France, which meant that the original intention of going overland via Petersburg had to be abandoned. After much debate it was decided they would travel by sea to Bombay, and then to Bushire on the Gulf coast of Persia from where they would go overland to Tehran; and in August Harford Jones was made a baronet.

James and Smith went down to Portsmouth at the beginning of September to make the final arrangements. HMS Sapphire had been allocated for what would be a lengthy voyage, and James was unpleasantly surprised to find it was a rather small 24-gun sloop in which his accommodation would be cramped. 'We shall all swing together, not on a gallows, but quietly in cots' he told his mother: 'I must own I was not prepared for such a treat, & I hoped to have some independent hole to have stowed my noddle in.' But Captain George Davis turned out to be a pleasant enough man, a 'little Welsh Captain ... [who] has none of the airs of a desperate fellow, but is very polite & good natured' with a scientific turn of mind and a knowledge of French.[2] James also got on well with Smith, a Persian scholar who helped him with his study of that language. Sir Harford, however, was delayed in London and they had to kick their heels for several weeks without even an explanation from him, or any indication when to expect him. James became disgruntled 'at being detained at this celebrated though infernal place'[3] in a 'very disagreeable inn'.[4] Whether from bad food, over indulgence in alcohol, or a combination of the two, his liver gave him trouble and he told his mother he was going to wean himself off drinking wine:

> at most it is but an artificial want, & the body can well subsist without it, for we see that to be the case in many nations whose habits of life are infinitely more laborious than ours, & amongst those peoples who drink wine habitually we find that there are many more vices which spring from such habits only, which to non bibbers are totally unknown. As for instance, the liver complaint almost wholly proceeds from excess of wine ... and it is very certain that if the want of wine be a privation it will be felt when the man who is habituated to drink gets into a country where none is drunk. As such may be my case, I must own I should much like to leave it off entirely.

He had discovered, however that Captain Davis had laid in a great stock of wine for the voyage, and 'as it will appear unsociable not to help him out in it, I fear I shall find the temptation to join in the circle too great for my philosophy.'[5] Although there is no evidence that James ever became an excessive drinker, there is equally none to suggest that he ever succeeded, except when circumstances gave him no choice, in giving up such a pleasant indulgence. Nor did he let his disgruntlement at being stuck in Portsmouth kill his habit of shrewdly observing life around him. A convoy for India was assembling and he noted that:

> the place is full of E[ast] I[ndia] passengers: writers, lawyers, cadets, judges, ladies who are going for husbands & ladies who go to get rid of husbands, men with fortunes & men without fortunes, in short 'tis difficult to communicate the different characters who are going to the land of *milk & honey*.[6]

At a local ball he found all the beauty & fashion of Gosport & Portsmouth assembled:

> ... The great subject of admiration was a young lady from London to whom the country ladies seemed to look up to as the zenith of excellence, & all I could discover in her was that she was the summit of stupidity. It is not a little amusing to see how very powerful are the attractions of a stray London Miss among the good people of a country town, nor is it less amusing to observe how much this said Miss seems to feel the consequence her London bonnets & dresses give her.[7]

The party eventually sailed on 27 October 1807. By then James had begun to fear that the whole expedition would come to nought. Up to now British relations with Persia had been conducted by agents of the East India Company acting as representatives of the governor general of India, and it was in this capacity that a young army officer, Captain John Malcolm,* had been sent there in 1800 – when Bonaparte's invasion of Egypt was believed to be a prelude to an attack upon India. Malcolm had succeeded in concluding a treaty in 1801, in which the shah undertook to keep the French out of Persia, and to attack Afghanistan if that country should attempt an invasion of India, while the British undertook to aid the Persians should they come under attack from Afghanistan or the French. The shah had felt badly let down when Britain, in 1804, had declined to consider that this treaty obliged her to help Persia against the Russians, and by May 1807 the French had concluded the Treaty of Finkenstein with him, under which he was to denounce the treaty with Britain and declare war on her, and allow French troops passage through Persia to India. Sir Harford's detention in London had been caused by the discovery that

---

* John Malcolm, 1769–1833, although a professional soldier in the employ of the East India Company, developed his career mainly in civilian political jobs. Made KCB in 1815 and governor of Bombay 1826–30.

Lord Minto*, governor-general of India, had decided to send Malcolm back to Persia as his envoy, to try to prevent such a threat to India becoming a reality. Sir Harford had tried to stop this, as it would appear to make the king's representative subordinate to India, but in the end he had had to leave with orders simply to take detailed instructions from Minto once he reached India. Although his status as the king's representative was confirmed, James foresaw trouble, and he was right.

On reaching Bombay on 26 April 1808, they discovered that Minto – alarmed by the arrival in Tehran of a sizeable French military mission under command of General Claude-Matthieu Gardane – had decided he could not wait for Sir Harford. Only a few days earlier he had authorised Malcolm, promoted Brigadier for the purpose, to set off to make contact with the shah, and try to persuade him to expel the French and renew his friendship with Britain. Sir Harford was furious, suspecting that it had been a deliberate ploy to get the better of him when they must have known that he was only a few days' sail away. But he could only accept the situation with outward dignity. He and his suite had to spend the following four and a half months uselessly in Bombay.

It was an anxious time for James. By the middle of August he was still unsure whether Sir Harford would go to Persia, stay in India or return to England, but he told his mother that he had made up his mind to stick with him 'wherever he goes.'[8] A few days later they heard that Malcolm's mission had failed and he was on his way back. Minto now agreed that Sir Harford should have his turn. James was now cheered by 'the pleasure of activity [which] has dispelled all the gloomy thoughts we had of remaining here a long time unemployed', filled with admiration at 'the patience & temper in which' Sir Harford had borne not only his frustration, but also the news that he had lost a lot of money through the collapse of a business in which he had invested; but he still could not see that they had much chance of success.[9]

In fact the shah, once he discovered that the French had allied themselves with his enemy, Russia, was holding back on implementing the Treaty of Finkenstein. But Malcolm had made the mistake of arriving at Bushire with 500 Indian marines and soldiers and sending a message demanding, with implied threats, that the shah expel

---

* Gilbert Elliot, 1751–1814, created Baron Minto 1798, 1st Earl of Minto 1813. He had been minister plenipotentiary at Vienna 1799, then president of the India Board of Control before becoming governor-general of India 1807–13.

Gardane and his military mission. The shah had refused to receive him in Tehran, and Malcolm had refused to open discussions anywhere else. James thought it would be a miracle if Sir Harford succeeded in softening the shah's attitude after this. However, clearly as much under the influence of his chief's Welsh charm as ever, he felt that their hope lay in the 'virtues of moderation, disinterestedness & public spirit … [which] Sir Harford possesses to their fullest extent' – in contrast to the self-interest and jealous intrigues of which he considered Malcolm guilty.[10] The relationship between Sir Harford and James was by now very close and relaxed. 'He displays the sincerest friendliness towards me' James told his mother, 'and makes me the sole confidant of all his very secret plans. I can never praise Heaven enough for having thrown me, so to say, into a life such as I never dreamed of.'[11] James would let him read his letters from home (his sister Emily was staying with Lady Jones) and looked upon him 'as if he were one of my own relatives.' He did not 'make the smallest mystery to him of either our joys or our distresses, for he partakes in them all.'[12] Moreover, Sir Harford decided to appoint him 'Treasurer of Embassy', with an addition of some £150 a year to his salary. He therefore set off for Persia from Bombay in the best of spirits.

Sir Harford's approach was quite different from Malcolm's. Instead of a show of force he would rely on a combination of respect for the shah's majesty, and insistence on reciprocal respect for his own dignity as the representative of a powerful monarch. He would be lavish with gifts, but would take with him only a small escort of 40 native Madras cavalry. His suite was also small, comprising only James, Thomas Sheridan (nephew of the playwright) as political assistant, Captain James Sutherland as surveyor, Cornet Henry Willock in command of the escort, and a native Persian secretary. (Major Smith was delayed at Calcutta and did not sail with them.) They embarked in three ships on 12 September, Sir Harford, James and Sheridan in the frigate Nereide, the military in Sapphire and the Persian secretary and others in a small East India Company ship the Sylph. The Nereide reached the Bushire roads on 14 October, Sapphire four days later. Of the Sylph, however, there was no sign and when a similar ship, which had left Bombay later, arrived on the 29th, reporting an attempted attack on her by pirates, the worst was feared. Sapphire was despatched to investigate. However, the Nereide had already left to return to Bombay, and had come across Sylph while she was under attack by pirates on the 21st. She had been able to sink one of the pirate ships and drive the others off, but had been too late to prevent the murder of 22 of the crew. Fortunately the pirates had thought that the magnificently attired Persian secretary would be good for a ransom, and he was rescued alive, eventually reaching Bushire in another ship.

Although Sir Harford was not going to emulate Malcolm in a show of force, he was determined that from the moment of his arrival in Persia he should be afforded all the respect due to the representative of the King of England: reports of this would quickly reach Tehran and would influence the shah in deciding how to receive him, if at all. Consequently Sir Harford insisted on the local sheikh (whom he had known years before as a boy) coming to greet him on board before he was himself prepared to go ashore. Having insisted on this, however, he showed respect for the sheikh's own dignity by paying him the compliment of a 5-gun salute, two more than was strictly required. The marines were under arms, Captain Corbet personally handed the sheikh across the quarter-deck 'and assisted him with some difficulty to descend from the deck to the cabin by a steep and narrow ladder which, however, no attention could render convenient to a man encumbered with an immense large cloak and slip-shod slippers.'[13] He was received at the bottom by Sir Harford and, after the appropriate exchanges of courtesies and general conversation, he returned on shore with Sir Harford and his suite in the Nereide's boat to the accompaniment of a 15-gun salute. This much discomfited the sheikh's suite, who were embarking in their own boat right under the guns. On reaching the shore they were escorted 'in a cloud of dust, and through streets six feet wide to the sheikh's house, and at length entered it by a door so mean and ill-looking that it might more properly have formed the entrance to his stable.'[14] After more courtesies, this time in the Persian style of smoking several water-pipes (*qaleouns*) and drinking coffee, Sir Harford and his party moved to the house of the East India Company's resident representative, Mr Bruce, about a mile out of the town 'and then completed a day of full entertainment by an excellent dinner.'[15] The next day they were caught up in a local political crisis when a high official, Mahomed Khan, arrived from Shiraz with a body of men to arrest the sheikh who had welcomed them. He called formally on Sir Harford who then gave James his first diplomatic task by sending him, in uniform complete with cocked hat, to make the return call. The khan was:

> … encamped among some date trees; and living in the remains of a house which was all in ruins, but which he had screened up with mats to keep off the sun and wind. A clean mat was spread on the floor, carpets were arranged

all round, and his bed and cushions were rolled up in one corner: over the carpet, on which he sate himself, was a covering of light blue chintz. When [James and his escort] were within a hundred yards ... he seated himself in the place of honour, and did not pay us the compliment of rising when we entered. I made him a civil speech in Turkish, and he ... seemed, indeed, much pleased with the epithet of *Effendi,* which I used frequently in addressing him, but which, as I afterwards learned, is never applied in Persia to any but very great men. His vanity was accordingly much flattered; and he exclaimed to his attendants, that I was '*Khoub Javani*', a fine fellow.[16]

Thus James inadvertently, in his ignorance, helped to create the best possible atmosphere for Sir Harford. A few days later the khan made a public announcement 'woe be to that man who shall be found guilty of giving the smallest offence to any Englishman or to any of his servants or to any thing that belongs to him.'[17]

They now settled down to await replies to the letters Sir Harford had sent to Shiraz and Tehran, announcing his arrival as 'Envoy Extraordinary from the King of Great Britain to the King of Persia in order to confirm and augment the amity which has so long existed between the two countries.'[18] James already had it in mind to write a book about his travels and the people of Persia, and he was keeping a detailed journal '*à la Chardin*',* writing down the smallest circumstances just as they occur ... [which is] the very best method, for all the histories of Persian intrigues between one another ... are happening most opportunely every day, & it is by them only that a good idea of the true character & genius of a people can be given.'[19] His first impressions of the Persians, however, were unfavourable:

They don't by any means carry as much respectability with them as the Turks. A Turk ... would see you at the devil before he would wait upon you, a Persian will do any thing for you, except eating pork. I never saw such a set of lawless, profligate fellows as they are. They are so far different to the Turk ... that they care not what they do provided they can gain a favour, if that is their aim ... speaking the truth is a quality that the most devout of them have not any pretensions to.[20]

This was a somewhat hastily drawn generalisation based on short acquaintance with a very limited section of the people, and an innate tendency to look upon foreigners with prejudice; but it was one which continued to colour his view of a country he never grew to like, even though he later portrayed it and its inhabitants with shrewdness and

---

* Sir John Chardin, 1643–1713, Protestant refugee born in Paris, travelled as a jewel merchant through Turkey to Persia and India 1664–70 and 1671–7 publishing his notes. Knighted 1681, FRS 1682, envoy to Holland 1684

humour in his novels. James, however, was not unhappy during the eight weeks they remained at Bushire. They could take long rides in the surrounding desert, and had a fresh water pool by the house for bathing. The members of the suite got on so well together that they called their temporary home Concord Lodge, and James enjoyed 'eating from morning to night ... mutton like that in England, fish, eggs, chicken & yaourt'.[21] As the weather got colder there were hunting expeditions, including one with hawks when they were accompanied by 'an old and keen sportsman ... one of the most picturesque figures on horseback [which James had ever seen]. He was rather tall, with a neck very long, and a beard very grey. His body, either through age or the long use of a favourite position on horseback, inclined forward till it made an angle of 45° with his thighs, which run nearly parallel to the horse's back; and his beard projected so much from his lank neck, that it completed the amusement of the profile.'[22]

On November 13 Sir Harford heard of the approach of an official from Shiraz, where one of the shah's sons was governor. As it was believed that this was the *mehmandar* (escorting official) they were awaiting, James, escorted by five troopers under Willock, was sent to meet him. He turned out, however, to be no more than an emissary sent by the prince at Shiraz to report on these new arrivals before a decision was made whether to allow Sir Harford to proceed. Fortunately he was sufficiently impressed by the way he was received and treated to make a favourable report, and a *mehmandar* of suitably high rank arrived on 10 December to escort them to Shiraz. James thought this was a momentous occasion. 'Cut off as we are from all European news' he had written to David on first learning that they were going to be allowed to proceed, 'we are totally ignorant of events which very probably have led' to it, and 'more than fortunate' to be at last on the point of penetrating a country which had 'been for so long looked upon in India as impracticable.'[23] He thought, in fact, that peace negotiations with France must have begun, or that Britain was again in friendly relations with Russia. Neither was the case: the shah had simply decided that he might be better off after all with the British than with the French, and that the sending of a personal representative of the king of England – and moreover one who knew how to behave towards him – was a good sign.

It was also a momentous occasion for James personally. Sir Harford, learning that Smith would not be rejoining his suite, now sent home a request that James be formally appointed public secretary. This meant that James would be left in charge of the mission if Sir Harford's application for home leave were granted. He wrote that James was 'the only person in my suite who I think can with advantage to the public be appointed chargé d'affaires. I entertain the highest opinion of Mr Morier's abilities and zeal, and I am confident he will discharge with credit to himself and benefit to his employers the duties of any office to which he shall be appointed.'[24] James had already been filling this position de facto, and in telling his mother of this development he explained that

'our first operations have of course caused a great deal of writing, & as I am *secrétaire en chef*, so I have the chief part of the business'; and he thanked 'my friend Sir Harford for the blessings I enjoy in the situation I hold, & really when I conceive that without much presumption I may advance much farther, I do not know in what terms to tell you how happy I feel at the idea of being useful to my family.'

But he excused himself from giving details of his work: 'I adhere to the literal significance of *secrétaire*, for which I am sure no one can blame me.'[25]

⊕

Although lacking the large military force which Malcolm had taken with him, Sir Harford's caravan was not inconsiderable. As James told David, 'travelling here is worse than in Turkey in so far as relates to furniture & baggage. I must have three horses, four servants & a dozen mules at least to myself.' To the suite that had come from India were added the company's resident at Bushire, Bruce, and a Dr Jukes, 'a little clever man who has been created Persian secretary & special interpreter to the mission.' In addition they had two Swiss valets and a Yorkshire groom, the bodyguard of 40 native cavalry, and 'about 100 Persian servants of one description or other, and horses and mules innumerable.'[26] There were also an English and a Portuguese tailor, and half a dozen Indian servants.

Wishing to show his understanding and respect for Persian customs, and at the same time demonstrate his belief in the success of his mission, Sir Harford asked the local astrologers to fix the most propitious time for his departure on 17 December, so they set off at precisely 11.15 in the morning. The cavalcade was headed by ten horses, each led by a groom splendidly attired, followed by a group of *shatirs* (running footmen). Then came Sir Harford mounted 'on a choice Arab horse' with a particularly fine *shatir* at his stirrup. The 'gentlemen' of the mission rode behind Sir Harford and the military escort brought up the rear.[27] In the rougher terrain the party inevitably became less formal, but whenever possible, and always when approaching and leaving villages or towns, Sir Harford was careful to present a picture of dignity and importance. He wanted to emphasise in every possible way that he was representing a sovereign, not simply the governor-general of India, and to reinforce this he made great show with the box containing his credentials from King George III. This was carried in a richly decorated litter escorted by troops with drawn swords. At every stopping place Sir Harford would dismount and follow the litter on foot, passing between two lines of troops presenting arms. Harford and his suite would ostentatiously bow whenever they passed the litter.[28] It was treated, so to say, like the 'ark of the covenant', a deliberate act in a country where James now began to note the close similarity between many local customs and passages in both the Old and the New Testaments.

It took thirteen days to reach the outskirts of Shiraz, a distance of some 250 miles covered in daily stages varying between about 12 and 25 miles, depending partly on the terrain and partly on the length of time needed for ceremonies on arrival at and departure from towns and villages. They would normally dine an hour or two after sunset, and the state dining tents, in which local dignitaries would be received, would then be dismantled and taken forward to the next staging post to be made ready for ceremonial use when the party reached it. Each 'gentleman' had his own sleeping tent and at day-break these too would be dismantled and taken forward, with the baggage, while they breakfasted in one remaining tent. They rested on Sundays, always having divine service, conducted by James. 'Nothing' he wrote 'excites a better impression of our character than an appearance of devotion and religious observance. If, therefore, there were no higher obligation on every Christian, religious observances are indispensable in producing a national influence. We never omitted to perform divine service on Sundays; suffered no one to intrude upon us during our devotions; and used every means in our power to impress the natives with a proper idea of the sanctity of our Sabbath.'[29] But there was no excessive sabbatarianism in their conduct. Christmas day happened to be a Sunday, and they feasted on the plum puddings they had brought with them which the East India Company's Persian agent at Shiraz, who had come to meet them, was more than happy to share.

Their ceremonial entry into Shiraz was arranged for the morning of 30 December, when Sir Harford insisted, with success, that those who came out to meet him, even though they were related to the shah, must dismount before him, and that he himself would dismount for no one other than the prince's chief minister. They all wore full uniform and Sir Harford, in order to emphasise his status, wore also a Persian cloak of a kind normally allowed only to princes. On New Year's Day

1809 they were received by the prince himself, Ali Mirza, son of the shah and reputedly the favourite after the heir apparent, Prince Abbas Mirza. Although only 19 years old he had already fathered eight children, and James thought him 'an engaging youth of the most agreeable countenance and very pleasing manners', but he 'appeared to be under much constraint during the ceremony of our audience.'[30] During the next few days there were lengthy exchanges of formalities with others, including a feast and entertainment given by the chief minister which lasted several hours, all endured rather than enjoyed by James and his companions. The feast was preceded by acrobatic, musical and firework displays, James being particularly impressed by the performance of a negro who drank what seemed to be about two gallons of water and then ejected them from his mouth like a fountain during a full five minutes. The musical performances he found to be in parts 'extremely noisy', in others 'not unpleasant even to our ears', but generally 'of the roughest kind.' The 'most ingenious and least discordant' performance was that by the man who played three wooden spoons – like a an old-fashioned busker outside a London theatre. The meal itself consisted of at least 'two hundred dishes exclusive of the sherbets', eaten with fingers and without conversation, which James liked: 'The silence, indeed, with which the whole is transacted is one of the most agreeable circumstances of a Persian feast. There is no rattle of plates and knives and forks, no confusion of lacquies, no drinking of healths, no disturbance of carving, scarcely a word is spoken, and all are intent on the business before them.'[31] James always considered food almost more important than social graces, and he told his mother that Persian food was 'the most delicious and attractive you can imagine' the only snag being that of having to eat it sitting uncomfortably on their haunches on the ground.[32]

Sir Harford now found himself in a delicate and difficult position. He received a despatch from Minto, ordering him to leave Persia and telling him that a military expedition under Malcolm was being prepared to occupy Kharg Island off Bushire. Minto had, in fact tried, to stop Sir Harford leaving Bombay for Bushire because of this, but his order had arrived two days too late. Now Sir Harford was horrified at this development, not only because an armed attack on part of Persia would completely ruin all chance of success in his mission, but because to obey the order to leave Persia would suggest to the Persians that the governor-general was superior to the king. He declared that his Welsh blood would never allow him to support such a notion, and he sent a despatch to the Foreign Office refusing to obey Minto's order.[33] To James this was nothing more than the result of 'the jealousies, intrigues and evil politics of certain personnages who never cease from looking to their own ambitions in the rout and failure of our plans.'[34] But Sir Harford then discovered that the prince already knew about the proposed military expedition, and that therefore it would soon be known to the French in Tehran, who would of course use the information to their own advantage with the shah. He managed, however, to persuade the prince's chief minister that this development should not be allowed to delay his onward travel from Shiraz, and two days later, on 7 January 1809, he actually had a request from the prince to mount a display before him by the Indian cavalry, during which the prince publicly showed great friendliness towards him. He was much comforted by this demonstration of support, and also by an incident of personal importance to himself: his natural son turned up in Shiraz to greet him, coincidentally with the receipt of a letter announcing the birth some six months earlier of a legitimate son to his wife in Hereford.

Before leaving Shiraz they all received presents from the prince, those for the 'gentlemen' being costumes of gold brocade with sash and shawl. James thought their appearance, when they donned them for their final audience with the prince, 'very ridiculous.' They simply put them on over their normal clothes, wound the sashes round their waists and fastened the shawls to their cocked hats, their ceremonial red stockings and green high-heeled shoes showing incongruously below. Quite improperly – such gifts from the prince should have been worn for at least three days – they discarded this uncomfortable dress as soon as they left the audience. As James put it 'an Englishman just invested with an Order would hardly throw off the ribband at the gate of St James's'; but, fortunately, the court officials took no offence.[35]

The party finally left Shiraz on 13 January, conducted by a new *mehmandar*. They were able to spend Sunday the 15th exploring the ruins of Persepolis, where James made many drawings. From here onwards he was often allowed to leave the main party for a few hours to do the same at other ancient sites they passed, and he was also helping Sutherland make maps by taking noon sights with a sextant to determine their latitude. The weather became more wintry, and sometimes they had to trek ahead of their tents because these could not be dismantled until the overnight frost in them had thawed. They were often caught in heavy rain and violent winds. Several tents were blown down on Sunday the 22nd, but 'notwithstanding the fury of the tempest,' wrote James 'we did not omit to put up our prayers and thanksgivings for all the blessings bestowed upon us; and the storm around only added, I hope, to the solemnity of our devotions.'[36] One of the blessings was the news which had reached them a few days earlier of British military successes against the French in the Peninsular War. This would, of course, further weaken Gardane's position.

Sir Harford became unwell just before they reached Isfahan and, to his disgust, had to join his credentials in the litter. He was determined, however, to enter the city in proper style, and remounted his horse for the last few miles. These were covered with some difficulty through a large crowd come to escort him, which included the Armenian bishop and his clergy. The bishop presented Sir Harford with a New Testament bound in crimson velvet. The mission, after the formalities of meeting the governor, were taken to quarters in a large, once magnificent and beautiful, building.

A few days later Sir Harford received news from Bombay that Malcolm had been there since 30 November 1808, assembling his force for the invasion of Kharg Island, and had planned to set off with it about the middle of January 1809. Sir Harford did not know that Minto had by now cancelled this expedition and, assuming that Malcolm was on the way, he decided that they must leave at once, travelling with all possible speed, in order to forestall him by concluding a treaty without delay. The intention was to cover the 235 remaining miles in six days. They set out in the early afternoon of 7 February. Three days later Sir Harford was forced to take to the litter again, but he nevertheless insisted on long marches of nearly 40 miles a day. On the 11th it rained and blew a gale, and they were still travelling after dark when the mules carrying the litter slipped into an irrigation canal and he was nearly drowned – and almost lost the precious box containing the king's letter. The baggage train had become scattered so, that night, they had only one tent between them. Sir Harford was by now in a pitiable state of fever and dosed himself with large quantities of rum and hot water until he fell asleep in a stupor and sweated it out. He was weak, but clear of fever, next morning; but everything was in such a state that they could not move off before midday. Sir Harford insisted on having only a short halt at a *caravanserai* before continuing through the night, much against the wishes of their elderly *mehmandar* who, by now, had had more than enough. He deliberately pretended to lose the way in the dark so that they had to return to the *caravanserai*. This delay meant that they did not reach Tehran until the 14th, a day later than intended. This was a pity, since the shah had already demonstrated his friendship by arranging for

Gardane to leave, as it were, by one door while the representative of
the king of England entered by another. Gardane, not surprisingly, did
not delay his departure beyond the 13th, thus at least diminishing his
public humiliation and denying Sir Harford his ostentatious triumph.
But this did not detract from the success of his negotiations, which
were completed in a remarkably short time.

Sir Harford had already achieved much. His previous service in the
Levant had made him many friends, some of whom were now in high
places, and able to exert influence behind the scenes. By his style of
diplomacy he had convinced the shah that Britain was not trying to
impose her imperial might, but wanted Persian friendship on terms of
equality between one sovereign and another. And the fact that all was
not going France's way in Europe also helped, as had his own offer to
surrender himself to the shah for whatever punishment was thought fit
– even execution – should any British force actually mount an attack
on Kharg Island. Nevertheless, even Sir Harford, convinced though he
was in his own self-assurance that he would succeed in his mission, was
surprised at the readiness now shown to conclude a treaty without
delay. For had they been so inclined, the Persians could have kept him
waiting a couple of weeks or more before doing any business with
him. The mission had arrived just at the beginning of the 10-days,
known as Muharram – ceremonial mourning for martyrdom, in 681,
of Imam Husain, grandson of the Prophet Muhammad – during which
no official business was normally conducted and no public function
took place at the court. Nevertheless, detailed discussions with ministers
on the terms of a treaty began the next day, and it was only Sir
Harford's ill health that made it necessary to postpone the first audience
with the shah until the 17th.

In the circumstances of the official mourning this audience was not
a public one; but it was nevertheless accompanied by much public
ceremonial as the mission was conducted to the presence through the
streets with pomp and parade. James was surprised, however, that the
final approach, after passing through various splendid courtyards, was
through 'a small and mean door which led us through a dark and
intricate passage … [and then through] a door still more wretched and
worse indeed than that of any English stable.' But beyond this was
another courtyard 'laid out in canals and playing fountains' in front of
a room, at the back of which the shah was seated on the peacock
throne, although dressed sombrely because of the mourning. James

later described him as 'aged about 45, a man of pleasing manners and an agreeable countenance, with an aquiline nose, large eyes and very arched eyebrows … his face obscured by an immense beard and mustachios … his voice … harmonious, though now hollow and obviously that of a man who had led a free life.'[37] Sir Harford presented the king's letter in its special box, James the gifts – consisting of a picture of the king set round with diamonds, a diamond of 61 carats which had cost £20,000, a small box with a lid on which a picture of Windsor Castle was carved in ivory, a box made from the oak of the *Victory* with a picture of the battle of Trafalgar carved in ivory, and a small blood-stone mosaic box for opium. During the next few days the mission attended various ceremonies commemorating the death of Imam Husain, including the final one, on the 25th, when all those who had performed in the ceremonies were supposed to parade before the shah (a spectacle on which James later drew for part of chapter IX of *Hajji Baba of Ispahan*). On this occasion the man who had represented Husain was too frightened to appear, having heard that, in a nearby village, when the drama was being presented the actor taking the part of Husain had actually been beheaded by an over enthusiastic 'executioner'.

Meanwhile long nights were spent in discussion with the pleni-potentiaries apppointed by the shah to reach agreement on the text of a treaty. The chief minister, Mirza Shefi, 'an old man of mild and easy manners who displayed more knowledge of general politics than any other person' they met in Persia, had already shown apparently genuine desire for everlasting friendship between the two countries by pulling a diamond ring from off his finger and putting it on one of Sir Harford's, begging him 'to accept this as a pledge of my friendship for you'[38] (an act which may have inspired the similar incident in chapter LXXVIII of *Hajji Baba*, where the ring went in the other direction). But there was still a French chargé d'affaires in Tehran with a small staff, and much intrigue behind the scenes. The shah was not going to burn all his bridges with France before he was absolutely sure that an alliance with Britain would serve him better. The Persian negotiators would mix friendly joviality with contentious arguments over small points. They would prolong sessions with long discussions of irrelevant matters, even deliberately falling asleep for an hour or two. Sir Harford patiently played their game, even succeeding on one occasion in turning the tables on them by prolonging one long night's session with a lengthy but irrelevant lecture on the geography of Europe and the various royal families, which won him a rueful compliment from the chief Persian negotiator. Finally, however, agreed texts in Persian and

English of a preliminary treaty intended to be the basis for a permanent one to be negotiated later were signed on 12 March and exchanged on the 15th.

⊕

This treaty now had to be taken to London. When Sir Harford had asked the Foreign Office, in December 1808, to give James the appointment of Public Secretary, he had intended going home himself with the treaty, leaving James in charge in Persia. Now, however, he decided he must remain in Persia to deal with a serious conflict which had developed between him and the governor-general of India, threatening the destruction of all he had achieved. The details are another story in themselves, and their only relevance to the history of James lies in the indirect effect they had later on his personal relations with Sir Harford (see chapter 12). It is sufficient here to explain that Minto's hostility culminated in his taking the extraordinary step of attempting to annul Sir Harford's appointment and all his actions as the king's envoy, of refusing to authorise the honouring of his bills of exchange and of announcing his intention of sending Malcolm to take his place.

It was, therefore, James who now returned to London, but not immediately. Six weeks were spent in Tehran (which gave him time to make many more drawings) while the shah decided whether to approve the preliminary treaty and send his own representative to London to negotiate the definitive treaty. There were several moments during this time when the whole agreement (which included a promise of financial help for the Persians in their war with Russia) was in doubt, culminating in Sir Harford's discovery that, contrary to what he had understood to be a Persian promise, the French were not being expelled. Gardane, on being told to leave Tehran, had moved only as far as Tabriz. Although annoyed that the shah had allowed a chargé d'affaires to remain in Tehran, Sir Harford had understood the need for time to close down their mission. When he had concluded the treaty, however, he had understood this to mean the final departure of all Frenchmen. He now decided that he must force the shah to prove his good intentions towards Britain by expelling them all. An audience was held on 31 March to present James before his departure for England, and a few days later the shah sent James a 'dress of honour' (*khal'at*), consisting of a brocade coat that covered him from neck to feet, a small outer coat trimmed with fur over the shoulders and down the back, a brocade sash and, a mark of particular favour, a sword which the shah himself had worn and which had his name engraved upon it. Sir Harford, however, did not allow this signal honour to divert him from protesting at the shah's failure to sever all relations with France. After a series of fruitless exchanges of letters with the shah's plenipotentiaries, he sent James to see them with a virtual ultimatum.

James, after being kept waiting some five 'long and melancholy' hours with no more than a dish of lettuces for refreshment, was unexpectedly taken to see the shah himself. The shah was seated in a garden which had recently been watered, so that having to stand before him unshod (as was the custom) 'on a wet brick pavement' was most disagreeable. The shah, who had by then studied Sir Harford's written communications, launched into a long and at times bitter lecture, accusing the British of trying to buy his friendship instead of providing the material help he needed in his war with Russia, and implying that the French might still be better allies. If Sir Harford did not have the authority to promise him troops, he said, 'let him send Mr Morier to England [for it] and wait here for the answer ... It is not money I want – no – Money I have got enough everyone knows ... I should disgrace myself if I sent the French away for money.'[39] Sir Harford, when he received James's report, knew just what to do. Exercising what would now be called brinkmanship, he sent a curt message to the shah that he was having his tents put up outside the city limits, preparatory to leaving next day. As no doubt he had known it would, this produced a conciliatory message from the shah, on whom he and James called the following day. The atmosphere was now quite different, and the shah promised to send the French packing, asking only that they be given reasonable time, to which Sir Harford agreed, saying 'I take it for granted that His Majesty's Government never wishes an enemy even to be treated with unnecessary harshness.'

All was now sunshine again. James thought the Persians showed great delicacy towards Sir Harford in the difficult position in which he had been placed by Minto, and that the shah treated him

> with the most gratifying evidence of his protection and individual favour: and his Ministers united in displaying the greatest personal kindness towards us. Throughout the whole management of a new and very delicate situation their proceedings were so plain, so upright, and so cheering; so eager to show respect and confidence to the Envoy that we regarded them with the liveliest gratitude; and felt relieved by finding among strangers all the heart and principle of countrymen and brothers.[40]

Although it might be thought that this was a deliberately flattering opinion for publication in his travel book, it was in fact quite genuine at the time. James had written to David in Constantinople in February, bursting with happiness and enthusiasm for the way they had been received and treated in Tehran, euphoric at the way his own fate had been changed from being 'destined to buy and sell Turkey figs' for ever to being 'appointed heir to this embassy' (this was when Sir Harford was still expecting to take the treaty to England himself).[41] He had promised David that he was no longer guilty of the 'sulleness that you have so often teazed me about.' These few months in Persia with Sir Harford had completely changed that, and the day he wrote this letter was 'one of the happiest days I ever passed.'

On the 18th, James was summoned to receive from the shah's hands a flowery letter addressed to King George III, arrangements were completed for a Persian envoy, Mirza Abul Hasan,* to accompany him to England. The last of the French left Tehran on the 29th. James and the mirza set off on 7 May, and thus began a friendship and experiences which led, fifteen years later, to the creation of Hajji Baba.†

---

* 'Mirza' as a prefix to a name denoted a scribe, a secretary or an educated man. As a suffix it indicated princely rank.

† The 'introductory epistle', with which James began his first novel shows that ever since his few months at Constantinople in 1807 he had had it in mind to write a book about 'oriental manners' based on his knowledge of life in Turkey. It was now that these but half formed ideas began to crystallize round his experiences in Persia instead

CHAPTER NINE

David 1807–1809

'I am anxious to do my duty well.'

When James had returned to England with Harford Jones at the end of 1806 – 'as fat & as merry as ever' according to his sister Emily – he found David, who had arrived from Constantinople in August, thinner than ever and looking unwell: 'He is not like you and me, strong fellows who don't know what physicking means' he told his brother William.[1] In fact David was probably suffering more from low spirits than physical ill health. After making his reports to the Foreign Office he had been unable to get any decision out of them about his future. Nor had he had any news from Jack since August. He had begun to feel that the Moriers, while useful for carrying out the sort of rough and sometimes dangerous jobs that he and Jack had been employed on, were of no great interest to the aristocrats of the Foreign Office. He did not take offence at this, at least not overtly; but it rankled and led to a loss of confidence in himself. Moreover, although he loved his sisters and mother dearly, life cooped up with them in a small London house, after his experiences in Greece, seemed almost oppressive. In January 1807 Lord Radstock – ever sensitive to the welfare of his sister-in-law Clara's family – realised that David needed a change, and got a friend, Mr Park,* to take him on a trip to Oxford, Bath and Bristol.

On his return to London in the third week of January, his morale fully restored, David set about trying to extract a decision about his future (and Jack's) out of the Foreign Office. He had no idea then, any more than the Foreign Office, of what was happening in Turkey, and he wrote in disgust to his brother Jack on finding that Straton, who was off to Stockholm, was to be replaced in Constantinople not by

---

* James Alan Park, 1763–1838, called to the bar 1784, at this time Recorder of Durham. He became Attorney-General of Lancaster in 1811 and was knighted 1816.

Jack, but by 'the young marquis':*

> When you know that the real marquis W[ellesley] is in high favour with the
> government you will not be surprised that his interest should have carried
> every thing before it, & when interest is in the case, the greatest inefficiency
> on the part of the protégé, and the most excellent merit of the less supported
> competitor, can have no sort of influence in deciding the fate of either ...
> Surely never was a post of such importance at the present moment so vilely
> prostituted ... Mr A[rbuthnot] I am assured has for the present no intention
> of leaving his place, so that it is to be hoped for the good of the nation that
> the honour of it will not yet be compromised by the follies of a child ... If
> I am not mistaken, I think you will feel less disappointment at the frustration
> of your own expectations, than at the unworthy cause of it, and I am
> persuaded that could you obtain a temporary relaxation from the barbarous
> service, you would return without disgust to it.[2]

David had strong egalitarian instincts, which told him that an
aristocratic family background should not be a God-given passport to
diplomatic eminence – particularly in the case of one so young and
when Elgin had written to him to say that he could not 'conceive a
hesitation in appointing your brother, having had so long a conversation
on the subject with Lord Howick [then Foreign Secretary].' David
thought Jack would agree 'that S[traton] has behaved to you in a most
— manner after the intimate correspondence which passed on the
subject between you; and A[rbuthnot]'s conduct is not much better
considering what he has also wrote [sic] home on the same.' This was
certainly unfair to Arbuthnot, who could have had no say in the final
choice, and probably unfair to Straton; but it was a natural outburst
from a brother who hoped to rejoin Jack and 'share in all your fortunes,
and rejoice in the reflection that we have done our duty.' Instead,
however, David now embarked on adventures which were the start of
a distinguished diplomatic career.

It was March 1807 before the news of the ignominious withdrawals of
both Arbuthnot and Duckworth from Constantinople reached London
– just after the change of government which brought George Canning

---

* This was Henry Wellesley, 1791–1866, illegitimate son of Richard Colley,
  Marquess Wellesley at that time governor-general of India. He was young, even
  by the standards of those days, for such an appointment; but, although he joined
  Arbuthnot in Constantinople, the break in relations with Turkey halted this career
  as a diplomat.

in as foreign secretary. Learning that the Russians were sending an emissary to treat with the Porte, he also decided to send an envoy there both to support this initiative and to try to restore British relations with Turkey. He chose Sir Arthur Paget, brother of Henry, later 1st Marquess of Anglesey, then 35 years old. His instructions from Canning, dated 16 May 1807, made it clear that he was

> to endeavour to accommodate the differences which have broken out between the Ottoman Porte and the Russian Government, and to bring back the Porte to a just sense of the expediency of renewing and maintaining its former engagements as well with Russia as with this country, and of throwing off that predominant influence which is now exercised over the councils of the Divan [cabinet] by France.[3]

This was a difficult assignment, lightened, however, by the happy chance that Sir Arthur was an intimate friend of the Russian emissary, Pozzo di Borgo, whom he had known in Vienna. Canning was also worried about Ali Pasha who, in the event of peace between Russia and the Porte, might look to the French if he felt he could not rely on the British. Paget, however, was instructed not to actively seek contact with him, but simply to respond with caution to any overtures. It was intended that he should attach Jack (now known to be at Malta) to his suite for use in any such contacts. David was to travel with Paget as Jack's deputy, ready to take over as consul general in Patras should Jack go to Ioannina.

David arrived at Portsmouth on 28 May 1807 to await Paget, not without some apprehension. He had written to his brother William that he was

> in a situation to feel the importance of resolution and constancy. I am on the point of being left entirely to my own guidance and discretion, a circumstance which I can hardly be said to have been in hitherto ... How I may acquit myself I must not presume to decide, but this I know, that I am more than ever diffident of myself and therefore more earnestly anxious to do my duty well.[4]

When he got to Portsmouth he found Arbuthnot just arrived. He now learned at first hand of the shameful events at Constantinople, and of the defeat of General Fraser by the Turks in March at Rosetta. He was horrified. 'What gives me real concern' he wrote to his mother 'is the certainty that this failure has completely ruined our reputation in the Levant, and no less than a complete victory over the French in Poland and everywhere else, or a great miracle, is needed to regain a half or even a quarter of the influence we used to have.'[5] But he remained optimistic, looking forward to his new adventure.

David found that he was to be in company with Bartholomew Frere.* At first he was a little doubtful about him, but was soon telling James that he 'gains upon me as I know him better; but there is not that warmth and openess of heart about him which inspires that unreserved confidence that is the delight of real friendship.'[6] He must have sometimes seemed almost threatening to others in the way he expected instant intimate friendship simply because of the generosity of his own extrovert personality. Frere had a more restrained character and was not going to open up in that way until he was sure of the other. David thought that 'though he may not possess the jovial qualities which Vaughan admires in others, he is not the less congenial to my general way of thinking. It is all very well to laugh, joke and be as merry as you please, but it is still better to keep out of dirt.'[7] And once they had been at sea together for a few weeks, Frere's defences came down: by the end of July David was describing him as a crony and, punning on his name, a real brother. The friendship endured for life.

Paget was delayed in London, and David had almost a week in Portsmouth before they sailed on 3 June, during which he was included in an invitation to Frere to dine at Lord Holland's.† He wrote to James that:

> They are the most amiable people that one can meet anywhere, and Lord Kinnaird# and his nice wife did not at all spoil the party ... After dinner the ladies went out in the barouche and *we* climbed up to the huge gothic outlandish chateau that Lord Lansdowne⁰ is building on a spot that commands a panoramic view of all the chimnies and surrounding country of Southampton. I am, as you may suppose, very well pleased to have found so pleasant an *acquaintance*. I will not call it connection, because I confess that there is a certain *ton & manière de penser* which does not precisely tally with your and my ideas on some important points. The true *foxite* spirit, *free & easy* but perfectly *good humoured* reigns throughout.[8]

Both James and David recognised the advantages of becoming known to the aristocracy, and were prepared to go to some lengths to fit in; but even David's two years at Harrow had not encouraged him to think he could be fully accepted by them, or even want to be in their company – except with his contemporary there, George Hamilton

---

* Bartholomew Frere, 1776–1851, son of John Frere (antiquary and fellow of Caius College, Cambridge) only graduated from Cambridge in 1806. He subsequently served as a diplomat in Spain and Constantinople.
† Henry Richard Vassall Fox, 1776–1851, 3rd Baron Holland and his wife Elizabeth Vassall, the couple famous for their salons at Holland House in London.
# Charles Kinnaird, 1780–1826, 8th Baron.
⁰ John Henry Petty, 2nd Marquess of Lansdowne

Gordon, Lord Haddo later Lord Aberdeen, with whom a lasting friendship had been formed. David, to the end of his life, remained the most unpompous of men. While never actively seeking the company of high society for social reasons, he yet accepted friendship from its members in an uninhibited way if, as often happened, it was offered without condescension. He was wary, however, of those who gave themselves airs, particularly the young, and he was now scathing about two 'young lords' who were in Paget's suite – and wickedly delighted that they had been relegated to travel in HMS Excellent with, so to say, the second eleven. 'I am not at all grieved' he told James 'to be without the company of the noble sucking Socs as you call them. My friend has a shocking *testa di piombo* [is a block head]; as for the other, he seems to have acquired habits and talents in the 4th Regiment of Dragoons which would do honour to the arrantest ostler that ever curried a horse.'* But he was equally scathing of the private secretary and interpreter engaged by Paget (also relegated to *Excellent*), a Mr Berthold whom James knew from Smyrna to have a questionable background and reputation. 'I have seen [him] sporting a pair of highly polished yellow breeches in High Street.'[9] David thought it unlikely that Berthold and Paget would make a successful team – and indeed, Berthold was sent packing the following year.

Thanks to the influence of Lord Radstock, David and Frere were allocated berths with Paget in HMS Montague. They even had a cabin each, and David found his comfortable, despite having 'a pounder' in it, with the particular advantage 'for such a long mackerel backed fellow as I am' of having good headroom in which he could stand upright between the beams 'even with my hat on.' He was critical, however, of Paget because although he 'seems to have laid aside all stiffness of ambassadorial dignity, it is still perceivable that he rather endures the society he is in than that he is pleased with it.'[10]

They sailed on 3 June and, on the 18th, joined up with Admiral Collingwood's squadron off Cadiz, where David was able to go aboard HMS Ocean and meet his brother William and his cousin Granville Waldegrave (both of whom were serving in her) and to spend a night

---

* This was Lord Fitzroy James Henry Somerset, 1788–1855, youngest son of Henry, 5th Duke of Beaufort, who became a cornet in the 4th Light Dragoons in 1804 and the 1st baron Raglan in 1852 under which name he is well known for his part in the Charge of the Light Brigade during the Crimean War. The 'block head' has not been identified.

on board. They called at Gibraltar for a few days, and then at Palermo, where David's Protestantism was revolted by the display of Catholic superstitions and the sale of indulgences. 'I am more than ever surprised,' he wrote 'that people who have two grains of common sense can have any respect for the mummery and absolute impiety of such a degraded and corrupt worship as that which is performed in these churches.'[11]

David arrived in Malta on 13 July, where he found Jack far from well. Paget, when he realised the state of Jack's health, decided he should return to England and formally hand his consular functions over to David, who thought it was wise of Jack to acquiesce in this, not only for the sake of his health, but because he would 'have had nothing to do out here [and] the Ambassador's character is such that my brother would have found him insupportable.'[12]

The next few months were not easy. They sailed on 15 July for the Dardanelles, and then had to hang about off Tenedos while Paget tried to get negotiations with the Porte under way. David was not involved in these talks, and he simply did not know what to do with himself, cooped up in a ship and unable to get his clothes properly washed. 'Had I not managed' he wrote to his sister Emily 'to get a shirt off the Captain I should have been reduced to the most unpleasant & disagreeable *shift* of wearing on a *Sunday* the same shirt I had had on for near ten days.'[13] He might have been comforted had he known that Paget was also writing to his mother 'it is by the bye well that I took the stock of linen I did, … It is I dare say generally thought that we are all living in clover; be assured that the reverse is as much the case as possible.'[14] With Frere he was able to go on shore on Tenedos to shoot partridge, and spent happy hours making sketches of the Asiatic coast with accurate compass bearings; and at least the climate was agreeably fresh. But he was shocked at the sight on Tenedos of the damage caused by the fighting that had taken place between the Russians and the Turkish garrison, and by the wanton damage the Russians had wreaked before leaving. He wrote to his mother describing the scene:

> Imagine a town completely in ruins, the inhabitants fled, vineyards and fields deserted, mangled corpses everywhere of those killed by one side or the other. All the descriptions in the world have not given me a more terrible idea of what war means than what I find in Tenedos.[15]

The Turks were not cooperative. They produced flimsy excuse after excuse for not producing someone with full powers to negotiate. But when Paget learned, late in August, that the Tsar and Bonaparte had signed a peace treaty at Tilsit at the beginning of July, he realised that at least he could now concentrate on trying to conclude a Turco–British peace treaty without being obliged to have regard for Russian interests. The Turks, however, took the view that, as there had been no formal declaration of war between the two countries, there was no need for a formal peace treaty. They proposed a simple truce for three months to give them time to settle their relations with Russia, during which time they expected Paget to remain ready for a summons to Constantinople for discussions. Paget, although angry at such treatment, reluctantly agreed to a truce of six weeks, provided he could be assured that after this he would be received in Constantinople for formal negotiations and that, in the meantime, all the British prisoners taken at Rosetta would have been released. The next day he sent David off to Egypt to agree the arrangements for their evacuation with the Pasha of Cairo.

On arrival at Abukir, David found that General Fraser* 'one of your good blunt, honest sort of men' had already organised the evacuation. He joined the general on the shore in a last conference with the pasha who, explaining that his tents had not arrived from Alexandria, simply sat 'on the burning hot sand close to the water.' David left them there, smoking their pipes together, and

> strolled about the beach amongst a crowd of the strangest and most unseemly figures I ever saw collected together. There was a mixture of miserable one-eyed Arabs, Ethiopian negros, Turks, Mamalukes [sic], and my old acquaintances the Albanians. These all formed the suite and attendants of the Pasha and were taking care of horses and camels that were disposed over the sandy desert which lines the whole of this coast. What surprised me most of all was to see the Arabs digging holes in the sand not two feet from the sea and finding muddy troubled water, mixed apparently with seaweed, which they drank up with great avidity out of their hands.[16]

David had mixed feelings on finding his mission thus aborted. Having been given some discretion by Paget to negotiate a deal over the prisoners, he was disappointed at losing an opportunity of making a mark with government. He was not unhappy, however, at 'escaping this time the innumerable crowds of fleas, bed-bugs, scorpions & all the horrors which the plagues of Pharoah have left in Egypt.' So he simply carried out the remainder of his instructions, which was to make his way to Malta to await the outcome of Paget's negotiations.

---

* Alexander Mackenzie Fraser, 1756–1809, professional soldier, son of Colin Mackenzie and assumed the name of Fraser in 1803.

On his passage in HMS Glatton, in company with the 78th Highlanders 'whose officers are fine men', he saw a comet* which he thought 'a magnificent spectacle which I imagined to be a world like our own which had caught fire in which the inhabitants were being burned (as we will be one day) for their sins. At least that is as reasonable a conjecture as any other on things we know not.'[17]

David reached Malta at the beginning of November. By that time Paget's mission had failed and he was on his way back to England. One of his last acts before leaving Turkey had been to obtain the release from captivity of Captain Leake, who had been caught unawares in Salonika by Arbuthnot's departure, and had been incarcerated in a noisome cellar there. He ordered Leake to go and see Ali Pasha. He had also sent David instructions (which he found awaiting him at Malta) to go to the Morea to promise the Greeks British assistance, and to take Leake's place if his health was not up to going to Ioannina. David complained to Jack of 'the harum scarumness of such instructions which put one in mind of the fable about the rats consulting about tying a bell round the cat's neck,'[18] and was advised by Sir Alexander Ball, the Governor, that 'without orders and substantial instructions from home such an expedition could be the height of absurdity.' So he wrote to Canning to suggest that to do as he had been told by Paget would, in view of the presence of numerous French emissaries in the area, 'only be needlessly exposing my life to inevitable destruction in pursuit of an inadequate object', explaining that instead he would get a ship to take him up the coast of Albania with a view to making secret contact with Ali Pasha.[19] In the end, however, even this plan was dropped when he discovered that Leake had already made contact with the pasha.

Further orders were a long time a-coming and although David had the pleasure of being reunited with his father, he began to find Malta a depressing place. As an antidote he decided to 'fag very hard at turning Thucydides into modern Romaika [demotic Greek] by way of preparation for any Greek operations;'[20] but it is clear that he found it difficult to concentrate on any particular course of study, even though he thought he should be improving himself because so 'many people

---

* This unnamed comet with two tails was first observed over Sicily on 9 September 1807 and disappeared from observation a few weeks later. It is not expected back until about the year 3507.

of my age are a thousand times more advanced in knowledge than I am ... which makes me sigh for the loss of the five or six years I spent in the counting house.'[21] Considering he was capable of writing in English, French, Italian, Latin and Greek, he was being hard on himself. But he was desperate for some proper occupation and, in March 1808, he wrote to Frere in London, who was also awaiting further orders:

> I don't understand what further use there is in the world for such characters as ambassadors or their secretaries and all the inferior train of consuls, agents, deputies and so forth ... We must convert our quills into swords and join in pulling down that great bully Napoleon ... You see to what a desperate pass I am come when the mere idea of the army as a resource can come to my mind. If you can recommend me any thing better, where there is less chance of a broken head and hard drinking, I will be much obliged to you.[22]

And in June 1808, just a year after he had left England with the Paget mission, he could find nothing more cheerful to write home about than the funeral of the 'poor young Prince of Orleans ... [who] was only 29 and came to this island in the hope of restoring his health which had been undermined by consumption caused, it is said, by the life he had been leading with the Prince of Wales. He is not the first that this man has killed with his friendship.'[23]

During this period of demoralising idleness David, it seems, may have been tempted from the moral high ground he had been brought up to keep. He was fond of dancing, which he did well, and his tall, Byronic good looks were an obvious attraction for young ladies. (On one occasion later in Constantinople he was given 'a pretty purse by a young lady I have never seen ... accompanied by a Greek letter entreating me to accept of the work of one of my slaves.'[24]) From between the lines of his letters emerges a picture of one who was certainly not driven by sexual appetite, but who felt the need of feminine company as an escape from boisterous masculinity and loneliness. That he found this during his enforced stay in Malta is clear, though with whom and just how far the affair went or might have gone is not; but it disturbed his conscience enough to induce him to make some confession to his mother, who had been assuring him that she was not worried at his lack of employment because she knew that he had 'the will and the desire to put all [his] time to good use.' David thanked her for the compliment, but begged her not to be under the illusion

> that I am more perfect than others, for I tell you frankly that unemployment can be as fatal for me as for others ... I have had to undergo a severe test which I cannot flatter myself I would have passed with all the necessary

Plate 1   James Justinian Morier in 1819 by Martin Seagrave

Plate 2 David Richard Morier circa 1820.

Plate 3 Mirza Abdul Hassan Khan

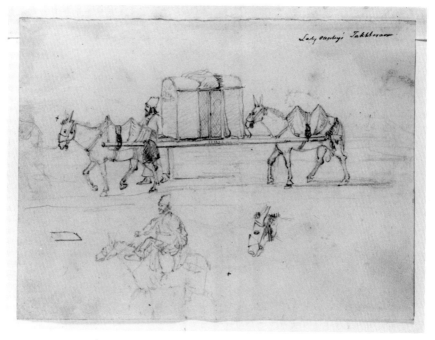

Plate 4 Lady Ouseley's litter sketched by James Morier. (By kind permission of the Master and Fellows of Balliol College, Oxford)

Plate 5 Bushire in 1811 sketched by James Morier. (By kind permission of the Master and Fellows of Balliol College, Oxford)

Plate 6 James Morier's sketch of his summer house at Damavand, near Tehran in 1815. (By kind permission of the Master and Fellows of Balliol College, Oxford)

A PERSIAN BREAKFAST.

Plate 7 James Morier's etching of a Persian breakfast from *A Second Journey through Persia, Armenia and Asia Minor to Constantinople between the years 1810 and 1816*

14.

The dress in which I travelled from Tehran to Constantinople in 1815. an english drab great coat, persian sheepskin Cap, a turkish Cartouch belt, & English Boots.

Plate 8 James Morier's sketch of himself dressed for a journey from Tehran to Constantinople in 1815. (By kind permission of the Master and Fellows of Balliol College, Oxford)

Plate 9   Captain Gaspard Deauville sketched by James Morier. (By kind permission of the Master and Fellows of Balliol College, Oxford)

COURDISH CHIEFS.

Plate 10 Kurdish chiefs drawn by James Morier

stoicism if the object had not been removed from my sight for ever. I render thanks very sincerely to God for having removed this temptation from me, and it is with all the fervour I am capable of that I pray never again to be exposed to the like. I do not fear, my dear mama, to make this confession to you, for you must know the human heart too well to suppose that just because I am your son I am spared the weaknesses and passions of other men. On the contrary, I fear that I have them in too great measure and that it is only the religious principles which you have instilled in me that have enabled me at my age to avoid the wildnesses for which perhaps only the opportunity has been lacking. See now, my good mama, if I am not justified in my impatience to be rescued from this terrible state of idleness and suspense. That I be given some work is all I ask.[25]

Rescue came not long after this outburst, when Canning appointed another emissary, Robert Adair,* to reopen negotiations with the Turks, and instructed David to join him as his secretary when he called at Malta on his way to Constantinople. When David heard of this his first thought was of the step this would be, 'small as it is, towards the improvement of our fortunes, for as we must look upon ourselves as each forming part of a small political society, so we must conclude that the welfare of one of its members cannot but contribute to that of all'; and, as he waited in August 1808 for Adair to arrive, the only cloud was the news that his brother Jack had been thrown out of government service without even a pension. 'Who the devil' he wrote to his mother 'would risk his life, his peace and every thing *pro bono publico* if he can look forward to no other remuneration than the memory of his service?'[26] But the euphoria generated by the news of this appointment evaporated somewhat when Adair turned up early in September in HMS Sea Horse. David discovered that his new chief had 'quite set his face against' any immediate communication with Ali Pasha, 'so that for the present I am a perfect cypher.' And his first reaction to Adair himself was one of wary suspicion: he 'is very polite to me, I may say kind if that epithet could be applied to the habitual smiling manner of a man of the world who is *made up*'.[27] He soon, however, overcame this first impression, and told his mother: 'He is a man of the world, very sociable, with much wit and knowledge and, having lived much in the turbulence of politics, his conversation is not only

---

* Robert Adair, 1763–1855, was a close friend of Charles James Fox, 1st Baron Holland, and had served in Vienna before this appointment. He was made KCB in 1809.

very amusing but instructive for young diplomats.' His only remaining reservation was a doubt whether Adair was at heart a man of morals, although he could not but be 'wholly content with the way Mr A treats me personally.'[28]

Of greater importance, however, was the intimate friendship which now developed between David and Adair's public secretary, Stratford Canning, cousin of the foreign secretary, whom he found to have

> all the qualities you would suppose incompatible with [this connection] for, instead of being proud, full of vanity and arrogance, giving himself the airs of a great politician ... he is the most amiable, well educated young man with the highest religious and moral feelings you could find ... He is only 21, but with all the liveliness of that age he has a good sense which would do honour to a man of 40. He is full of Greek and Latin but makes no parade of it, and he has such a sense of humour and fun that he makes a delightful companion. I blush ... that he knows more in his little finger than I know in my whole body.[29]

Such feelings were reciprocated in full measure, and they remained close friends for life despite the wide gap in professional status that opened up between them. Years later Stratford in his memoirs referred to David as one:

> whom I had already learned to esteem not more on the ground of his moral character than by reason of his talents and literary achievements. He was my constant associate, my never-failing resource during two eventful years [at Constantinople].[30]

Although David had a horror of using such a friendship to gain favours, it was not long after they sailed from Malta that he was unburdening himself to Stratford over the injustice he felt Jack had suffered. 'As young men soon become confidential towards each other' he told Jack 'I have communicated very openly to him all our consularian concerns.' Stratford seems to have had the measure of his rather austere relative, for 'he without any circumlocution told me that he is convinced that there is no man more ready to do justice to the claims of merit than his cousin, but that in no instance would he ever depart from precedent'.[31] (Perhaps, however, Stratford did put in a word, for Jack did eventually get a pension before being reemployed in 1810.)

Adair approached his assignment with patient subtlety – and quickly made use of David. Arriving off Tenedos on 23 September, he decided to test the waters by concealing his own presence on board Sea Horse, instead sending David ashore with a letter from Captain Stewart to the

Capitan Pasha pretending that, in Malta, he had met the negotiator
sent out from England, had seen his full powers and

> that the only thing which prevents his immediately approaching the
> Dardanelles is his desire to be assured that ... a plenipotentiary [of the
> Ottoman government] is ready to meet him in order to settle a treaty of
> peace, and that a convenient place has been fixed upon for the negotiation.[32]

The gun brig Saracen was detached for this mission and, after making
contact with the fort at the entrance to the Dardanelles, David was
invited to come ashore after dark to deliver his confidential letter. A
small boat was sent for him. What followed was 'cloak and dagger'
farce of a high order.

The instructions with the boat were that David should be in disguise,
and he had first to submit to the attentions of two Turks who 'after
enveloping me in a ponderous scarlet beniche were employed near a
quarter of an hour rolling up about twenty yards of muslin which was
to serve as my head piece.' It was then found that no skull cap had
been provided to form the base of this turban so 'one of the officiating
Turks very kindly accommodated me with his own *fesch* all reeking
with the effluvia of his own scalp (happily bald) which nothing on
earth would ever have induced me to put upon my head but the
urgent necessity of the occasion and the most ardent zeal for the
public service. I had the precaution, however, to turn this same skull
cap the wrong side out.' David was then rowed for some miles in
serene moonlight which almost made him fancy himself Diomedes
accompanied by 'the wily Ulysses [his dragoman] engaged in the secret
expedition to explore the Trojan camp and carry off the horses of
Rhesus.' It was after midnight, and the moon had set, when they
arrived opposite a house by the edge of the water. David was asked to
disembark 'which I found rather a difficult matter, for what with my
legs being quite benumbed with sitting for 3 hours and more, and
what with the unusual cumbersomeness of the thick drapery I was
involved in' he nearly fell into the water. In total darkness he was then
taken up to his ankles in mud and 'through half a dozen intricate
passages and chambers where I believe people were sleeping' to a
room 'half furnished, with a solitary candle in the corner.' There he
smoked a pipe with a Greek speaking secretary before being conducted
through more dark passages to meet the pasha, 'a huge, unwieldy,
broad lump looking for all the world like a monstrous toad' in a small
'closet' measuring 8 feet by 6. At the end of a conference, which lasted
nearly two hours, David understood that the new government in
Constantinople was very ready to enter into negotiations with any

envoy that might be sent from England. The return trip seemed less romantic; and as dawn was breaking before he got back to his ship David felt he made a ridiculous figure climbing back on board in his absurd costume as though returning from a fancy dress ball. But he experienced a glow of satisfaction at having performed an important diplomatic function with success.[33]

Adair's patience was now severely stretched: it was 17 November before he was able to make his first trip ashore to meet a Turkish plenipotentiary. For the next month messengers rode back and forth between them and Constantinople with texts and counter-texts for a treaty until, on Christmas Eve, Adair decided he could no longer be kept waiting in this way. He announced his intention of sailing for England on 31 December. On the 30th, after visible preparations for sailing had been made, he went ashore for a final but fruitless interview. It was by now too late, in an almost complete calm, to set sail and Adair therefore agreed a few hours later to an urgent request for another meeting next day, making clear, however, that he would certainly not delay his departure beyond 10 am. Next morning another counter-proposal was received which Adair found unacceptable, so he sent the Turkish messengers back with an unequivocal statement that unless the text he had proposed was accepted he was off. Half an hour later the messengers returned with an agreement to this, and the treaty was signed on 5 January 1809.

David was now sent overland to obtain from Constantinople the necessary *firman* authorising Sea Horse to go there and assuring Adair a proper reception. His journey took four adventurous days, in company with a king's messenger who was to carry overland to England duplicates of the despatches being sent home by sea. This messenger was somewhat of an encumbrance for David, who described him as 'very heavy and fat, and not knowing a word of any language other than his own' and as being 'totally incapable of looking after himself.' The road, after prolonged heavy rains, was a quagmire and, right from the start, the king's messenger was in trouble. They were moving at night and his horse, at the rear of the group, became stuck in a deep morasse. David spent half an hour 'in the most piercing cold I have ever experienced' while they pulled the poor animal by tail and ears and finally extricated it. But only a few hours later the same thing happened. This time they abandoned the beast to its fate and mounted the messenger on another. After that they travelled by day, but their nights were passed in miserable wayside shelters where they were unable to get properly dry or fully thawed out.[34]

The party struggled into Constantinople on 11 January, tired and filthy, but without any apparent ill effects. David even thought the experience might have done him good, and his reception was heart-warming. He was lodged for three days by the reis effendi himself, given a present of a tobacco box decorated with diamonds worth 2000 piastres and 'treated like a sultan.' The Turks he met were clearly delighted to be once again on good terms with the British, although they were still fearful of the punishment this might bring down on them from the French. Shortly after David had obtained the required *firman* the French chargé d'affaires called and, in his presence, lodged a protest at the news he had heard of the conclusion of a treaty with England. The reis effendi blandly assured the Frenchman that the signature by the Turkish plenipotentiary had not been authorised, a lie which filled David with astonishment and admiration, finding the Turkish 'diplomatic finesses no bad lessons for us young beginners: the French fully deserve to be thus grossly deceived as they have only been paid in their own coin.'[35]

Adair arrived in Constantinople on 26 January. The splendid new English palace, so flamboyantly designed and begun by Elgin, was not ready for occupation, having suffered depredation from both weather and human intervention during the period when relations had been broken. They had to be content with the house of the chief English dragoman, Pisani. David, however, wrote Jack that he couldn't be more comfortable 'having a snug room to myself and being on the most friendly terms with all my companions.' He felt, indeed, that this was probably preferable to being in the palace, which he thought 'a melancholy monument of the blunders of diplomatic *architecturising* [which] will one of these days, I am afraid, become a subject of enquiry in Parliament [it did, as other similar projects elsewhere in the world have done at intervals ever since] for the expenses are not by any means over.'[36] David was now about to spend the next three and a half years in Constantinople, apart from a period of ten months when he took James's place with Sir Harford Jones in Persia.

CHAPTER TEN

James 1809–1810

'I am every day making friends
that will be useful to me.'

Four months after David reached Constantinople in January 1809, James set out from Tehran in the company of Mirza Abul Hasan on the seven-month journey to London. Then only three months short of his 27th birthday, he had found his time in Persia interesting, and had made copious notes of everything he saw and heard; but they had not given him any desire to prolong his stay, still less to return for further duty among a people whose attitudes and manners he found distasteful. He was looking forward to getting home with hopes that, with Sir Harford's influence behind him, he would obtain a diplomatic post in Europe. He was not looking forward to several months as a sort of servant to a Persian who would, undoubtedly, expect him to show obsequious respect to the personal representative of the shah. To his great surprise, however, he soon discovered that his companion was a man of wit and culture, 'a perfect gentleman, even to our taste in his manner & conversation,'[1] who treated him as a friend, as ready to talk freely about his own life and Persian customs as to learn as much as he could about the English. And what James learned fascinated him, providing him with material of which he made much use in *Hajji Baba*.

Mirza Abul Hasan was a striking contrast to James. Tall, handsome, a lush black beard below his beautiful dark eyes contrasting with the dazzling white of his teeth, he towered above the rotund James, seven years his junior. He was born in Shiraz in 1776, son of a minister to the previous shah. His maternal uncle had been vizier to the first Qajar ruler, Aqa Muhammad, and it was his influence that had assured the succession of the present shah, Fath Ali. Abul Hasan had married one of his uncle's daughters. One of his brothers-in-law was a son of the shah and another the second vizier. But Abul Hasan had experienced a precarious life in the turbulence of Persian politics, indeed he might never have been born.

Abul Hasan's father had incurred the displeasure of Nadir Shah in 1747, and had been condemned to be burned alive. This shah, however, was assassinated the night before the execution was due, and Abul Hasan's father's life was spared to continue in high office until his death from natural causes. But Abul Hasan himself faced a similar fate some years later, when his uncle fell foul of Fath Ali Shah and was put to death. At that time Abul Hasan was governor of Shushtar, but as a member of the disgraced family he was arrested, brought naked and bound, before the shah and taken off for immediate execution. He told James: 'I was already on my knees, my neck was made bare, and the executioner had unsheathed his sword to sever my head from my body when … a messenger in great haste announced my reprieve.' A friend of the family had successfully persuaded the shah to pardon him. Not, however, putting any faith in the endurance of this leniency, Abul Hasan disobeyed the order to retire to his home city of Shiraz and returned to Shushtar where he was personally popular. There he was given 7000 piastres by public subscription, which enabled him to flee to Calcutta. He spent some two and a half years in India before receiving an assurance of the shah's forgiveness and returning to Persia. Although he then enjoyed the shah's favour again, and was able to play an active part in court affairs as aide to his brother-in-law, the second vizier, he could never be sure that he would not again fall out of favour. His appointment as envoy to the court of the English king was an important distinction, but he knew that unless he fulfilled it in a way that satisfied the shah he could, once again, be in trouble.

In India Abul Hasan had learned something of English ways. He was also blessed with a sense of humour which matched James's, and the two quickly became relaxed in each other's company. They travelled under the care of a *mehmandar*, but otherwise relatively simply. The mirza had less than a dozen in his suite and James himself only four, comprising Sir Harford's natural son Howell, a French valet previously in Sir Harford's service, and two Persian servants. They shared many discomforts, for the small villages at which they stopped could seldom produce more than rudimentary shelter, and more than once they were forced to spend a night in the open. James began to give English lessons to the mirza, who proved a quick learner, and to satisfy his consuming curiosity about England.

They left Tehran on 7 May 1809. Fifteen days brought them to Tabriz, a distance not far short of 400 miles. For the first time since setting out they could here enjoy comfort again, James himself lodging with the governor of the city which was the seat of Prince Abbas Mirza, the shah's presumed heir apparent. (No succession could be guaranteed over his brothers, but it was expected.) James declined a suggestion that he should request an audience with the prince, on the ground that he was simply in transit with no official business to transact at the court; but he spent some time with the prince's first vizier, whose son invited him to a dinner, at which he met 'a number of young and pleasant men who would have enlivened any company.'[2] After nine days of leisure in Tabriz they set off again on 1 June. At first James was delighted with the beauty of the countryside and the freshness of the climate, but on the 5th, just after they had pitched camp in order to avoid staying in a village believed to be in the grip of the plague, they were subjected to the fury of a violent thunderstorm with hailstones an inch across. Despite this, James found camping was preferable to staying in towns and villages where they invariably suffered the ravages of fleas.

They entered Turkish territory on the 8th, and soon began to meet with many difficulties. Here the *firman* they carried from Prince Abbas was effective only to the extent that local pashas or agas felt themselves more likely to suffer from Persian displeasure than to be under the protection of the authorities in far off Constantinople, and their reception varied from the hospitable to refusal even of entry into villages, so that they had to camp in the open. They reached Erzerum on the 15th, having covered some 300 miles in two weeks from Tabriz. Here they were politely received by the governor, who invited them to dinner; but between towns travel was dangerous. Bands of disgruntled soldiers were roaming the country – apparently owing allegiance to no one unless, from time to time, a pasha would employ and feed them to help him in his quarrel with a neighbour – demanding food and shelter with menaces from isolated communities and threatening travellers. Although James and the mirza were not themselves attacked, they were in constant fear of it, and sometimes had to make diversions when they heard of a band of marauders ahead of them. As James put it in a letter he sent ahead to David in Constantinople, since coming into Turkey 'we have led the life of dogs ... the country is in great confusion: everyone commands, some obey, & between the kicker & the kicked we have come in for a good share of the blows.' He was tempted to break away from his Persian companions and complete the journey at high speed on his own with his own small party, but he resisted, partly from a sense of responsibility towards the mirza and partly from fear of the possibility of being robbed and losing the despatches he was carrying.

But he begged David to come some of the way to meet them, and to send a messenger out with a *firman* from the Porte, by which they might hope to get better treatment from the local governors on their route.[3]

The dangers of travel through this area led to their agreeing, on leaving Erzerum (on the 21st), to take under their wing an extraordinary lone traveller who wanted the protection of a large group. He was a Bosnian wearing, for his protection, 'a coat of mail under his clothes and a burnished helmet on his head, and was armed with two heavy rifle guns, a pair of pistols, a long [dagger] and a sword, besides a variety of powder flasks etc, which altogether made him weigh thirty stone.'[4] He was a drolé character given to whiling away the tedium of long days' treks by singing doleful patriotic songs. James noticed that they were usually drenched by a rain storm every time he did this and, rather unkindly, told the credulous Persians that this singing was a well known Bosnian way of calling up rain. The result, of course, was that every time the poor man tried to break into song after this he was forcibly silenced.[*]

Between Erzerum and Amasya – a distance of some 400 miles which they covered in seventeeen days – they had to spend many a night in the open, sometimes in heavy rain. They did however find rare hospitality at one small town, where they were lodged in the aga's own house and welcomed as guests of honour at a dinner to which their host invited local leading men, such as the schoolmaster and the priest, who 'arrived with very good appetites for the feast; for no sooner were they seated and the lamb placed before them, than every one had his right hand in the dish at once, tearing off as large pieces from the animal as his strength and dexterity would admit.' Perhaps it was the contrast with the unfriendliness they had experienced in so many other places that led James to comment that:

> although such a meal may be repugnant to the delicacy of those who have been accustomed to a civilized mode of eating, yet there was a species of wild and generous hospitality in the manner of these people that I could not help admiring; and a few ingredients of which would add extremely to the delights of a modern table.[5]

At Amasya – where he was particularly struck by the beauty of the unveiled women – James finally decided that he could no longer put up with their slow progress. On 10 July he set off on his own with only

---

[*] It was suggested by Bernard Bevan, great-grandson of William Morier, that Lewis Carroll may have read James's travel book and got from this incident the idea for the White Knight in *Alice Through the Looking Glass*. It is an engaging thought which would have appealed to James.

a *tatar* and a *janissary* as company. By dint of hard riding in all weathers, often through much of the night, he covered the remaining 500 miles to Constantinople in seven days. As *tatars* enjoyed a protected status as carriers of the mail, and were usually well treated at any stop for refreshment or a night's shelter, James decided to conceal his true identity, something he could do easily, for 'my appearance bespoke very little of the master ... my black skin cap was become very dusty; my silk trowsers were all torn; my Persian boots were soaked with rain and twisted under the heel; whilst my coat and great coat were all in dirt and in rags.'[6] So he pretended to be a poor Persian travelling under the protection of the *tatar*. It amused him to let the *tatar* give all the orders – and get the better share of any comfort going – especially as in this way he had to pay only a fraction of what would have been demanded of him had his true identity been known. He even took pleasure in finding how hardy he had become and 'how little food and how little sleep are necessary for health and strength.'

To his great disappointment James reached Scutari too late on 17 July to be able to cross over to Constantinople that night, having, as he wrote, 'completed the journey from Tehran in two months and ten days in which time I had not once slept out of my clothes.'[7] He did so very early next morning, hoping to surprise his father (who had returned from Malta in April) and his brother David, who had not come to meet him on the way. He found his father absent, so he sent the servant round to waken David with a message that there was someone who wished to see him, 'he believed a Jew with business to discuss.' David guessed who it might be while he hastily dressed and, sure enough, at his father's house he found 'Mr Jem dressed as a Persian with a red beard which would not have disgraced a pharisee.' Sadly for posterity, David had no chance to make even a quick sketch of this figure before a barber was called and the beard was off. Under it David found James quite unchanged except that he was fatter and more rotund than ever, despite his hard travelling, and now had a deep copper complexion contrasting with the white where the beard had been so that it was 'difficult to decide if he was more like a negro who was turning white or a white who was turning black.'[8]

James now established himself in a house of his own in Pera, and he and David spent many a happy hour together while he waited for Abul Hasan to catch him up. They went together to meet him, three hours' journey out from Scutari, on 3 August – seeing on the way columns of volunteers coming to reinforce the sultan's army challenging the Russians on the Danube. David was surprised to notice that these columns consisted mostly of priests, inspired by religious zeal which, he hoped, would be sufficient to make up for their lack of arms. 'One would have two sabres and a pistol, the next a pistol and a pipe, another only his pipe'; but their discipline and courageous bearing was impressive as they went 'to meet whatever destiny their Prophet had assigned them.'[9] The mirza and his party were then lodged in Scutari. Adair was very attentive, giving parties and balls in his honour. James was amused by the reactions of the mirza's companions to finding unveiled women at such entertainments, and seeing western style dancing (something Abul Hasan himself had already seen in India). Although James may have wished to introduce some compliments to the Persians in his travel book, there is nevertheless an air of sincerity in the way he expressed his admiration for their readiness to adapt to the customs of those they were with, such as eating with knives and forks. 'In the national character of Persians' he wrote, 'the most striking difference from that of the Turk is perhaps the facility with which he adopts foreign manners and customs ... I am sure that if the Persians had possessed as much communication with Europeans as the Turks have had, they would at this day not only have adopted many of our customs but, with their natural quickness, would have rivalled us in our own arts and sciences.'[10]

The problem now, however, was how to get the mirza to England. There was no suitable naval vessel at Constantinople. After some delay it was arranged that HMS Success would be sent to Smyrna for them and James went ahead to make all the arrangements. Travelling overland he arrived at the top of the pass above the city on 22 August, a couple of hours before sunset, and was overwhelmed by all the memories the magnificent view awoke. But his arrival in the city itself was almost as tumultuous as when his mule had dashed into consul Hochepied's parlour in March 1804 (Chapter 5). It was dark, and at the narrow entrance to Frank Street, he came face to face with a party of friends who were leaving for the country. The noise and confusion was memorable as the respective *janissaries* shouted for passage, the friends tried to exchange news and the horses 'began to fight, kick and screech in the most discordant manner.' James was welcomed warmly by all his relations and friends, both in Smyrna and at Sidiköy; but his meeting with the Wilkinsons was fateful. He had to tell David that 'the old folks talked to me of their daughter in such manner as would really have melted a heart of stone, protesting that I stood arbiter of her misery or happiness in this life. Said I – I'll marry your daughter

the first moment I'm able, and I'll do all I can to make her happy –
to which they have agreed, and I will with God's help do all that in
my power lies to keep my word.'[11] How much this was the result of
having his passions reawakened by seeing Maria again, and how much
it was simply the reaction of an honourable man is unclear. There was
little sign of joy in that letter to David, yet there is later evidence that
he did continue to believe he was genuinely in love with her – although
in the end there was no marriage.

The mirza and his party joined James at Smyrna on 5 September,
and all went on board next day to a salute of 15 guns – a signal honour
which gave the mirza great pleasure – and the cheers of a large crowd
of onlookers. The ship was small, but Captain Ayscough received them
with all courtesy and kindness, and ensured they had as much comfort
as could be contrived. Abul Hasan soon 'accommodated himself to the
manner of a ship, sleeping in a cot and eating with knife and fork.'[12]
He had even, with good humour, submitted himself and his companions
to James's instructions to have a thorough scrub in the baths before
embarking 'as next to the French the navy have no greater enemy than
a louse.'[13] Going to sea was a totally new experience for the mirza's
companions, but they too showed great adaptability, although filled
with wonder at how it was possible to find one's way out of sight of
land, and at the ability of ships to communicate with each other by flag
signal. At Malta they transferred to the larger and more comfortable
HMS Formidable, but were not allowed to go ashore because of
quarantine regulations. As they neared England the relaxed mood of
the Persian party was affected by the rougher seas and the greyness of
the weather, and the mirza himself began to show signs of tension as
he wondered what kind of reception would be extended to him. He
knew that his reputation with the shah depended on this, for if it was
not of the highest and most magnificent order, thus showing proper
regard for the shah's own status, he would be blamed. While he
personally took pleasure in the informal atmosphere on board ship, he
could not help wondering whether the English really understood the
importance, when he would be in the public eye, of treating him with
the respect and dignity due to his sovereign. Unfortunately, although at
first all went well, his worst fears were later realised and James found
himself with a very different, and difficult, person on his hands.

James had taken the precaution of writing to the Foreign Office from
Malta, stressing the importance of sending a reception party to the

Downs, where they were expecting to land, and ensuring that there would be no delay in their getting ashore and on to London. To give credit where it is due, this was arranged; but weather conditions forced Formidable to make her landfall at Plymouth, on 25 November, where no arrangements had been made. As a result it was the 30th before authority could be obtained from London to release the party from quarantine and allow them ashore. The mirza seemed to realise that this was an accident of the weather, and took it in good part, accepting without question the specious explanation that 'not even the king himself' may leave a ship for four days after arrival at an English port' and being consoled by 'the sight of the flowers and trees on the hillside by the harbour.'[14] While they waited the mirza was also mollified by the presents delivered to him from the city dignitaries, while musicians and dancers were sent on board to entertain him. He was surprised to find a crowd of women coming on board who, as he wrote in his journal:

> with bewitching guile and seductive glances captured the hearts of the seamen … [and] … of certain deprived Iranians. Sounds of the seamen's carousing and love-making reached even the ebony wheel of heaven and the din of their music and singing so excited my comrades that they were overcome by a desire to worship the vine.

He recorded without comment Captain Fayerman's possibly teasing explanation that

> if these harlots were not allowed to relieve the crew of their money, to empty their pockets as clean as a glutton his plate, the shipowners might be faced with a shortage of labour for the next voyage.[15]

The mirza remained in relaxed good humour when the party was eventually able to disembark, and he was received by a military guard of honour and salutes from the Formidable's guns. Once installed in the best inn, the Golden Lion, he was called upon by the admiral of the port, the general officer commanding the garrison and many ladies of local society anxious to see this exotic visitor. A whole suite of rooms had been prepared for him, and a magnificent meal was awaiting him in a room lined with mirrors, a feature which, in Persia, was considered fitting only for royal apartments. The mirza had realised that the journey to the capital would take a few days: indeed, such was his misunderstanding of the distance that he was fully prepared to find himself a couple of weeks on the road, and, therefore, all the more delighted and astonished to find that the *caravanserais* were so luxurious.

The next day was spent seeing over the naval and military establishments of Plymouth, while some of the mirza'a servants were sent ahead, piling into a coach fully armed and insisting on sitting cross-legged on the floor. The mirza and James followed on 2 December, spending two nights in Bath and another at Hartford Bridge, where they were met by Charles Vaughan – now private secretary to the foreign secretary, Lord Bathurst* – and the under-secretary of state, Terrick Hamilton. They had brought three official coaches for the remaining stretch to London, which they began on 5 December. Thus far the mirza had been content with the attentions paid to him, and delighted with the comfort and speed of travel on English roads. But James then experienced, as he put it in a letter to Sir Harford Jones,

> one of the most disagreeable days I ever past [sic] in my life ... [The mirza's] spirits were excellent as far as Hounslow, but began to droop extremely as he approached Brentford; he saw no crowds, no soldiers, there was no *isteqbal* [official high level reception party] announced, & he only replied to our assurances that public entries were never granted to ambassadors on the first day of their arrival at our capital by the most virulent language, & by upbraidings that no honour was paid to his king's name ... Nothing would convince him that he was not slighted, & his king's name disrespectfully treated[16]

The mirza felt that he was being 'smuggled into town more like a bale of goods than a public envoy'[17] – and his reactions were understandable. In Persia it was the custom for a distinguished person, particularly the representative of a king, to be met some way out from the capital city by an official of high rank and a guard of honour, and for his entry to be through crowds of onlookers showing their respect – as had been the case with Sir Harford. The mirza would have to report in detail to the shah on his reception, and was liable to be disgraced (or worse) if it seemed he had belittled his sovereign by submitting to such undignified treatment as was being shown to him now. Even the magnificence of the house at 9 Mansfield Street which was to be his residence, and the banquet awaiting him, failed to raise his spirits or improve his temper. He also discovered that it might be weeks, in the normal course of English protocol, before he would be able to present his credentials to the king, and that ambassadors from other countries were ahead of him in the queue. Such a delay would not have occurred in Persia and the mirza, despite all explanations, considered it another insult to the shah. He flatly refused to stir from the house until he had been received by the king, and threatened to return at once to Persia

---

* Henry Bathurst, 1762–1834, a close friend of Pitt's. He became 3rd Earl in 1794 and was foreign secretary for only three months at the end of 1809.

if this could not be arranged within five days. As James wrote to Sir Harford, 'if every part of our etiquette & court customs had been explained [to the mirza] previous to his setting out from Persia it would have done away an uncommon deal of the difficulty which has taken place in making him understand them.'[18] The trouble was that neither James nor Sir Harford had any experience of the way these things were done in England, so had been in no position to provide such warnings.

After the trouble that had been taken to cultivate Persian good will, and Sir Harford's success in concluding the preliminary treaty of friendship, the mirza's threat was an alarming one which had to be taken seriously. The Marquess Wellesley* was due to replace Lord Bathurst as foreign secretary next day, and James was taken to see him to explain the situation. James found him full of understanding, and he immediately had Sir Gore Ouseley† officially gazetted as the mirza's *mehmandar*, ordered James himself to attend on the mirza as a sort of private secretary (and live at Mansfield Street) and set about doing what he could to arrange an early audience with the king. Moreover, he decided that the mirza, who had been described by Sir Harford as a mere chargé d'affaires, should be called envoy extraordinary and referred to as ambassador. James thought the appointment of Wellesley at this moment to be the greatest good fortune, for 'had any other person been in office … nobody would have known how to treat the mirza.'[19] He was not overjoyed at having to move into Mansfield Street: he would much rather have stayed with his mother, his brother Jack and his sisters at his mother's house in Devonshire Street after such a long absence abroad. But his reward was the further insight this gave him into Persian manners which he used to such effect in his second novel, *The Adventures of Hajji Baba of Ispahan in England*.

Wellesley went even further, calling on the mirza personally on 11 December and getting the prime minister, Spencer Perceval, to do the same two days later. And he managed to persuade the king to receive the mirza in public audience with the minimum delay, with the full panoply of an escort of Horse Guards, thus going well beyond what even a fully accredited ambassador could have expected in normal circumstances. Unfortunately, however, it would have taken some time to arrange this, and the mirza preferred to cut further delay and be

---

* Richard Colley Wellesley, 1760–1842, eldest brother of Arthur, Duke of Wellington, had been Minto's predecessor as governor-general of India until 1807. He was foreign secretary 1809–12.

† Gore Ouseley, 1770–1844, oriental scholar with a deep knowledge of Persian literature, had been ADC to the Nabob of Oudh and made baronet in 1808.

satisfied with a private audience and less pomp. Even so, this was an occasion which gave him much pleasure and attracted great public attention, so anxious were people to get sight of an exotic eastern potentate. According to contemporary press reports, crowds gathered outside Mansfield Street from an early hour on 20 December to watch the mirza, gorgeously attired, come out 'carrying his credentials in his hand in an elegant gold casket upon a silver salver covered with crimson velvet' to enter one of the king's carriages pulled by 'six beautiful bay horses with the servants in their new state liveries and dressed in every respect as if to attend his majesty in state, except having hats on instead of caps.'[20] With Sir Gore and James beside him, followed by two other carriages with his own staff, they processed through New Bond Street where 'the windows of the stores in the principle storey were all thrown open [despite the falling snow] and crowded with elegantly dressed and beautiful females'[21]: the streets and St James's Park were so crowded with onlookers, all cheering lustily, that the carriages were frequently held up. At Buckingham Palace (then known as Buckingham House, the Queen's House or the Queen's Palace) the mirza was allowed to enter by the main door. He was then surprised to find the king waiting for him all alone 'in a small gilded room.' In Persia an ambassador would have been received with awesome ceremony, having to remove his shoes and bow to the ground, at a distance, before a shah surrounded by courtiers. The mirza was impressed and captivated by the simple friendliness of the king, and recorded him in his journal as having flattered him by saying: 'Until today we have seen no ambassador from any monarch so young and so learned',[22] a compliment no doubt embellished in Sir Gore's elegant translation into Persian. On his return to Mansfield Street, the mirza only managed to get from his carriage to the front door through the cheering crowd with the help of the 'Bow-street patrole'.

The mirza was now happy, particularly as he had been given, at his request, an official letter to send to the shah explaining the cause of the delay in getting this audience and that it was neither his fault nor indicative in any way of disrespect towards his monarch. All the expenses of his establishment at Mansfield Street were met by the British government. He had a permanent private box at the opera. During the next six months he became, from time to time, impatient at the delay on the part of the British government in giving consideration to the treaty he had brought with him; but he was so flattered by the way he was lionised by society, and by royalty itself (he was received in private audience by both the queen and the Prince of Wales, both gave receptions in his honour, and both the Duke of York and the Princess of Wales invited him to private dinners) that his protests at this only once had any real force. He was made much of by the City and the East India Company, and scarcely a day went by when his activities were not reported in the press. Women of every class and age vied for the attention of this handsome, exotic man and were enchanted by the pretty compliments he paid in his quaint English, in which, thanks to James's tuition, he became quite fluent. He himself was frank in his journal about losing his heart to many a pretty girl, particularly the foreign secretary's niece, Emily Wellesly-Pole. And Mrs Calvert* recorded in her journal that 'this fiery Eastern potentate showed such warm admiration of the lovely Isabella [daughter] that we were at one time troubled lest he should make proposal for her hand.'[23] There were some (though not of the best society) who threw themselves at him and begged to be taken back to Persia. Perhaps he was tempted. Years later James, in the notes he made in his copy of Samuel Bagster's Treasury Bible – comparing passages in the scriptures with scenes and customs he himself had observed in Persia and Turkey – wrote with reference to Genesis chapter 31 verse 50 that the mirza, although allowed under Mohammeden law to do so, felt he could not take a second wife, for fear of the reactions of her powerful relatives, even though the one he had was older than he 'and no longer attractive.'

After the strict separation of women in Persia, the freedom of society in England was certainly heady for Abul Hasan and his entourage. Even in his *Hajji Baba in England* James, however, gives little away as to how these visitors coped with all the temptations. In a letter to Sir Harford he wrote that:

> … a few of [the mirza's] servants have got with the doctor's list, having made some acquaintances in Suffolk Street that have not turned out much to their advantage, altho' they have gained something by the connection which will be lasting & which they may stand a chance to hand down to their posterity.[24]

But he refrained, at least in surviving writings, from any comment on the mirza's own behaviour in this respect. Abul Hasan himself records in his journal the occasion on 22 June 1810, when he was out walking and

---

* The Hon Frances Pery, 1767–1859, wife of Nicolson Calvert.

... two women came up to me and asked if they could call on me at home.
I agreed and in the evening they both came to the house. One of the women
was younger and better looking than the other and I was more attentive to
her than to the other. The second woman became jealous and started to
make a scene ... I was alarmed and fled from the room ... Mr Morier, who
was asleep in his bedroom, was awakened by the uproar; finally he went
into the drawing-room in his white night-shirt and eventualy managed to
get them to leave.[25]

This was an incident of which James made good use in chapter 32 of
Hajji Baba in England. The woman who claimed in a letter to the gutter
press that she was pregnant by the mirza, however, was apparently
well known as having also claimed to have had children by all the
royal princes, so could be dismissed as living in a fantasy world. But
what of a Miss Rankin who lived at 45 Foley Street? She did not use
the press, but she wrote to Sir Harford claiming that the mirza was

... so determined for me to come [to Persia] that we agreed I should procure
sailors dresses for myself and servant [but could not persuade the captain of
the ship] to represent me on board ... as his son – which was the wish of
the Meerza [sic] – unless Sir Gore Ouseley would give his consent.[26]

Her allegations were serious enough to involve even the prime minister
in efforts to buy her off.

James, although not always included in the party when the mirza
was invited out, had to spend a great deal of his time with him or on
his business, which could be irksome. He did, however, derive much
pleasure and advantage from being thus thrown into prominence in
the press and high society, telling Sir Harford 'I am every day making
friends that will be, I hope, one of these days useful to me.'[27] It says
much about his character that, despite having been in almost
continuous intimate company with Abul Hasan since May 1809, and
despite his natural wish to spend time with his own family and friends
now he was back in England, he seems to have managed, with only an
occasional hiccough, to remain on the best of terms with the Persian
throughout the eight months of their time together in London (and
indeed thereafter). His family too made much of the mirza, who
recorded in his journal for 14 December 1809: 'As they kindly did
every morning, Mr Morier's sisters came to see me. Because I was not
feeling well they arranged for a doctor to attend me.'[28] The mirza
often visited the Morier home, where he became devoted to Clara
(who gave him a miniature of one of her daughters which he
cherished), and thought that 'Mr Morier's sisters sang English songs
prettily.'[29]

There was the occasional friction, however. Once, in February 1810,

James, believing that the mirza was angry with him, got the idea that his presence in the house at Mansfield Street was an irritation. The mirza recorded in his journal that he had 'summoned Mr Morier and said: "I am amazed! How little you seem to know me. I thought our journey together on land and sea had been sufficient test of our friendship." Mr Morier agreed and apologised.'[30] On another occasion, in May, the mirza was angry with James for overstepping the limits of intimacy in public; and in June James had to be reprimanded when the mirza complained of his entertaining friends at Mansfield Street when he himself was out.[31] But the journal also contains evidence that they enjoyed much intimate fun together, during which James, to the mirza's delight, sometimes told vulgar jokes (although apparently no worse than some told by the Duke of York).[32] And James was evidently as keen as the mirza himself on flirting with society beauties: the mirza comments on 4 April 'Mr Morier is in love with Miss Hume,' a talented amateur violinist, daughter of the art patron Sir Abraham Hume, who in fact married the 2nd Baron Brownlow later that year (and died four years later).[33] Miss Rankin, however, may have been exaggerating when she claimed that when James

> ... was sent to me to tell me I could not go to Persia ... he pretended to fall in love and made to me advances wich [sic] I seriously repulst [sic], and indeed such was his conduct that had I not bin [sic] a woman I should have shown him battle on the business ... Indeed Morier's conduct and behaviour to me from first to last was gross, ungentlemanlike nay unmanly.[34]

In fact, James was evidently still in love with Maria Wilkinson, or at least believed so. In a letter dated 2 March 1810 he thanked Sir Harford for having 'written me the kindest letter I ever received, under the title of the Romance at Smyrna,' evidently containing advice about his passion for Maria, and perhaps, though this can only be deduced from James's reply, urging him to marry her. 'This subject' James explained to Sir Harford

> ... as it comprehends the happiness or misery of another, has weighed upon my mind more than words can express for now past three years, because I find myself drawn by so many different claims of duty both in the adoption or non adoption of the line of conduct you prescribe. As far as my own happiness is concerned, I would not hesitate to marry Maria tomorrow if I could, both of us standing in the same shoes we now stand in, but I have most seriously reflected, on what I look upon as a much higher concern, the situation of my own unprovided family.

He went on to write of the probability of his father's having to return to England with no income, possibly to die, in which case

... what is to become of my mother & her three daughters totally unprovided for? It is these considerations which must make me determine to sacrifice the desire I have to be committed to the woman I love, in order that I may provide for those who have such far greater claims upon [me] for subsistence. I only need place the accumulation of misery which must of necessity accrue to my family, by bringing another member & perhaps many more to add to its wants, before your eyes, to make [you] agree with me that it is better not to marry under such circumstances.[35]

Even given the high minded morality by which James was generally guided, that hardly suggests an overwhelming passion for Maria from which nothing could divert him – and it appears, from a passage in a letter to David the following year, that he may even at this time have been contemplating matrimony, as a result of 'a transient affection', with someone whose 'fortune would have put us all above want', but whose mother evidently later decided should not be tied down to someone likely to be in Persia for several years.[36] Indeed, James may have had a number of amorous adventures at this stage of his life. William, the youngest brother, wrote to David in 1812: 'Old Jem has let me into a secret or two, one of which has astonished me very much, the other comes in the course of every man's life. Indeed both of them do more or less.'[37]

This time in London with the mirza was a turning point in James's career, and also an important stage in his progress towards becoming an author of renown. He and Sir Harford had talked of writing a book together about their adventures since they had set out for Persia from England in October 1807. James now had with him in London the 'manuscript journal in as bad an order as ever'[38] which he had been keeping. He showed this to Robert Inglis,* who persuaded him in April to have it published immediately rather than wait to produce something jointly with Sir Harford later. Together they managed, despite James's other preoccupations, to complete most of the editing before he left again in July. Thus was born the first book of his travels in Persia, Armenia and Asia Minor – eventually published in 1812. He asked permission to dedicate it to Sir Harford, telling him he intended it 'as the forerunner of another of much greater size & more solid

---

* Robert Harry Inglis, 1789–1855, son of Sir Hugh Inglis, Bt, director in the East India Company, from whom he inherited the baronetcy in 1820. For a few years, while training as a barrister, from 1806 he was private secretary to Henry Addington, 1st Viscount Sidmouth.

materials, which is the book we so frequently have called our book, so I hope I shall have all your materials to add to those I shall glean during my next stay in Persia, & then cook them up quietly on my return.'[39] But before the first was published the friendship between James and Sir Harford broke up. The dedication never appeared, and the second travel book, published in 1818, was again James's own work. But as he left England to return to Persia in July 1810 – in the suite of the new ambassador Sir Gore Ouseley – James had no inkling of the troubles that were in store for him in his relations with Sir Harford.

CHAPTER ELEVEN

David 1809–1812

'My ambition is to be so placed
that I can do something worthwhile.'

Early in January 1809 David learned that Jack had at last been awarded a pension, and had taken himself off to Cambridge for some quiet study*. Jack now planned, if he could find the right wife with money, to take up farming. David wrote to his brother:

> ... I think £400 p annum for a single man who is not extravagant will make him very comfortable, and the manner in which you propose to spend your time ... really makes my mouth water. Were it my own case I should for the present prefer the cultivation of the muses to that of a farm, and I think you will find yourself to be rather too young and active for the occupation of a retired husbandman, whilst among the libraries of Cambridge your mind will find the most delightful exercise.

He was glad that Jack would not again be

> ... embarked in the thankless office of Albanian Pasha baiter, for neither fame or fortune is to be acquired by it and it is too great a sacrifice of one's best years to spend them among savages from whom nothing can be learnt than either to be brutal or melancholy.

But it looked as though he himself might be doing just that. Adair, once he was sure of Turkish goodwill after concluding his treaty, decided that contact with Ali Pasha should be resumed and was thinking of sending David to Ioannina. 'Do not think that I grumble at the prospect' the latter told Jack

> ... for I assure you that I am just now quite pleased with the idea of the active life ... and particularly with the hope that in the intervals of the journeys and business I may have to make I shall be able to give myself up entirely to my propensity for the classics, of which I intend to carry about

---

* Cambridge University have no trace in their records of Jack's having been following a recognised course of study.

with me a small select set, without any other books but my bible and prayer book of which one can feel the true value of only in a separation from one's friends like that I am likely to endure.

He had sent to Sidiköy for James's old faithful Greek servant, Stasso – 'with him at my heels I shall feel myself ready for any work' – to replace his 'present squire, a precious Maltese blockhead improving daily in blunders and stupidity.'[1] And he assured his mother that he was

> ... getting used to the idea of passing several years of my life in these countries, and as I am young I should have no complaint provided I have occupations to take me from the fatal leisure to listen to the passions of my age. I fear I am hardly in a career where one makes a fortune, but that is something that doesn't concern me for the present, my object being to get used to acting alone according to my own strengths and my own lights, because I feel that so long as one has no responsibility thrust upon one, one remains chicken-hearted and irresolute, or rather one doesn't know one's courage and resources.[2]

But David was not destined for Ioannina after all. Adair had to get Foreign Office approval for re-opening contact with Ali Pasha, and in March he learned that Leake had already been sent to Ioannina for this purpose. He then suggested sending David to join him, but Leake made it clear that he would not welcome having someone from the mission in Constantinople on his patch. David viewed this with mixed feelings, on the one hand not sorry to be spared the hazards and discomforts of such a journey, on the other frustrated at being deprived of the chance to show what he was capable of. There was in prospect another way of showing this: Adair, who had asked to be allowed to return to Vienna, had recommended to the Foreign Office that David be made Secretary of Embassy when his successor was appointed. David, however, saw little chance of its being approved unless his friend Lord Aberdeen were to be given the post (a possibility of which he had heard a rumour) in which case, as he told James,

> ... I have a chance of something you know. I am not very ambitious ... but I must confess that I am anxious to be put in a place of responsibility, because I am sure that is the only way of learning business and acquiring confidence in oneself which I want of very much, having been for the last two years in little better than a state of inactivity.[3]

But for the present he still had no clear cut job of work to do, and, in his frustration, he proposed to Adair that he should go off to the Turkish army then confronting the Russians on the Danube, as Jack had done in Egypt nine years earlier. 'I feel' he told Jack 'that the

personal inconveniences and dangers of such a life as one must lead
in a Turkish camp are at all hazards to be preferred to the miserable
apathy of a Pera life ... which is the very perfection of moral
vegetation.' He was doing his best to occupy himself in learning Turkish
and reading books designed to fit him for the diplomatic career he was
hoping to achieve, but it was a struggle:

> ... What with the keeping up what little I have of [classical Greek], with
> improving the modern, with scraping together a little Turkish, and with
> becoming master of my business, and what with governing the little republic
> of my passions amd preventing their forming a league with the indolence
> and listlessness which ... are so apt to creep into one's habits, I have enough
> to occupy my thoughts by day & my dreams by night for as many years as
> I may be doomed to reside in this — country. I leave you to apply what
> epithets you think most adapted.'[4]

Here again, however, David was frustrated: the Turks never agreed to
his joining them at the front.

Early in July Adair received from London the ratification of the
treaty he had concluded in January, and his formal appointment as
ambassador. But for David there was disappointment: George Canning
was not prepared to promote him to Secretary of Embassy. 'I am
dissatisfied' he wrote to Jack 'because I feel my own present insignific-
ance'; but, modest as ever, he added 'I don't know that I deserve to be
better placed – but I want to be good for something, which it is most
likely I never shall be in this line', and showed no bitterness that
Stratford Canning, although younger, got the job.[5] Nevertheless he was
now set on making a career in diplomacy. Sir Alexander Ball had
offered to get him appointed private secretary to the naval commander-
in-chief in the Mediterranean, but 'both my inclination and habits' he
told Lord Radstock 'would lead me to prefer [diplomacy] however
inferior in point of gain, to all the pecuniary advantages of any
situation at sea.'[6] What really irked him was the lack of useful
occupation. 'I am more idle and useless than ever' he wrote to
Aberdeen, privately: 'You would ... do me a particular favour by
pointing out to the Secretary of State how improper it is to give away
sinecures in this country – for really I can't give my present post any
other name.'[7] But his escape from this situation came when James, on
his way through Constantinople with Mirza Abul Hasan, suggested
(and Adair readily agreed) that David should be sent to Persia with
despatches and stay there as long as Sir Harford Jones could make use
of his services.

⊕

David set out from Constantinople with Stasso on 30 August. It took
them 44 days to reach Tabriz, longer than expected. In the first 23
days he managed only 200 hours on horseback, having frequently to
spend 24 hours, occasionally even 48, bargaining for changes of horses.
He was fortunate, however, in falling in after the first day with a minor
Turkish official travelling in the same direction – as this meant that
between them they had an escort of twelve armed guards with which
to face any attacks by robbers (of which in fact none materialised). On
James's advice, David had dressed himself in *tatar* fashion, all except
the enormous tall hat which these messengers always wore, preferring
instead a turban of white muslin as he had worn for his midnight
assignation with the Turks at the entrance to the Dardanelles a year
earlier. He had shaved his head and allowed his moustaches (but not
a beard) to grow until with his 'wide trousers, boots, three or four
belts, turban, pistol, daggers, sword and whip' he began to look like
Don Quixote.[8] Whether it was sensible of him to travel thus dressed
may be doubted, for it appears to have confused local chieftans over
his true identity.* He carried a *firman* describing him as *Elchi Bey*
(honourable envoy), which meant he was addressed with respect and
even received with honours; but the hospitality was not always
generous, and respect and honours not always what they should have
been. He was accommodated by one pasha in the house of an
Armenian maker of iron grills in a gallery open to the air and the
smells of a cow. Here he was constantly subjected to the importunities
of crowds demanding money because he was an *elchi bey*. Fetched to go
to an audience with the pasha he noticed some men erecting a sort of
giant blunderbuss in the courtyard of the house 'pointing exactly to
the corner where the privy stood' which, when they put a light to it,
went off with an enormous explosion bringing down quantities of
plaster and mud and all his possessions and clothes in his 'room'.
Recovering from this 'salute', David was then taken on horseback, not
as he had thought to see the pasha, but to spend an hour with some
unidentified local official eating melon and smoking a pipe. After
returning to his now damaged lodging and waiting there some time,
David was again fetched and – escorted by 'a mob of knaves' preceded
by one wielding 'his ceremonial rod of office to which were attached
little chains making a tinkling noise like a child's bell' – was again
placed on a horse, this time to go to the pasha's 'palace'. In his honour
as he supposed, and perhaps to impress him with the severity of the

---

* James must have got from David's experiences on this journey some of the ideas
  for Lord Osmond's experiences in his novel *Ayesha Maid of Kars*.

pasha's governance, the route was strewn with the heads of recently decapitated thieves. On arrival at the 'palace' he was met by a man of fearsome appearance '6 or 7 feet high who performed leaps in front of me twirling his monstrous moustaches and uttering shouts as loud as cannon fire.' The pasha received him politely enough, but on his return to his quarters he was once again pestered on all sides for money by those who claimed to have been instrumental in procuring him the audience. And when he tried to satisfy them with a few piastres his money was thrown to the ground with imprecations as being insultingly small.[9]

Once into Persia David had an easier time, and he found a haven of peace for two days with the Armenian Christian community of Uç Kilise ('The Three Churches') at Ecmiadzin, which he reached after an all night crossing of a very cold desert. The monks received him

> ... with the greatest hospitality. My carpet was spread out under the porch of the church and fruits were brought to refresh me. I never enjoyed a greater luxury in my life. To find myself all of a sudden transported from among mussulmen to a monastic retreat was such happiness.[10]

Accompanied by Stasso, he answered from here a summons to attend on Prince Abbas Mirza, who had been engaged in hostilities against the Russians and was camped nearby. David was greatly impressed by the prince, and the prince in his turn was clearly impressed by what must have been a striking pair. Stasso matched David's height, being

> ... tall and erect, of the finest proportions, of great strength and agility, and dexterous in all manly exercises. His face was peculiarly handsome, his nose aquiline, his eyes full of intelligence, and when fully dressed and armed, he was a most imposing personage ... He possessed all the astuteness of his nation [and] was brave as a lion.*

They were received with great friendliness. The prince 'desired me to be seated and we talked politics for about a quarter of an hour with as much composure as if [the prince] had been a private gentleman of the country and I his equal.' David was captivated by this man whose 'qualities of every kind ... are so good and extraordinary for such a land as this that he deserves to be noted as one of the remarkable men of the age.[11]

The prince was about to return to Tabriz, so David was allowed to follow at the back of his train. He reached the city on 13 October, having 'just time to eat a good English dinner, drink some famous

---

* James, in a footnote in his novel *Ayesha Maid of Kars*, made clear that this description of Lord Osmond's servant was a portrait of Stasso.

madeira & have a good night's rest in Jem's old bed' before being whisked off next day by Sir Harford for the 3-day march to the shah's camp to hand over a letter from Adair. Here, wrote David to his father, 'the king in a most gracious manner ordered Sir H J to come close to the foot of his throne, and me also. I thought His Majesty smiled very sweetly upon me.' The shah paid David the compliment of exchanging a few words directly with him, and David was struck by 'the remarkable beauty of the King's countenance, which is truly majestic.' But he was even more struck by 'the very great familiarity with which the conversation was kept up by H M, his two ministers and Sir H' which showed 'how the latter has got such a complete hold upon these people.' The letter from Adair to the shah was received with evident pleasure, and as a reward the shah sent David next day a magnificent coat 'of cloth of gold'.[12]

It is not surprising, after all this excitement following on an arduous journey, that David was now unwell for a couple of days and that, on return to Tabriz three days later, he had to take a purge 'to get rid of all the heats and humours contracted on the journey'.[13] But he had come well through this his first solo journey of any considerable length, and accomplished an errand of some importance. Before setting out from Constantinople he had written to Sir Harford to tell him 'how happy I feel at the prospect of something like active occupation after having been so long languishing in this vile place in such ignoble repose', and hoping that Sir Harford would consider him 'as the substitute of James in every thing that requires fagging & that you will therefore in this respect treat me without ceremony.'[14] To his delight Sir Harford, who treated him with great friendliness, decided to keep him until James returned, which he thought would be next spring. But this arrangement, for a period at least, turned out to be quite uncomfortable for David. Sir Harford was moody – disgruntled by the hostile attitude of the government in India – and anxiously awaiting news of the reception in England of his treaty, and the attitude of ministers there to him personally. He had no specific work for David and gave no thought to the domestic arrangements of his mission, with the result that David felt permanently hungry. By December it was only the prospect of getting home in the spring that enabled him to put up with his life 'of a hermit who practically never leaves his room all day, who rises and goes to bed with the sun ... occupies himself with the same things every day such as eating, drinking and yawning with great dictionaries before him.' He was trying to learn Persian, but had no opportunity for using it. He longed to spend some time in England again

> ... to profit from the conversation of those well versed in things and people,
> whose comments on politics, morals and such serious subjects would nourish
> and occupy my judgment and spirit ... [Here] one day replaces another ...
> and only Sunday is different when the Mission meet to say prayers.

He thought the Persians the most debauched people in the world, 'not
even hiding their vices behind a veil of decency', and that the Turks
with all their faults were 'to be preferred a thousand fold', although he
had to admit that there were some honest ones to be found and that
at least they all showed good manners. He now began to feel 'that this
diplomatic profession is not worth a damn and will never lead to
anything.'[15]

But David never remained long in such moods: something would
always crop up to restore his natural optimism, and by New Year's
Day 1810 he was once again cheerful. Sir Harford had heard that the
government in India approved of his treaty, and he told David that, as
soon as James returned with the British ratification, he would send him
to England as escort to the Persian ambassador he was sure would
then be appointed to London. David now told his mother that he
could not remember ever being so happy as he was then, and that he
would gladly, after being able to see her for a time again, return to
spend a year or two in Persia if asked to. By mid-March, however,
with no sign of James, David found himself in a quandary. He was
now happy in Persia, and ready to remain there until James turned up;
but he was needed in Constantinople.

Stratford Canning had learned that Adair was to return home, leaving
him in charge at Constantinople until a new ambassador could be
appointed. Stratford had no desire to be given this promotion but had
no choice, so he had written to David begging him to come back and
support him, suggesting that there seemed to be 'a general disposition
to leave me in the lurch.' David's conscience was touched, and he
feared that Stratford, whom he had already told of his expected return
to England, could quite reasonably charge him 'with the selfishness
which I am afraid had too great a share in influencing' his decision to
agree to Sir Harford's proposal. 'I cannot help thinking' he wrote back
'that I should deserve [your reproaches] if I did not disclose to you all
that has revolved, with no little agitation, in my mind since your letter.'
He explained that his first reaction had been to return to
Constantinople at once, and that Sir Harford, fully understanding the
reason, had approved in principle. But Sir Harford had doubted

whether Adair was really thinking of moving so soon, and had opined that his successor would get there before he left so that Stratford, as David wrote, would 'be spared all the cares and honours of pleni-potentiality and the aid of my long fingers will not be much needed.' David went on to confess, moreover, that if the occasion should arise for him to carry the Persian ratification to England before it was known when Adair would be leaving, he would 'not have the courage to resist the temptation of going home, the hope of which has become so fixed with me', even if it then became clear that Stratford would be left on his own for some time. Indeed, he was seriously thinking of not waiting for the ratification before returning to England because Jack, 'who you know is my wordly patron' was urging this on him. 'You know' he wrote 'what little chance there is for one who has so little interest as myself' of being officially attached to the mission at Constantinople; and he felt that he must 'one day or other make up my mind to quit this career altogether unless I get something of a more permanent and more official nature.'[16] He believed he should make the break without further delay.

This was one of those moments which from time to time occur in every young (and sometimes not so young) man's life, when the road ahead forks and there is no clear view round the corner of either alternative to help in the decision on which to take: yet a decision must be made and youthful impatience often takes it impetuously. David, however, hesitated. Deep down he wanted to choose the road that would keep him in the diplomatic line, even though there seemed to be so little chance along that one of finding security. He had, of course, known nothing else in adulthood, not having spent any years, like his brothers, in the Levant trade (to which Jack, little as he had enjoyed his time in it, was seriously thinking of returning). He trusted Jack and was prepared to follow where he led; but something was holding him back, and he wrote to Jack to explain:

> ... I have been all along of your opinion that this government service in which we are is a most precarious means of subsistence, but yet I shall never regret having engaged in it hitherto, on account of the opportunities it has afforded me of seeing a little of the globe we creep on. We must, however, look forward to what is ultimately to be got by it, & I perfectly agree with you that the prospect holds out nothing worth pursuing. But still, until we can fairly settle ourselves in another course of life, let us not relinquish all hold upon the present course in which there is always a chance of doing something in our way, as long as the Turkish Empire in Europe holds together, & as its crisis seems now absolutely at hand, we can't be kept long in suspense, & when the game is all up, then we may determine upon the

adoption of such scheme as may in the interval present itself to our deliberation.

Jack had evidently mentioned that there was just a possibility that he might again be sent in a consular capacity to Ioannina, and David assured him that 'I shall be glad to resume my ancient post under you'; but he thought that they should consider 'the general advantages of the whole family' and that it would remain to be seen 'whether I can be better provided for in a *wordly* point of view.' He believed that

> ... the interests of our dear mother & sisters require that one of the boys should fix himself in England & marry, not only that protection may be afforded them in case of any accident to our dear father, but because by the marriage of one of the brothers I think the sisters have a better chance of getting married too.

He thought that James was very likely to be returning to Persia with a secure position, but 'if not, why he must participate in our plans & we must all make it out as well as we can.'[17]

In some respects David had by now become the maturest of the three brothers, taking more thought than the other two for what might be in the best interests of the rest of the family, and showing a caution over taking decisions which could have long lasting results. He was very conscious of his father's precarious position as consul general in Constantinople, from which political developments might throw him out at any time, leaving him without income. He was beginning to think that he, the youngest of the three, might have to take responsibilty for the welfare of his mother and sisters. But circumstances conspired to keep him in the Orient for some time yet.

In May 1810, yielding partly to his longing to start making his way home and partly to further pleadings from Stratford Canning – and deciding that it was now going to be several more months at best before the British ratification of the treaty would reach Persia – David persuaded Sir Harford to let him return to Constantinople, unaware that Adair was already writing to advise him to return at once. 'If you stay so long in Persia' Adair wrote, 'you will run the risk of finding on your return to Constantinople no one of your former friends ... with whom you began this Mission', and there was a risk that the new ambassador would have little interest in him. Adair would be recommending him, but this would be only by letter and therefore not as effective as personal contact. On his return to London, Adair would write to George Canning 'entreating him to show you every countenance and to point out to the Ambassador when he arrives how useful you have been, and how much more useful you may become to the Mission since your residence in Persia.' Nevertheless, Adair thought David should be present in Constantinople while Stratford was still there and 'able to fix you with the Ambassador, and of course will add his own recommendation to every thing that mine can do in your favour.'[18]

David spent 36 days on the return journey to Constantinople, which he reached on 11 July, just in time to see Adair, who had handed over to Stratford the previous day, before he sailed for England. And, as is so often the case, it was not long before he was recalling his time in Persia with nostalgia. Now he looked back on what seemed to him the most tranquil time of his life in Tabriz, where he and

> ... the *youngsters*, for I was the oldest of all but one, used to beguile the long winter's nights in our mud-built room with dumb-motions [dumb-crambo], dancing, singing & a thousand other boyish pranks. In general I was the musician. I used to sing reels and country dances to the thump of my old slipper on a silver tray, while the others used to dance. On extraordinary occasions the trumpeter belonging to the troop of horse used to be called in to play upon a fiddle of his own manufacture. This ingenious little fellow was by birth a Hottentot and by *habit* a Mussulman ... I will solemnly assure you that had I the choice of remaining for any number of years in *Persia*, or for the same time in *Pera*, I would without hesitation prefer the former.[19]

But then, unlike his brother James, he had not had to conduct political business with the Persians – and he had received extraordinary attentions from the prince royal, Abbas Mirza. 'I swear' he told his sister 'that I believe nine tenths of the young ladies in England would lose their senses at the sight of my charming Prince' who had clearly himself been charmed by this young Englishman. He gave David a very particular mark of his favour on his departure. The prince had special responsibilty under his father for foreign affairs and the mission had been invited to a grand supper at the royal palace given by his chief minister, after which they were summoned, late at night, by the prince himself 'whom we found sitting alone in a little room.' They were invited to sit and David was then called forward to receive a long message for the Turkish ministers and Adair, 'nearly every word of which' he understood. David had noticed a handsome Persian sword in a corner which he had been warned was intended as a present to him, so he was surprised when they were dismissed without it. Next day Sir Harford was told that the prince had been ashamed to 'give such a shabby present' before so many people, and it would be sent

over. David managed to let the prince know that the quality and value
of the present was immaterial to him: the value lay in his receiving it
in person from the prince's own hand. So he was sent for on his own:

> ... I found him sitting in a beautiful summer house in the middle of a
> garden very busy with his grand vizier and another man. He made me sit
> down close to him, and when the two others were gone he pulled down
> from a shelf some prints of battles and portraits just come from Russia
> which I explained to him as well as I was able. You have no idea with what
> patience and good humour he helped me out when he saw I wanted a word
> to express myself. At last he produced the sword and, putting it into my
> hands, desired me to accept it as a mark of his affection which he said he
> was sorry he had not had greater opportunity of giving greater proofs of.[20]

David was expecting Adair's replacement to arrive soon, when both he
and Stratford would be able to return to England in their turn. But
month after month went by with no word of a new ambassador, and
even when it was announced in 1811 that Robert Liston had been
appointed, a year passed before he turned up, during which David felt
he could not desert Stratford, to whom he considered he owed a duty
of assistance and, indeed, protection. Stratford himself was thoroughly
fed up with his lot. He 'had no predeliction for diplomacy'[21] and
would have preferred to return to England and enter Parliament; but
his cousin, the foreign secretary, had insisted upon his staying, and
probably he needed the salary.

Stratford was in some respects a difficult person to work with, and
being an unwilling holder of the office did not help. Adair himself, in
a farewell letter from his ship, told him:

> ... I esteem you for the power of your mind, and I like you for your many
> virtues: among the first of which I class a proud and independent spirit ...
> [which] is to me so sacred ... that I cannot bear to check even its faults; for
> its faults are part of its virtues ... When these are accompanied with a warm
> and kind heart, which I know you to be in an extreme degree, I say in two
> words that I am content with the man formed of such materials.'[22]

David, replying from Persia to a complaint from Stratford at his
absence, had written: 'even at this distance I stand in awe of your lash.
Pray spare me on this occasion. Were it not for that single defect, for
it is a great one, you would be the best fellow I know.'[23] Stratford, deep
down, was probably not entirely sure of his ability to fill the post of
head of mission, and he would have compensated for this with
occasional curt assertions of his authority. He treated David officially

as a young subordinate, giving him hours of dreary work copying his verbose despatches, but virtually never drawing him into discussion of the political instructions he received from London or the tactics for carrying them out. In fact Stratford showed very considerable competence, despite his youth and limited experience. David, admiring him for this, nevertheless longed to be taken more into his confidence. However, he understood – and forgave – this behaviour. While he was unhappy at not being allowed to be a partner in making political decisions, he realised this was not because Stratford considered him too junior in rank, but simply because he was unwilling to show any sign of weakness. Off duty they were the best of friends and could relax happily together. David needed the warmth of friendship, and he understood that Stratford did too, so he could cope with 'the vexations arising from his responsibilities', as he put it to his mother.[24] So, although he longed to get home to her, he felt 'it would be a great sin in my eyes to leave him so long as I can be useful ... He is a young man whom I honour and whom I esteem in the highest degree.'[25] But he also confessed that

> ... I shall like him more cordially than I do now when we shall be together as friends in equality and not as Minister and Secretary, for in that relationship I experience from time to time vexations which break the uniform and tranquil course of the affection I wish to have for him always. It is as much through a sense of duty as through character that I overlook some things which cause me more irritation than perhaps a christian should feel; but I willingly pardon him the moment the first irritation passes, and I just hope for his sake that he will never have business with someone with as much spirit and the same humours as his own.[26]

It was not just affection for Stratford that now kept David in Constantinople for two years: he was not at all sure what he wanted to, or could, do elsewhere. He was at least comfortable where he was, living in the now habitable English Palace 'in a huge apartment where I can walk up and down at my ease without fear of breaking my legs, long as they are', with a salary of £300 a year and 'free board, lodging, laundering etc'; and he enjoyed being called *Illustrissimo Signor Secretario della Legazione Britannica*.[27] He knew that he ought to move if he were to make anything of his life; but to what? Various alternatives to staying where he was came under consideration, but none came to anything. Adair had told him he would be recommended for the post of consul general in Ioannina, which David thought 'too good a situation to be refused by a poor devil like me,'[28] but he had made it clear that he would not accept it so long as Stratford needed him – and in fact he would have gone there with reluctance. He was tempted by a suggestion that he take holy orders, but not so much as to desert Stratford. The one initiative he himself took came to nothing: he proposed himself as interpreter to the minister the Persians were expected to send to London once Sir Harford's treaty had been ratified. This was actually agreed to, and Lord Radstock held out to him the added attraction of a duchess (unidentifiable from surviving papers) ready to marry him; but Stratford still held him. 'The tempting prospect' he wrote to his uncle 'of leading a Duchess to the altar' was not necessary to induce him to return to England with the Persian minister; but 'were the advantages of such a plan ten times greater than they are (and I am aware that they are such as may never offer themselves again), I must renounce them ... As long as Canning is kept here, without any other assistance than what he derives from my fingers, I cannot think of leaving him.'[29]

What David really wanted, as he explained emotionally to his mother in one of his numerous letters during these two years, was 'to be with a woman who takes an interest in me and who by her counsel and her company can calm and pacify the spirit when it needs rest and consolation – this woman is you my dear mama, or my good aunt Henrietta [in Smyrna] who is so like you.' He wanted to be able to

> ... converse with [his mother] freely ... to tell you all my little secrets, to let you know of all the changes, all the trials through which my soul has passed, so that in telling you all you, as my father confessor, can reprimand me for any thing you find bad, encourage me in what you find good and finally give me an absolution so that I can begin with new energy.[30]

In other letters he worried about the lethargy that seemed to overtake him when he was free of his official work. He felt he was in a 'living tomb'[31] and wanted to escape from the

> ... apathy of soul and indolence of spirit ... I call in aid religion, reason, memories, anticipation of the future to needle myself into a better state of mind ... [but] one needs a great strength of character to improve oneself without the help of some external stimulus. Solitude is fine for those who have completed an honourable career, but for a young man it is the cradle of idleness and of all the evils which come from that.[32]

He even found living 'in this accursed hole' had frozen his heart. 'You know' he wrote to his mother

> ... that I have always thought myself guilty of being too susceptible to tender passions. Well here my heart has become closed and as cold as ice. Is this philosophy? Is it virtue? No, it is pure apathy, it is pure stupidity brought on by the situation in which I find myself. Day after day goes by in which I see no one whose company I want. Canning is only 24, I only 27, yet we lead

a life of two Trappist monks. I swear I would hang myself were hemp not so dear.'[33]

He wanted to escape from the routine of being a subordinate. This was not, he said, out of any ambition:

> I don't want brilliant rank because I have seen enough of the world to know that the higher one goes the greater the cares. My ambition is to be so placed that I can do something worthwhile on my own and can say to myself 'there is your métier, your profession, your goal, work at it.'[34]

But he was now convinced that diplomacy was not the profession for him: 'I must be on my own and independent of everyone else, for I am tired of only thinking and acting as ordered by a superior: there is nothing that so weakens and makes timid the spirit's abilities.'[35]

In the midst of all this uncertainty over his future, David suddenly fancied he had fallen in love with his cousin Mimi Chabannes. That family had returned to France from London in 1800, and he had been in the habit of writing occasional letters to her. Now she had taken to writing to him at length and affectionately. Her outpourings about the many vicissitudes suffered by the family since the Revolution touched him deeply, as did the evidence in her letters of her loving unselfishness. 'I verily believe' he wrote to his sister Emily 'that if I am not already in love with her, I should become so at the first sight of her.'[36] He was more definite to his mother, after learning that Mimi had escaped the 'frightful fate' of being forced to marry some general: 'If fate does not oppose it I shall not hesitate to ask for her as my wife.' He was in love 'with her character; as for her beauty, you know well that there are much prettier girls in the world; but I begin to realise that the impression made by a pretty face without other quality is only transitory.'[37] Later David came to realise that it was all a romantic dream, and the romance, of which Mimi herself was probably unaware, came to nothing – although the intimate friendship blossomed and endured for many years.

These emotional outpourings were only occasional windows into his inner feelings during a life which was often, perhaps mostly, full of interest and enjoyment. It may have had some faint resemblance to that led by British diplomats in Turkey during the Second World War, when they were living cheek by jowl with the diplomatic representatives of the country at war with their own – Germany. In David's time the enemy was France, and he had occupation in the business of countering French propaganda. But there was not much society to his taste. The Frank community was mostly French, and they were forbidden by their ambassador to fraternise with the British. There were small Swedish and Spanish diplomatic missions, with whom David found 'the amusement of the evening chiefly consists of conjugating the verb "to be bored".'[38] But there were occasional moments of pleasure. British travellers frequently spent time in Constantinople on their continental tours, and David enjoyed their company, even though he, as usual, felt some diffidence before such as Henry Gally Knight, writer on Norman architecture and nephew of Alleyn Fitzherbert, and even young Frederick Sylvester Douglas, son of Baron Glenbervie, who he thought at age 20 had 'so much learning as to make him seem twice that age'; and he

> ... trembled at the thought of finding himself in company in London with all these gentlemen who have been to university. I blush all the time at my ignorance, but I console myself with the thought that this fills me with true humility, for the more I know of the world the more it confirms what I have long held, that egoism is the source of all the crimes just as vanity is the source of all the follies of men.[39]

One visitor, however, was obviously not to David's taste, Lady Hester Stanhope.* It is significant that David, who seldom liked to say anything bad about anyone, makes no comment on her; but she herself shows that they did not hit it off. She was in any case prejudiced against young diplomats. Writing to George Canning from Turkey in July 1811 she had said:

> I have lived a good deal with diplomatic men, & can speak with experience of the risk a young man runs at best of vice from habit becoming natural; if it has not this sad effect, it makes a man unhappy by rendering him suspicious, & making him less agreeable, from his always being on guard respecting unimportant things.[40]

As this formidable, arrogant woman was making life difficult for Isaac with all her demands for vague consular services , David may well have been 'on guard' with her. Writing to General Oakes, Lady Hester explained that she would not allow Stratford Canning 'to introduce one person to me since I came here, but young Morier who I dislike extremely.'[41] The feeling was probably mutual.

In the long run these three years of rather unstructured life in Turkey and Persia did David no harm – indeed it was perhaps just as well that

---

* Hester Lucy Stanhope, 1776–1839, eldest daughter of Charles, 3rd Earl Stanhope, niece of William Pitt, travelled widely in the Levant from 1810 and finally settled on Mount Lebanon where she died in poverty.

he failed to take any firm decision then about the shape of his future career, for it left him available to be taken under the wing of his old Harrow friend, Lord Abcrdeen, in 1813 and from there to become a properly established member of the diplomatic service. He and Stratford were both able to leave Constantinople in the early summer of 1812 when Robert Liston at last arrived as ambassador. Their journey home together was a particular pleasure for David. He considered, as he wrote to his mother shortly before they left, that Stratford was

> ... the one young man in the world without the smallest *vice* ... His heart is as pure as crystal. He has faults, if you will – he is sometimes too sharp and impatient. But ... his position is in direct conflict with his character. He is the most open, the most frank, the most loyal, the most upright and at the same time the most sensitive person I know. He has to deal either with astute, false, dissimulating people, or with hard and obstinate heads on which all the missiles and catapults of antiquity would have made not the slightest impression. I suspect he has enemies who culumniate him. He assuredly does not deserve them ... I must tell you that we have never had the slightest argument together which has lasted 4 minutes.[42]

They visited Greece in high spirits. Going ashore one day on an open beach Stratford

> ... mounted on the shoulders of one of the sailors made for dry land, which he reached much sooner than intended, for a wave getting between the sailor's legs upset him, and His late Excellency was pitched forward, like a sack of coals, and lay for a few seconds in an amphibious state ... to the amusement of all present as well as of himself.

Released from the responsibilities and cares of diplomatic office they reverted almost to schoolboys, passing 'a very pleasant time on board in pelting and belabouring each other with cushions.'[43] Back in Portsmouth, on 27 September, their ways parted, though not their friendship. Stratford went on to become a distinguished man in politics and, despite his dislike of it, diplomacy.* It was to be a few months more before David, unexpectedly, went off to become involved in the final diplomatic stages of the Napoleonic wars and the Congress of Vienna. Meanwhile his immediate concern, typically, was over the fate of his brother James, whose relations with Sir Harford Jones had taken an unpleasant turn.

---

* Stratford Canning was plenipotentiary in Switzerland 1814–20, envoy to Washington 1820–24, to Petersburg 1824, ambassador at Constantinople 1825–27, 1831–33, 1842–47 and 1848–58. He was also three times an MP and was created Viscount Stratford de Redcliffe in 1852, and Knight of the Garter in 1869.

CHAPTER TWELVE

James and Harford Jones 1810–1811

'He really is a dangerous man to know.'

When James arrived in England with the mirza at the end of November 1809 he did not know whether he would be returning to Persia. He did not really want to go back, and he even told Sir Harford that he and David were 'in the idea that the diplomatic life is of too precarious a stamp to make us live like gentlemen by it.'[1] But, although he knew that Sir Harford was anxious to quit his post there as soon as possible, he believed that his best chance of making a living was to keep close to this man he so much admired and loved, who might well get a peerage, and whose interest on his behalf could be crucial. And he used his position as the mirza's confidential aide to good effect to improve his chances. He became very much *persona grata* with the East India Company (who paid him £750 in April for all his trouble, a pretty contrast to the tight-fisted Foreign Office who merely granted him the pay of a messenger). He dined several times with the foreign secretary. He was invited to dine and stay the night with Lord Melville* at his house in Wimbledon and, afterwards, could not 'recollect to have been so much in love with any man in so short a time as I am with him. There is friendship, kindness, business, patriotism, & a thousand other qualities are blended together in one of the most ardent frames I ever met with'[2] (a sentiment shared by Sir Walter Scott and others). He hit it off well with Sir Hugh Inglis (father of Robert), and was well connected at the Foreign Office. He knew, however, that he needed a patron; and although he was well aware that Sir Harford had his enemies, he was not wise enough to realise the danger of so obviously attaching himself to that particular star. It was only because the mirza was so fond of him, and kept insisting that he wanted him

---

* Henry Dundas, 1742–1811, son of Lord Arniston the distinguished Scottish judge and Lord Advocate 1775–83. President of the India Board of Control 1793–1801, created Viscount Melville 1802, First Lord of the Admiralty 1804–05.

to return to Persia, and because Sir Gore Ouseley, when appointed to replace Sir Harford, wanted to please the mirza, that James was chosen to be his Secretary of Embassy. Sir Gore was somewhat suspicious of James's attachment to Sir Harford, from whom he was expecting (and got) trouble, and also thought he was rather too pleased with himself. James achieved his next step up in life almost in spite of himself.

⊕

James was happily unaware of the impending quarrel with Sir Harford when he sailed from Spithead on 18 July 1810. He wrote to his brother William that

> during the [next] two years ... I hope to have laid the foundation of my future advancement in life in so secure a manner as not to fear any future necessity of flying to the last resort of tooth drawing, and to be able to forget about the possibility of having to sell cotton & figs all the days of my life ... [I now have] above £800 in my pocket clear & a certain pension after my services are expired.[3]

He did, however, have one regret, that instead of going to Constantinople and then overland to Tehran, he would have to endure another six months at sea and reach Persia via India, as he had done three years earlier with Sir Harford. Sir Gore, whose decision it was to travel by this route, flatly refused to let James travel separately, saying he could not do without his secretary, even though there would be virtually no occasion for political work before he reached Bushire (where James could have joined him). He just might have agreed had James not revealed that it was Sir Harford who was urging this on him, and that he seemed to feel more beholden to his former chief than to his present. But, as James was to discover later, Sir Gore knew that Sir Harford was not good for him and was already trying to save him.

It was a large party to be accommodated by Captain Heathcote in his 64-gun HMS *Lion* (the same ship that had taken Lord Macartney on his embassy to China in 1792/93). Sir Gore was accompanied by his (pregnant) wife and their daughter Mary Jane aged 2, plus five personal servants, as well as his brother Sir William (another noted orientalist) as private secretary, the Hon Robert Gordon (Lord Aberdeen's younger brother) as attaché, two clerks and James. They were joined by the mirza, accompanied by a clerk and seven assorted servants. James had one of two small cabins about nine feet square (Gordon the other) with an eighteen pounder gun in the middle, on the other side of which was a stall containing a cow, which he found less noisy than the adjoining Persian servants. But he was content with his lot. The purser provided him with pegs on which to hang his clothes and two extra beds which he used as a sofa. 'An honest tar by name Bob Watson was appointed to attend upon myself and Mr Gordon, to take down our cots in the morning, to clear out our cabins twice a week, & to do us all the service that we stood in need of.' He was much struck by the harmony which reigned between Captain Heathcote and his officers, who had a club 'that met every night in the cabin of the captain of marines & which was devoted to drinking grog, smoaking & singing.'[4] He found Gordon 'a very sensible young man' whose company was a great comfort.[5]

There was a brief call at Madeira – and during the ceremonies of crossing the line 'Neptune' tactfully forebore from instructing his minions to shave off the Persians' beards. They reached Rio de Janeiro on 14 September, where they spent a fortnight as the guests of the Portuguese Prince Regent. There was a battle of wills between Sir Gore and the local British envoy, Lord Strangford,* over who should call on whom first, which Sir Gore won, determined to establish and keep the highest possible status. He had already persuaded Captain Heathcote to grant him 'Royal Honours'; and when vice admiral Drury heard of this breach of naval etiquette he admonished Heathcote, who had to explain that Sir Gore had 'assured me that it was his due so soon as he should have left the mother country and I had no reason to doubt the word of a man in his very high situation.'[6]

On arrival at Rio, James was sent ashore to supervise the preparation of the house provided for them, and found

> a number of taylors [sic] & upholsterers fitting up the rooms with a profusion of silk curtains & gilded corniches ... much greater pains having [been] taken to provide rooms of show and ceremony than a room of comfort & convenience ... The beds were emblematical of the people. Their outsides exhibited [finery] ... but on turning up this finery we came to a bedstead made of common deal plank.

He was astonished to find 'a man of rank' in a 'uniform with a profusion of ribbands and stars' busily cleaning: he turned out to be the owner of the house. James, to his disgust, found that what could have been a pleasant escape from life cooped up in the ship was 'thrown away on grimaces and ceremony' as they exchanged protocol calls; and he strongly disapproved of Sir Gore's action in refusing to

---

* Percy Clinton Sydney Smythe, 1780–1855, 6th Viscount Strangford and 1st Baron Penshurst.

attend a dinner given by the foreign minister because that gentleman's wife had not called upon Lady Ouseley. James thought this particularly petty, as the foreign minister himself had set aside the strict rules of protocol and made the first call on the mirza because 'he was well aware that the agents of a court so ignorant & so proud as are all the Mohammeden courts would never understand the diplomatic usages of European courts.' He described the prince regent as 'a thick, fat, ill-shaped man with a large face without any expression on its features except that of good nature, with great unmeaning bloodshot eyes, & with much loose flesh about the lower part of it.'[7] There were opportunities, however, for horseback rides in the surrounding country-side, and for making many drawings; but James found the people generally dirty and uncouth. The natives had the habit of defecating publicly in sight of their residence, but when Sir Gore tried to stop this by having guards posted he soon had them removed because he was even more disgusted by their cruel treatment of the blacks.

They left Rio on 27 September, taking three and a half months to reach Bombay. It would not have been surprising if on such a long sea passage there were times when tempers became frayed. James, however, mentions only one, a particularly dramatic explosion from the mirza on 20 November, when some of his suite complained to him of being roughly treated by the ship's officers. The mirza took their part as they 'seized the opportunity of raking up every trifling grievance which had befallen them since they left their own country', and he 'flung himself violently out of the cabin, and followed by his men, retired into their berth, where he expressed his determination to remain for the rest of the voyage.' James was told by Sir Gore to try to smooth things over. 'Every mouth (Ambassador's and all) was opened upon me, and it was a full half hour before I could obtain a hearing', James wrote; but eventually he managed to soothe them all. The mirza later excused himself by explaining 'that if he did not appear to take an interest in the welfare of his people, they would not fail to misrepresent his conduct when they got into Persia, and would calumniate him as a Christian, and a despiser of his own countrymen.'[8] In fact the Persians seem on the whole to have endured this voyage with remarkable patience, although the mirza was unwilling to share James's inclination

> to hold a voyage on the sea as a most providential break upon the chain of our existence, as a suspension of the busy scenes of life, and consequently as a retirement in which the worldly man may have time & opportunity to sift the secrets of his heart, to look back upon his past conduct, & to form resolutions for his future life … When he stands upon the summit of a wave, a mere speck upon the surface of the deep, he … can despise the pride &

vanity of his former days of splendour ... When the mind is dead to the little follies, fripperies & intrigues of this life it can extend its flights to where it was intended by her divine Maker that it should be placed.[9]

The mirza took a more earthy view and 'would not allow that a sea voyage can be productive of any thing but misery, inconvenience & disappointment': he could 'contemplate the works of God just as well on his horse', and quoted from his favourite poet, Saadi, 'I had rather give one hundred *tomauns* than pass over even one wave of the sea..'[10]

The mirza's relief on at last reaching Bombay on 12 January 1811, after a voyage lasting five months and twenty-five days covering a distance, according to the ship's log, of 18,589 nautical miles, was manifest; and it was succeeded by even greater joy when he learned that the shah had so approved all his actions in England that he had rewarded him with the title of *Khan* (somewhat equivalent to baron in England) so that he was now Mirza Abul Hasan Khan and a man of considerable consequence. This so affected his ego that he insisted upon the governor of Bombay* calling upon him first, rather than the other way round as normal protocol demanded; but Sir Gore, with the best of motives, had already sold the pass by allowing the mirza to go ashore before him, and thus appear the more important. Two weeks were spent in Bombay sightseeing and attending banquets. The mirza had now decided to stop drinking wine, at least in public, ('even tho' champagne was offered him under the guise of grape water'[11]) so that, in his new dignity, he would not be suspected of having adapted too much to foreign ways, and he asked James to ensure that he was not offered it, lest he be suspected of having drunk it when in the west (a fact which James rather unkindly, and tactlessly, published in his second travel book). But James had no need for such abstinence and enjoyed himself in his new dignity of office (although bored by the local dances).

James, however, had been very upset to receive at Bombay a letter from Sir Harford Jones dated 31 July 1810 expressing anger because James had 'not been diligent enough in getting him an honour from the king for his services in Persia & because I have not rejoined him by way of Constantinople so that he could return to England.'[12] These were accusations which James simply could not accept as having any justification.

---

* Jonathan Duncan, 1756–1811, was governor of Bombay 1795 until his death.

Sir Harford had made clear to James in England that he did not want to remain in Persia as envoy once the treaty he had negotiated had been ratified; but he did want a good pension, a peerage and to be allowed to incorporate in his coat of arms the high Persian honour bestowed upon him by the shah.* He had expected James to exert himself in London on his behalf in all these matters; and, despite the difficulties of such a brief, James had done his best, as Sir Harford knew from his letters received by the end of July 1810. James had been able to tell him 'that the whole of your conduct has been most highly applauded ... [and] all your enemies humbled ... You have risen more than ever in the public mind ... [and] ministers have not scrupled to speak aloud of the shameful conduct of the Indian Govt to you.' He had assured Sir Harford that 'as far as my feeble voice can go I have never failed to cry out on the expediency & necessity that you should be invested with some striking mark of the king's favour ... I have never missed an opportunity to speak of it to my & your friends whenever I could do so with propriety', and that the mirza himself had taken every opportunity of speaking similarly.[13]

The king's agreement over the coat of arms had been obtained; but, it is true, James had then had to warn Sir Harford that as the king 'is very averse to foreign Orders ... [and] as there has been an uncommon deal of fuss made about the granting of this honour to you, I fear the Ribband from your own monarch is now become more difficult than ever.'[14] Perhaps James's mistake had been to express enthusiastic 'gratitude to Sir Gore Ouseley for his perseverance, his candour in doing every thing that lay in his power to see every justice done you; for the many truths which he alone dared to speak to Lord Wellesley, & for assisting me in every point which I have wished to carry for you,'[15] and generally to show his admiration for Sir Gore as a person. But he had made clear that he himself, despite his appointment as secretary of Embassy, had wished to travel by way of Constantinople but had been prevented by Sir Gore from doing so. Indeed the mirza too had wanted to take this route, and was trying up to the end to get the Foreign Office to agree.[16]

What drove Sir Harford to write this letter at the end of July 1810 is a mystery. It is true that, at the time, he was under strain from a renewed attempt by the government in India to sabotage his position.

---

* This was the Order of the Sun, which he had refused to accept from the shah because it had been bestowed upon Gardane. The shah, understanding this, then awarded him the unique distinction of allowing him to incorporate it in his coat-of-arms, which he could not do without the king's permission.

They had again sent Malcolm to Persia. But he had received James's letter, which had described how, when this intention had become known in London, even Wellesley (who was normally reluctant to oppose Minto openly) 'could not withhold his indignation when he heard of this new trait of perverseness in Lord M ... Be assured, my dear Sir H, that every body here feels extremely for you & that there is every disposition to do you justice.'[17] Perhaps Sir Harford was simply jealous of losing his protégé to Sir Gore. It is significant that years later, when writing his own memoirs after he had left public service, he recorded that James 'who before he went out with me [to Persia] had never been in any public employment, was all at once, from being my private secretary, taken into His Majesty's regular diplomatic service, and appointed secretary of Embassy in Persia; and the consequence to me was, that I who had been near thirty years in a regular service, and employed in several arduous and delicate affairs, was ultimately compelled, from a sense of honor and decency, to abandon that service, and was taken – into no service at all'.[18] Yet, even while writing so bitterly to James, he could write in August to David (by then back in Constantinople) with apparent concern for James's future, while careless of his own: 'I have dropped into a good sum of money by the death of Lady Jones's father & am therefore completely independent with a flowing sheet. *Rebus sic stantibus* & Jim provided for, I am indifferent as to reward for myself.'[19] Even as late as November he referred in a letter to David to 'your dear brother.'[20]

James, however, was unaware of this when, losing his grip on syntax in his agitation, he penned his reply from Bombay to Sir Harford's 'truly cutting' letter of 31 July 1810. Although he had received at the same time 'its antidote dated 2nd August', nevertheless he was 'pained by the very severe expressions you make use of to me' and impatient for an opportunity to give a face-to-face explanation of his actions in London:

> for until that explanation has taken place my mind can never be fully at rest. In the meantime, I will just recall to your recollection the strict injunction you gave never to do any thing or advance any thing without the concurrence or advice of your friend ... Sir Hugh Inglis – from that injunction I never deviated ... I can fairly say that it was not for want of my exertion that you have not received [the peerage] ... You told me at parting "wait to see what they will offer". I waited & no offer was made ... I made known your wishes & what was expected in Persia thro' a channel more efficient than mine, thro' the mirza. It is enough to say Lord Wellesley was in office ... and the ribband was urged with all the warmth the mirza is master of. He was put off & was told, as I was, that all should be settled at your return ... As for

my urgency about returning to you by way of Constantinople, I appealed to Mr Hamilton of the F. Office, to Sir Gore Ouseley, & to the mirza & to fifty others if you like, if I did not require it in the most urgent manner I was able. I asked to be sent by way of Aleppo – as well as I was able I pointed out the utility of it in a political view, and then asked it as a request from you.

James had also asked at Bombay to be allowed to go ahead of the main party from Bushire when they got there, because Sir Harford had said he was now determined to leave Persia at the latest at the end of February 1811, and had asked that James be sent on as a courier 'which', he told Sir Harford, 'I was most willing & most anxious should take place.' But Sir Gore, although professing to be 'very anxious to do every thing that could possibly give [Sir Harford] pleasure' was adamant, saying

he was new in the country, that he had only me to advise with, that it was on the score of my having been in Persia that he asked Lord Wellesley that I should be the Secretary to his Embassy, that it was on account of the utility that I should be to him that I received that appointment, that my proceeding before him would only make a difference of a couple of weeks or so ... With my hand on my heart I can honestly say that the greatest misery that could ever befall me w^d be to think that you suspected me of having neglected you, or of being unmindful of your great goodness to me & mine.[21]

For a short while James wrestled with his conscience, and his feeling of loyalty to and affection for Sir Harford: Gordon, indeed, believed he was going to resign his appointment to Sir Gore's staff and that he, Gordon, would replace him. But when James discovered that Sir Gore had it in mind to put him in charge of a sub-mission at Tabriz, self-interest won. As Gordon reported to his brother, with a touch of disappointed malice, James would thereby get 'double emoluments.'[22] James, however, found himself again torn when they reached Bushire at the beginning of March, for there he became caught up in a disagreement between Sir Harford and Sir Gore, and received further hurtful letters from the former, which, he replied, were 'really so distressing to me, that I can with difficulty express how strongly I feel the nature of their contents.' Sir Harford was apparently* still complaining that James (whose letter from Bombay had not yet reached him) had taken the part of those against him. 'It is that' replied James 'that revolts me, & makes me call you unjust. Can you conceive for a moment that if I could in any shape whatever have advanced those

---

* None of these letters from Sir Harford has survived.

wishes that you have expressed as necessary to your happiness, that I would have let slip an opportunity?' But James refused even now to believe that Sir Harford could really have turned from friend to enemy. He still hoped they would meet (which they did not, even though Sir Harford finally did not leave Tehran until 22 April and Persia until late May), but he had to explain that 'Sir Gore ... persists in requiring me to accompany him. Tell me, can I act in defiance of his requests?'; and he signed off 'Believe me my dearest Sir Harford your ever affectionate & grateful friend.'[23] And a few days later he even asked Sir Harford, who would be returning overland, to buy presents on his behalf for his family and friends (for which he would get his father to pay in Constantinople), urged him to visit his Van Lennep relations in Smyrna, and asked him on his behalf to explain to the Wilkinsons that he could not possibly afford to marry, saying 'I endeavour to smother the flame [of my love] as much as possible' and 'applauding the wisdom' of Maria who he had heard had 'made another attachment.'[24]

Sir Harford's behaviour towards James, however, was almost schizophrenic. Having received James's explanation from Bombay, he apparently wrote in a very friendly vein in March. But in May James had two of his letters returned, endorsed with 'a wish on the part of Sir H Jones to receive no more.' The quarrel between Sir Harford and Sir Gore had now claimed James as a victim, and only now were his eyes opened to the realities. In brief, Sir Gore, for his own good reasons, had declined to accept Sir Harford's offer to have his communications with the Persian government channelled through him. He had also refused to bypass, and arrange the dismissal of, the East India Company's acting representative in Bushire, Bruce – whom Sir Harford regarded as Malcolm's friend and his enemy. It had been bad enough, in Sir Harford's eyes, that James had chosen to obey Sir Gore and not go ahead to meet him. The last straw was his apparent failure to have nothing to do with Bruce. Yet James had, in his misplaced loyalty to Sir Harford, and at the risk of his relations with Sir Gore, deliberately kept his distance from Bruce. He had even twice refused invitations to dine with him. Sir Gore, although aware of this, and knowing the reason, had decided at first not to intervene; but on a third occasion, when Bruce had invited all of them to dine on the eve of Sir Gore's departure for Tehran, he had made James accompany him. In his journal he recorded that he had had to tell James, who had argued that he did not wish to offend his friend, Sir Harford, that

> he was no longer part of Sir Harford Jones's family and that I could not allow any member of mine to enter publicly into the dissentions of the former Envoy ... and that if he wished to mark his attachment to Sir Harford

Jones in a manner that I considered disrespectful to me I must consider it as a separation from my Embassy altogether.[25]

James had reported this to Sir Harford, explaining that although he was not obliged to regard himself as part of Sir Gore's 'family', because he held his appointment as secretary of Embassy from the crown, 'yet Sir Gore has most liberally been pleased to call me one of his family' and so he had felt obliged to fall in with his new chief's wishes.[26] But in another letter, a few days later, he had been unwise enough to remonstrate with Sir Harford over his attitude to Sir Gore which had 'given me the greatest pain.' He said he was 'not much honored with Sir Gore Ouseley's confidence – he does not wish to cultivate an acquaintance with me farther than displaying to me every civility & attention that one gentleman does to another'; but

> I think I have seen enough of him & his way of acting and thinking to be permitted to say, that your expressions about him are not founded upon justice ... It really hurts me to find you have taken so decided an antipathy to Sir Gore Ouseley ... I am certain it was never his wish to offend you ... I have now spoken my mind very freely upon a subject which I can perceive you are too warm to listen patiently to. It would be uncandid in me, were I to disguise my sentiments, & still more so not to say, that I am placed in one of the most distressing situations that a man can be placed in.[27]

This was one of the returned letters, showing that James, if he was hoping to make his peace with Sir Harford, had sadly misjudged his character. But at least he was now brought face to face with reality, for on telling Sir Gore what had happened he received 'some explanations', as he told his brother David, 'which his modesty or his delicacy had never permitted him before to avow to me.' Sir Gore now told him, assuring him he spoke truthfully, that far from owing his present position to Sir Harford, his connection with him had been 'the worst claim I could have to [preferment] with the Ministers & the E I Company,' that if it had not been for Sir Gore's request to have him as secretary of Embassy he would not have been given further employment. James now considered that 'this unparalleled act of illiberality towards me' of returning his letters 'cancels all my obligations' to Sir Harford. As he explained to his brother, he now found

> ten thousand things turning up every day that shew how little we ought to build upon the suspicions of Sir Harford Jones. Poor Willock is in the same scrape as I am. Sutherland complains of the ungracious conduct of the Envoy to him, & from every one I hear nothing but remarks of his sourness & crabbiness. He talks of all he has done for the young men about him, but sift the matter to the bottom, have they had any thing more than what he

complains to have received himself from Gover', fine words? ... In short ...
after all my long acquaintance with Sir Harford Jones I am led to make this
distressing conclusion about him, that as long as a man is useful to him he
will cherish him, but the moment that man gets into other trammels, adieu
the friendship, adieu the fine words, adieu every thing, & the man may go
to the devil for what he cares.[28]

James felt badly betrayed. Sir Harford had been, for four years, a sort
of father substitute. Did a little iron now enter his normally happy-go-
lucky heart? Certainly he appears never again to have formed such a
close friendship with anyone in the public service from whom he might
gain preferment, and there is indeed little evidence of his having
thereafter any really close relationship with anyone outside his own
family. The experience did not kill his inborn sense of fun and humour;
but perhaps it introduced the edge of cynicism into his manner of
observing and commenting on the world and the people in it which
provides much of the zest in his Hajji Baba books and other writings.
At first he wanted to keep good relations with Lady Jones, and asked
David and his family to try to get her to understand that he was not
at fault. David himself tried to bring Sir Harford round, writing to
him from Constantinople when he got James's letter, that he could not
'believe that James is capable of any thing in the shape of ingratitude
or even indifference towards his best friend and benefactor ... His
heart is, I will answer for it as for my own, unchanged and unchange-
able ... He would be ready to throw himself in the fire for you.'[29] But
Sir Harford did not respond, and James not only gave up all effort to
mend the breach, but became determined never to have anything
more to do with the family. The last straw was when he found that Sir
Harford had not even thanked his mother for the present of a copy of
his travel book – 'It is over this that Mr Author is really angry' James
told his mother, adding 'never has a man been to more trouble and
expense to please another and never so failed.'[30] Even then, however,
he yielded to pleas from Lord Radstock to send through him a letter
of reconciliation to Sir Harford; but he did so only with the greatest
reluctance, believing that when his uncle was fully aware of all the
circumstances he would agree that it was not for James to make the
first move. His belief was justified. He learned in June 1812 that his
letter had not been delivered because

Lord Radstock had finally seen the conduct of the fulminating little Baronet
towards me in the same light that I do. I do not wish to renew my
acquaintance with Jones – and let him take what steps he chooses to cackle
me up again (for the fellow is quite capable of it) I shall ever be most cool
& reserved towards him. He really is a dangerous man to know ... I think

I am lucky to have *washed my hands* of him – he w^d always have kept me here in *hot water*, as I should have remained *saddled* with all his little dirty, paltry intrigues to the great detriment of my happiness & comfort during my stay with Sir Gore Ouseley.[31]

All this was in sad contrast to the enthusiasm with which James had written to his mother about Sir Harford from Bushire in December 1808: 'I can safely say this, that as far as it will be in his power he will ever befriend us. I can repeat to you what he has frequently said to me, that all his intent & abilities will, when he can be useful, be employed for us.'[32] But if all Sir Gore had told James was the truth, it was as well for him that the friendship did break up. However, James's stay with Sir Gore in Persia was not as full of happiness and comfort as he was expecting.

CHAPTER THIRTEEN

James 1811–1812

'I am sick of Persia and every thing belonging to it.'

When James, in May 1811, finally realised that he could no longer count on Sir Harford Jones as a friend, he and Sir Gore Ouseley had been in Persia for over two months and had already progressed as far as Shiraz on their way to Tehran. Sir Gore too had had his problems. His arrival at Bushire on 1 March had created a considerable local stir – especially when the governor and his suite, on coming aboard to welcome him, had been introduced to his wife in her own cabin in the presence of the nurse and two of her personal female servants: they thought he had four wives, thus establishing him in their eyes as a man of great substance and power. It was not so easy, however, to get the Shah to recognise his status, for Sir Harford in Tehran, to say the least, was not being co-operative.

At Bushire the Mirza went ashore first, at three hours after sunrise on the 3rd, the auspicious hour chosen by the astrologers. There being no usable landing stage, everyone had to be carried the final few yards from the ship's boat, and the Mirza, wishing to pay a compliment to those who had so safely brought him thus far, spurned the Persians who rushed forward to offer their services for this honour, and chose instead British sailors. Sir Gore and party landed two days later, to the same noisy and dusty reception experienced by Sir Harford and James in October 1808. They were accommodated not in houses, but in their own tented camp nearly two miles outside the town where they then spent over three uncomfortable weeks in a strong, hot, dusty wind, which even blew down some of the larger tents. It was a trying time, but Sir William Ouseley considered that at least they ate well, for they were

> abundantly supplied with mutton and lamb; veal, poultry and eggs. Some beef offered for sale appeared so disgusting that none of it was ever placed on the Ambassador's table. But this want we scarcely felt; for the neighbouring sea furnished a great variety of excellent fish. The prawns were larger than any which we had seen elsewhere.[1]

The delay in starting the trek towards Tehran was caused by problems of protocol. Sir Harford, as requested, had sent two of his officers and some soldiers to act as escort. He had failed to ensure, however, that a *mehmandar* of appropriate rank was with them. Sir Gore considered that, as a full ambassador representing a sovereign, he was entitled to a *mehmandar* appointed personally by the shah, and he had specifically asked Sir Harford to arrange this. But all that Sir Harford had done was to arrange for one Mohammed Zeki Khan to be sent from Shiraz, and even he had not yet set out from there. Stiff messages from Sir Gore produced assurances from Tehran that the shah himself had approved of the choice of Zeki Khan, and from Shiraz that he was now on his way. Despite this, Sir Gore felt his dignity had been slighted, and to show his displeasure he deliberately set out without waiting for Zeki Khan to arrive – instead forcing the local governor at Bushire to act as his *mehmandar* for the first part of his journey. As Lady Ouseley, by now seven months pregnant, had to travel in a litter, their progress was slow, which irritated James who also complained to Sir Harford of Sir Gore's parsimony, so that he 'does not go thro' the country with half the comfort that you did.'[2] He was impressed, however, with the 'patience & resignation' with which Lady Ouseley put up 'with every thing with exemplary goodness.'[3]

The governor of Bushire was sent back when they met up with Zeki Khan on 1 April. Sir Gore at first refused to meet him personally, sending James to call on him to explain the insult he felt he had received. He knew, however, that the comfort of his party on the journey ahead was largely dependent on establishing good personal relations with his *mehmandar*, so once he had made his formal point, and Zeki Khan had tendered suitable apologies for what had happened, his attitude changed and they became friends. For Sir Gore could exercise great charm and, if he chose, behave very informally. For instance, that very day he played an April Fool joke on the Mirza, sending him a message that James was dying and wanted to see him urgently. The Mirza rushed over, half dressed, stepping painfully on a thorn in his unshod feet, only to find James emerging from his tent in full dress to make his call on Zeki Khan. Although this April Fool practice had been explained to the Mirza in England, he had failed to notice the date and was well and truly caught – apparently without taking offence – and Sir Gore was delighted.[4]. This mood of jollity evaporated at Shiraz.

⊕

When the party reached Shiraz on 7 April, Sir Gore learned that Sir Harford had no intention of awaiting his arrival at Tehran before himself leaving. As an unseasonable drought meant that it would be almost impossible to get food and fodder if they continued their journey at once, Sir Gore gladly used this excuse to delay their departure until Lady Ouseley had given birth; but he found his three months there 'in many respects disagreeable.'[5] For much of the time he and Sir Harford were exchanging a quarrelsome correspondence over the latter's attempts to interfere in the way the former wished to conduct his relations with the Persians. So irritated did Sir Gore become that he began, as James told David, to regret 'that an embassy has ever been sent, and thinks that all the treasure we are spending here, will be so much thrown to the dogs.'[6] His instructions were to negotiate a definitive treaty with the Persians to replace the preliminary one concluded by Sir Harford, but he told the Foreign Office that he doubted whether it was really worth trying to do this, and certainly not worth buying one: 'The giving of money except to servants' he wrote 'I have totally abolished, and what presents I think it absolutely necessary to give are selected with the hand of prudence and economy.'[7]

James, however, although uncomfortably placed between these warring envoys (and not yet aware that he was going to be thrown over by Sir Harford), was at first quite happy. He told his mother 'the life that we lead here is more like the pastoral life of our first fathers than that of our modern gentlemen.' The Ouseleys had established themselves in a little house belonging to the prince governor, the rest were in tents. His was roomy, consisting 'of a little salon which serves me as boudoir, audience chamber, bedroom etc, & is surrounded by a canvas wall which forms a vestibule for my people.' As valet he had 'a fine chap, active, intelligent, in a word a perfect sailor', who had been given him by Captain Heathcote of *Lion*, and amused him by his efforts to learn Persian. He also had a couple of Persian servants, a groom, and two horses. He was able to go riding every day, and he visited Persepolis again to make a detailed study and drawings of the ruins.[8]

Although very hurt when the break with Sir Harford became final, James's natural ebullience seems to have quickly overcome the bitterness in his letter to David (see chapter 11). It was not long before he was telling David that he was going to use the time at Shiraz for building up his knowledge both of Persia, ancient and modern, and of 'the duties' of his profession, although perhaps for a while he did so with less than full enthusiasm. 'I intend' he told David to study Persian, not because I take any delight in it, but because it is a sort of thing expected from a man who has lived in Persia, that he should be conversant in its literature. My object in reading its best authors … will be to have the power of judging whether they really possess those excellencies that our oriental scholars are so eager in giving them … From what little I have seen of Persian literature, I must own that it does not repay the trouble one has in learning it, & that its poets & historians would never bear the test of close criticism – at least according to our northern & logical ideas of excellence.

And although he had good intentions of studying political economy from *The Wealth of Nations*, this book was 'till now laid very snug in my book trunk.' He had also thought of reading Malthus on population, but had found the copy available in Bombay too expensive. 'However' he told David, 'I do not intend to increase the population of this country myself' relating in this context an amusing story that had come to his notice:

Mirza Abul Hasan brought with him a certain quantity of silk stockings from England, & having exhibited them before the Prince, he said that the Franquis generally put them on when they went to bed, & hinted that they were great promoters of that sort of vigour which as people so debauched & sensualized as this, are ever so anxious to acquire. The Mirza's stockings of course became the property of the Prince, with which the latter immediately hastened to the harem to try the experiment. He returned covered with glory, & immediately sent to the Mirza for more silk stockings.

Such stockings now being in great demand, James hoped 'a fresh impetus will be given to our manufacturers & our trade having a new article of exportation to the East'; and thought the hosiers should erect a statue to the Mirza and send him a personal supply gratis.[9]

In May, with Sir Harford now off the stage, Sir Gore acquired greater leverage with the Shah, who decided to show him some respect by sending his fourth Minister from Tehran, with an escort of 40 horsemen, to be his *mehmandar*. Sir Gore nevertheless determined to continue to stand on his dignity. He made a formal call on this *mehmandar* as soon as he reached Shiraz, but declined his later invitation to breakfast with the excuse that 'he always got wind in his stomach if he stirred from home without his breakfast.'[10] He also made it clear that he was not going to stir from Shiraz until Lady Ouseley had been delivered of her child. A daughter was born on 13 June, but even then they were not ready to start their journey to Tehran until 10 July.

The summer heat, with day-time temperatures often exceeding 100° fahrenheit, had also been having its effect, and James was beginning once again to find Persia a most unpleasant place. His travels in the environs of Shiraz and to Persepolis had brought him into contact with the ordinary people of the countryside, and he was much affected by the misery of their condition. 'It is impossible' he wrote in his journal 'to see the situation of the wretched, destitute peasantry of this country without being filled with compassion at their hard & helpless lot, & execrating the unfeeling and hard-hearted tyranny of their government.'[11] To David he wrote that it was beginning to look as though Sir Gore might decide to quit and leave him in charge, a position for which he had 'no great ambition ... particularly in this rascally, beggarly, b-gg-rly country'[12] where if the state of anarchy under 'this pitiful government' went on much longer 'the poor people must either die of hunger or rob in the high way.'[13]

The day-time heat also meant that the mission now travelled mostly at night. They would all be roused by a trumpet call not long after midnight and, after dressing as best they could in the dark and cold, the 'gentlemen' would ride over to Sir Gore's tent. Another trumpet call would announce that His Excellency had mounted, and off they would go. The whole party, tents having been sent ahead, would stop about mid-morning, and remain in the new camp for the rest of the day. It was a painfully slow way of travelling, seldom more than 15 miles a day, but at least it gave the 'gentlemen' a chance sometimes to go riding off into the countryside and perhaps enjoy a little hunting of game.

Even though they travelled mostly at night mother and child suffered much. Lady Ouseley had been unable to secure the services of a wet nurse because of the unwillingness of Muslim women to nourish an infidel child. She could not satisfy its appetite, and supplies of cow's milk were difficult to obtain. And night travel brought its own problems. Passing through an area where their Persian escort feared they might be attacked by Bakhtiari robbers, they all had to be crowded together the more easily to be guarded. 'There was an end' wrote James

> to all order and distinction of persons. Every body seemed at once to claim the privilege of talking; and an hundred different voices, speaking almost as many different languages, were elevated at one time, which joined to the neighing of horses, braying of asses, and the jingling of the bells of the mules and camels, worked up the confusion to its height.[14]

Needless to say, James, with his contempt for the Persians, was very doubtful that their escort would have been any defence had they been attacked.

They reached Isfahan on 29 July. The Mirza had gone ahead some time before, and came to meet them two days out. James found he had 'become as fat as a priest but as always gay and in good humour' and was able to give him a letter from Lord Radstock which so delighted him that he called his compatriots round to witness how he had not been forgotten by his English friends, exclaiming: 'You Persians do not know the meaning of real fidelity.'[15]

They were met on the outskirts of Isfahan with all ceremony and the 'succession of personages, whose rank increased as we approached the city' reminded James of the Book of Numbers, chapter 22 verse 15: 'And Balak sent yet again princes, more, and more honourable than they'. They were escorted to one of the royal palaces built by Shah Abbas the Great, and dismounted

> at an immense open hall, the roof of which was supported by twelve wooden pillars, inlaid with looking-glasses, and its interior superbly ornamented with paintings and gilding. Here was spread on the ground a collation of fruit and sweetmeats, piled up in China bowls, and ornamented after the Persian manner with cotton and gold leaf. When every person was seated, and the usual ceremony of smoking and coffee had been performed, a breakfast of Persian dishes succeeded, and the whole scene was performed in the presence of the rabble who had accompanied us from the beginning ... It was indeed a novel scene, and must have been very amusing to them to observe our agony at being seated in tight pantaloons on the ground, and our awkwardness in eating with our fingers.[16]

James now began to show a spirit of independence and non-conformity; a determination to make Sir Gore treat him less like a mere employee, and more like a colleague with his own rights. But his first action, of suggesting that the 'gentlemen' might be accommodated in what had been the harem of the great king, caused Sir Gore to reprimand him 'severely' because it would have offended the Persians.[17] Instead the women were lodged there 'living in Persian style entirely excluded from the profane sight of we men', who were allocated 'a small pleasure house called in Persian, *nemekdoun*, or *salt box*', into which they were 'packed like so many birds in a cage.' This did not suit James, who did not fancy being crowded up with the others. He took himself off, like Achilles, to live alone in a tent 'in the middle of a large garden belonging to the Shah ... from which I can enjoy the view of trees ... and hear nothing but birdsong.' There he had little to do except read and meditate. Every morning before breakfast and every evening before dinner, he was able to bathe in cold water 'which, with the exercise on horseback which I take fairly regularly, gives me an appetite to beat any I had before.' Letters from his mother had, as usual, contained much preaching, so he replied with assurances that he had read 'with enthusiasm' all she wrote to him on the subject of religion, finding it a great misfortune 'to be deprived of the help you have in Christianity', but at the same time glad that

> the life I live here, the distance from which I view the temptations which surround those who live in the great world, the solitude which allows me to reflect continually on my past life and my future destiny, all conspire to give me a sobriety of spirit which makes me enjoy the benefits of spiritual pleasures.[18]

James was a gregarious man, not given to seeking solitude; and he wrote at this time, to a friend in Malta, that he would 'like to be surrounded by a little population of my own creation instead of that constant succession of bearded muzzles that have so long been my companions.' Nevertheless, he also felt then that he did have the company 'of a number of agreeable people' and that Sir Gore was 'an amiable man & his lady a pattern of a wife'[19] (sentiments which were to change before long). For a few weeks after arriving in Isfahan he was fairly content to be in a contemplative mood. His pious sentiments were by no means false or forced. Like all his family, he had a genuine love of the bible, which he would read for pleasure, and of which he had a thorough knowledge; and it was now that – taking as his model, he said, Thomas Harmer's *Observations on various passages of Scripture* and Samuel Burder's *Oriental Customs* – he began to accumulate his notes comparing local customs with biblical passages, which he later transcribed into his copy of Bagster's Treasury Bible, and with which he peppered his second travel book.

The various official visits and banquets they had to put up with were born with patience; but one gave real pleasure. This was an invitation from the Mirza to his

> little Persian-style room prettily decorated in white and gold. In the middle of the floor were platters piled with pyramids of fruit, in the centre of each of which was a collection of bottles of Madeira wine and glasses. After serving us a Persian-style dinner (but each of us being provided with plate, knife and fork, and napkin) he took us to his English Room where he had an English sofa, two chairs, all his little writing boxes, his English books, and on the walls his portraits of Lord and Lady Arden,* the little portrait of Emily as a child which Lord Radstock had given him, and the patent making him an honorary member of the Board of Agriculture.[20]

---

* Charles George Perceval, 1756–1840, brother of Spencer Perceval (Prime Minister 1809–12) inherited the title Baron Arden in 1784 from his mother. His wife was also his sister-in-law, being the older sister of Spencer's wife.

⊕

Sir Gore decided to stay at Isfahan until the summer heats were passed, and they did not set out for Tehran until 10 October – arriving on 9 November. Here Sir Gore, once again, chose to stand on his dignity and demand special attentions from the shah. He insisted upon a royal tent being pitched five miles out, in which he could receive the *isteqbal*, which was then led by a relative of the shah's. Thereafter he was temporarily housed in the same quarters which had been used by Sir Harford and James in 1809, until two of the royal houses were made available. There was further 'gamesmanship' by Sir Gore over his first audience with the shah, which was granted after a wait of only two days, but which, in deference to Sir Gore's insistence, was held privately at four in the afternoon instead of publicly in the presence of the whole court at midday. (This was the normal practice, so as to make the handing over of presents look like a tribute from the foreign emissary). Moreover, in defiance of normal Persian court protocol, he insisted on handing both his credentials and the royal presents personally into the shah's own hands. He was also allowed to sit some five or six yards nearer the shah than would have been normal (cf chapter LXXVII of *Hajji Baba*). Perhaps the shah had been impressed by the Mirza's description of the intimate way he had been received by the English king, and wished to reciprocate. Sir Gore, however, felt he was getting the benefit of the stand he had taken at Bushire, which he thought had 'not only established our national character and independence on the highest grounds, but induced the display of greater condescension, honours and distinctions than have hitherto been ever shown to the representative of our own or any other monarch.'[21] James, alone of the suite, was allowed to accompany Sir Gore on this occasion and reported (with evident pleasure) that he had 'renewed acquaintance with my old friend the King of Persia, who to do him justice is as fine an old gentleman as I ever saw; I say so particularly because he called me *khoub javani*, or in plain English a very fine fellow.'[22] Indeed, surprisingly given his usual rather jaundiced view of the Persian rulers, James told his mother that the shah was 'a man who plays the part of king quite naturally & who, without lowering his dignity too much, can display an affability which is very attractive.'[23]

Despite this clear indication of the shah's favour, Sir Gore had some difficulty in persuading the chief minister, Mirza Shefi, to show similar respect to the representative of the king of England. It took three weeks and, he heard, a direct order from the shah, before Mirza

Shefi would agree to make the first call. But he was not particularly well disposed towards the British, preferring the French, while the shah was desperate to secure British support and practical help in his war with the Russians – who had seized Georgia and other parts of his territories. He quickly agreed to the exchange of ratifications of the treaty which Sir Gore and the Mirza had brought with them from London, and, on 30 January 1812, Sir Gore was able to report that the shah had ordered the immediate start of negotiations for the definitive treaty in the hope that he would thus be able to bind Britain firmly to secure for him the return of his lost territories from the Russians. Although this was signed within six weeks, on 14 March, it did involve some tiresome negotiating because of Persian unfamiliarity with European practice: 'Whatever demand we made' wrote James, 'however clear and self-evident, they always thought it had, or might have, some recondite meaning which they could not understand, consequently they never acceded to it without discussions so long and violent as frequently to end in quarrel'[24] – something James was to have further experience of in negotiations with the Mexicans, a dozen years later.

It helped the negotiations, however, when news was received of an important victory over the Russians in the north on 13 February. British troops being used to train the Persian army had played a distinguished part in this success, and two British sergeants lost their lives. This removed all Persian doubts as to whether Christians would be prepared to fight Christians on the side of Muslims, although James thought it 'mortifying to be under the necessity of settling such a doubt' in this way. He got some quiet amusement, however, (and some material for chapter XLII of *Hajji Baba*) over the way the Persians exaggerated the extent of their victory by claiming 2000 Russians killed and 12 guns and 5000 men captured, when the true figures were 500, 2 and 300. Their excuse for this absurd claim was that 'if we did not know that your stubborn veracity would have come in our way, we should have said ten times as much … You would not surely restrict so glorious an event in our history to a few dry facts?' Sir Gore was present when the Grand Vizier was dictating a letter concerning the victory, and instructed the scribe to put down 2000 dead and 1000 prisoners out of an enemy strength of 10,000, explaining blandly to Sir Gore: 'this letter has got to travel a great distance, and therefore we add in proportion.'[25]

During the mission's first six months in Tehran, James seems to have had little official work to do. Even during the treaty negotiations he was little more than a note taker. 'Our days' he wrote 'passed away in dull uniformity, with little to attract us beyond our house. We established a fives court, we rode much on horseback, and took exercise in a considerable enclosed garden attached to our residence.'[26] He was here living with the other 'gentlemen' of the suite, but it seems he had his own apartment at the top of the house, for in a letter to his mother he referred to 'a little room with this advantage over the others, that it looks over the roofs of the surrounding houses so that I can see the mountains in the distance.'[27] But they seem to have had little to do with the Ouseleys. Gordon wrote disapprovingly to his brother, Lord Aberdeen, that the ambassador had thought

> it necessary so far to agree with the customs of this country as to keep Lady Ouseley to himself as much as possible. He consequently lives with his wife & children in a perfectly distinct house on the opposite side of the street from ours, I mean the one in which Morier, Sir William, myself, a Bombay surgeon and an officer in the Madras army reside. We cross the street twice in the day to breakfast and to dine with Sir Gore & Lady Ouseley and twice to return to our own apartments.[28]

At the beginning of May the first reviews of James's travel book reached him. He was delighted with them, but apparently reluctant to claim all the credit. Gordon, asking his brother for his opinion of it, wrote:

> Perhaps you have not heard that although the matter of which it is composed is exclusively Morier's, the merits or demerits of the style in which it is written are attached to Mr Hugh [actually Robert] Inglis, who may be said to have given to Morier's material a form, shape & utterance ...

He added that Morier 'from motives of policy' had 'painted this country in warmer colours than it deserves', anticipating its translation into Persian.[29] To his mother, however, James wrote[30] that the news of its good reception 'made me very proud. To tell you the truth, I couldn't decide if I'd been foolish or wise in publishing it. Now I am inclined to think I did well, and have set myself on the road to authorship'; and he asked her to send copies to Lady Arden, to Lady Alvanley* and to 'Lady Stafford† because one day at the [royal] Drawing

---

* Widow of Richard Pepper Arden, Baron Alvanley, 1745–1804, who herself died in Edinburgh in 1825.
† Countess of Sutherland, wife of George Granville Leveson-Gower, 2nd Marquis of Stafford (and later 1st Duke of Sutherland).

Room she promised most graciously to be a patron of my book'. He thought the publishers were supposed to let him have 50 copies gratis, and he also wanted copies sent to friends such as Vaughan and Walpole, as well as to the Duchess of Leeds,* and two sent out to Persia, one for Sir Gore and one, specially bound in leather, for himself. He gave his mother carte blanche to distribute copies to others at his expense 'for good friends are always worth more than money.' (It seems, however, that the publishers were not as generous with free copies as he expected: a few weeks later he was complaining that 'these devils of publishers are going to make a fortune at my expense.'[30]) He reassured his mother that this success would not lead him to give up his diplomatic career. 'Do not worry. I am not preparing to quit Persia, & I shall suffer and remain as many years as they want provided this is to the advantage of my family. I begin to think that I'll be the richest, and the fattest, of the family and so I am ready to be the one who makes the biggest sacrifices.' He was expecting Sir Gore to return to England in the spring of 1814, and to be left as Minister Plenipotentiary 'which wouldn't be bad'; but he considered that 'a miserable Court like this one here' did not justify more than an Envoy, and asked his mother to pass this opinion privately to Hamilton. To his sister Emily he wrote with humorous irony:

> the feelings of an author when his vanity has been gratified by the applause of his readers is greater and more exquisite than you can conceive ... At one time I was taking it into contemplation whether I would any longer deign to hold converse with the common heard of mortals of this life, but thank God my fit went off in a few days and left me to my plain flesh & blood as usual.[32]

Sir Gore had arranged for a special baggage train to follow them with presents for the shah, consisting of 'several carriages, looking-glasses, a grand piano forte, a large mahogany dining table, and many other heavy pieces of furniture.' This caught up with them on 10 May. The largest items, including the carriages, had been dismantled, and were carried on men's backs the 620 miles from Bushire. But, to ease the loads, the men had had the habit of putting them on gun carriages which were allowed to run freely downhill, with disastrous results. Of the 70 mirrors, only a third arrived unbroken, and almost everything else was damaged in some way. The carriage destined for the shah could be assembled and made serviceable, but 'it was first necessary to knock down part of the wall of our court-yard to get it into the street.' It was then dragged, with difficulty, to the palace, to be formally

---

* Widow (2nd wife) of Francis Osborne, 5th Duke of Leeds, 1751–99.

presented to the shah. He inspected it carefully 'and then got inside, leaving his shoes at the door, and seating himself with much satisfaction upon the velvet cushions. The Mirza ... chief executioner ... some of the secretaries of state, and other personages of rank, all in their court dress, then fastened themselves to it, and dragged His Majesty backwards and forwards to his great delight.' Despite the shah's apparent pleasure at this gift, however, it was bricked up in a warehouse and never used.[33]

⊕

Sir Gore at this time had really only one wish, to give up his mission. Their infant child had died (from undernourishment according to James) and been buried in the royal garden. James read the funeral service and designed a memorial stone. Sir Gore, by now, probably shared James's private opinion that he had been most unwise bringing his wife with him and, being himself unwell, all he wanted now was to get back to England. James too wanted this, but realised he would have to remain to take charge of the mission. He told David that his

> (material) prospects in life appear to me to be as satisfactory as those of any fellows of my age ... I only require to be upheld in my resolution of remaining in this infernal country, which I leave to you, and the rest of my friends to do, for I am too diffident of my own fortitude, to be able to trust entirely to myself in carrying all these fine plans through.[34]

He was worried, however, that after the stay of five years he saw in front of him he would

> return an old boy in all the meaning of that term, caustic, obstinate in my opinions, opinionated, full of bizarre ideas, and as autocratic in my humours & manners as the emperor of Japan. There is nothing that so ruins the character of a man as to live in a barbarous country having round him only self-seeking and small minded people who never stop flattering his caprices and humours. It was certainly that which gave our friend [Sir Harford] his tone of haughtiness and despotism ... [so that] he finished by believing he had emerged from Jupiter's loins ... Truly one has to surround oneself with all one's good sense with these Persians for they are such fine flatterers and clever courtiers that they make one believe in the end that there is no one to match you in the world.[35]

But Sir Gore could not yet give up. He had been instructed to get the shah to agree to his joining with Prince Abbas Mirza to negotiate peace between Persia and the Russians (who at that time were Britain's allies in the war against Bonaparte). The shah had been reluctant, but had at last given way, perhaps influenced by the gifts. So, at the end of May, they were on the move again, – this time with Abul Hasan as their *mehmandar*. As before they moved mostly at night, and reached Tabriz on 19 June, after being met two days out by an escort of horse artillery sent as a compliment by Prince Abbas Mirza with his own carriage, described by James to his mother as 'one of those old things which you will have seen in pictures of the time of Queen Anne. It is Russian made, a gift from the Empress Catherine to the Armenian Patriarch of the Three Churches, and from him to Prince Abbas.' James was astonished at the transformation in the appearance of the cavalry, who had been persuaded by their English instructors to ride in the English style with long stirrups, English bridles, and boots and spurs, and even to shave off their beards (apparently after one of them had his badly singed when a gun fired prematurely). James thought they made as fine a show as any European troops, and put it all down to the enlightened views of Prince Abbas Mirza, the 'young prince ... who will perhaps be the means of pulling this country out of the barbarism into which it has sunk.'[36] They were received formally at the gates of Tabriz by a solemn little 8-year old, the son-in-law of the prince, and a band of fifes and drums (again trained by the English) playing God Save the King 'in a style not unworthy of that sublime tune', followed by traditional English military airs.[37] There was then another argument over protocol, when Sir Gore made it clear that he would be offended if the prince delayed receiving him, as was proposed. According to James, the prince then said 'For God's sake let him come how or when he pleases. I am too much indebted to him in a thousand different manners that there should be the smallest etiquette between us.' And, at the meeting, James was as impressed with the prince as David had been. He thought he had

> the most fascinating smile which gives play to a countenance that even in civilized countries would be pronounced as the mirror of a perfect & well organised heart & mind ... There is a sort of habitual affability that some men are gifted with & which it is the good fortune of this prince to possess in a superior degree ... [A strict Muslim, particularly with regard to wine, he is] equally temperate in the indulgences of the harem & strictly punishes that horrid offense against nature of which I have mentioned some abominable instances in the government of his effeminate, vicious brother of Shiraz ... On the whole he must be allowed to be an extraordinary instance of goodness in a nation where (with very few exceptions) all are bad.[38]

James now became involved in some practical diplomacy. When Sir Gore had concluded the treaty with the shah he had insisted that it be endorsed by the prince (so that its continuity would be guaranteed on the succession) and he had therefore brought it with him. The prince had duly agreed to this, and Sir William was sent off to England with it on 1 July. Meanwhile there was the matter of negotiations with the Russians to attend to. On their arrival at Tabriz they had found a Russian officer sent by the commander-in-chief in Georgia, General Rtischiff, with a letter for Sir Gore requesting his participation in negotiations for peace with the Persians. Prince Abbas Mirza had not been enthusiastic, but had agreed to Sir Gore's sending Gordon to Tiflis to get more information on Russian intentions. Gordon had by now sent back word that Rtischiff had full powers to negotiate, and was proposing an armistice during which he and Prince Abbas Mirza could meet on the frontier. Sir Gore sent James off to discuss this with the prince, who had moved to a camp with his army some 30 miles away. The prince was highly suspicious of Russian intentions, and would go no further than agreeing to meet an emissary in Sir Gore's presence. Although the prince was more than amiable towards him personally, James was thoroughly fed up on his return to Tabriz, writing to David that he detested Persia 'most cordially, that I hate its inhabitants with the most insurmountable hatred, and that I should think myself the most happy of all beings could I be quit of it.'[39]

James had little time to brood on this. On 7 September he and Sir Gore set off to join the prince at Aq Teppe, and await the arrival of Rtischiff. On the 22nd a general turned up to arrange precise details for a meeting between Rtischiff and the prince, but the latter was so incensed at the general's refusal to remove his boots in the royal presence that he would agree to nothing, and sent him packing. A further message then came from Rtischiff proposing that each side should send a plenipotentiary to Aslanduz, on the bank of the River Aras which formed the frontier. The prince agreed to this, and appointed his vizier as his plenipotentiary. James was then sent off to explain this to Rtischiff and, it was hoped, to escort a Russian plenipotentiary to the meeting place. He had an uncomfortable journey in bad weather, and had to cross the river 'in the trunk of a tree scooped out by way of a boat.' But on the other side he was met by a troop of Cossacks and on arrival at the Russian camp he found a tent already prepared for him. 'In full cap & feather' he wrote to David

> I made my visit to General Ritschiff. I found him an open hearted, liberal, friendly man, in person not unlike our friend Sir H Jones, particularly his grey hair & long upper lip, & in manner that of a plain well bred soldier. As soon as I arrived I was plied with coffee & tea & towards 9 o'clock (in the evening) his great officers came in to supper. Half a dozen generals all stuck

out with crosses, stars & ribbands, lots of colonels & abundance of Georgian princes. We then went to the long tent, in which was a table that reached from one end of it to the other. At the head sat old Rtischiff, & by his side the abovesaid great worthies, not forgetting me, who was placed next to him. At the bottom were all the tag rag & bobtail of the camp, aides de camp, doctors, clerks, greasy Lieutenants & lousy Cossack officers. The General first bailed out the soup out of a large brazen tureen to all the party. All the rest of the dinner was handed round by the servants, dish after dish – nothing but the soup being placed on the table. Then the General gave all sorts of toasts, the King of England, the Emperor of Russia, me, & other great men. I must not forget a speech that he made at table which is worthy of the most heroic ages. He said, pointing to all the officers that lined his long table "You see all these gentlemen – we have all one God, one sovereign, & one heart." Indeed a more excellent hearted old fellow I never yet met with, & one for whom during so short an acquaintance I have felt such esteem.[40]

On this mission James collected some useful background for chapter XII of book two of his novel *Ayesha Maid of Kars*, But, after a meeting with the vizier, the Russian plenipotentiary declined to agree to the Persian proposals, and hostilities were later resumed.

James got back to the prince's camp at Aq Teppe on 11 October. Although he had been unable to persuade the two plenipotentiaries to make peace, he was now in an altogether happier and more confident mood – having actually been given some responsibility. He was also pleased to find that Sir Gore, whose wife had had a miscarriage, had now decided definitely to leave Persia as soon as possible, and was sending home a plea to be allowed to return home on grounds of ill health, and leave James in charge. 'You must do all you can' James wrote to David (now in England)

to get it [the permission to leave] sent out immediately because then he will most probably go home next year, and then … I shall have acquired a step towards returning myself. I don't dread the moment of entering into business by myself so much as I did, since I have made a trial of myself with the Russians & Persians in the late business: thank God I feel a confidence that I shall be able *de me tirer d'affaires*.[41]

He and Sir Gore set off three days later to return to Tehran – arriving on 17 November. James was quite seriously ill for most of the journey, having to finish it in a litter. He told his mother he had become 'a veritable skeleton … able for the first time in my life to count my ribs.'⁴² But what really upset him was the death, en route, of his English sailor servant, William Hollingsworth. In his journal he wrote:

> Gentleness & courage, simplicity of heart & good plain sense, honesty & generosity were never more finely blended than in the nature of this excellent creature ... My feelings were never so much affected on hearing this good creature the day before his death pour forth his soul in prayer, repeating those forms his rude education & self instruction had taught him with the most unfeigned sincerity, forgiving his enemies & blessing his benefactors.'⁴³

And on top of this they learned, on reaching Tehran, that Sheridan had died at Shiraz; that Major Christie had been killed in action against the Russians at Aslanduz, where the Persian army was soundly defeated by the Russians in an engagement in which Prince Abbas Mirza, according to James, 'behaved like one of the most arrant cowards that is recorded in history'; that the missionary Henry Martyn had died on the road to Constantinople – 'a most able, zealous, pious young clergyman, who had just finished a translation of the New Testament into Persian ... He was a most shining pattern of every Christian virtue' – and that Major Stone of the Royal Artillery had died of a fever. There was only one thing to cheer him. A copy of his travel book had arrived. *'Pas si mal pour un débutant!'* he wrote to David: 'Here it reads very heavy, but in England I can conceive the novelty of the subject might have created some little interest ... Had I been in England I could have managed the embellishments much better ... the choice of subjects [of illustrations] is bad. I could now add a million little curious details.' But generally he was thoroughly depressed, longing 'to get away from this infernal place ... I am sick of Persia & every thing belonging to it, and I don't think I shall ever have a wish to write again about it.'⁴⁴

CHAPTER FOURTEEN

James 1813–1814

'I need someone to whom I can pour out my heart.'

In January 1813 the news reaching Tehran was that Bonaparte was on the point of totally defeating the Russians. The Shah became alarmed at this, convinced that it would mean an imminent invasion of his kingdom by the French. In his panic he went, metaphorically, on his knees to Sir Gore to beg for British help. He virtually offered to hand over his own power to him. He could offer troops, but no money, he said. He could have 100,000 men ready in ten days and another 100,000 in twenty. Sir Gore reported him as saying:

> I do not want to have any thing to do with the payment of these troops, or in fact meddle in any shape with them ... Pay them yourself, discipline them, arm them, command them yourself, and bring such English troops as can be spared from India, to shew them the road to and ensure victory ... In short, do in Persia exactly as if it belonged to you.

So astonished was Sir Gore by this outburst that he took the precaution of checking with the chief minister that his own note of the meeting was accurate before reporting it to London.[1] And he warned James to be ready to make a hurried journey to Calcutta, to coordinate arrangements with the government of India should news come of Russian surrender at Moscow.

This prospect appealed to James, particularly as the winter in Tehran was bitterly cold. He had recovered his health after getting back there from Tabriz in November, and had been able to tell his mother:

> Your son begins to recover his normal paunch; his cheeks are filling out, his calves are rounding out again, his ribs which formerly showed only points and sharp angles are no longer so visible. Before the New Year he promises a certificate from all the doctors in Persia that he again has the right to his title of fat Jem ... able once more to eat anything laid before him.

But he was still dissatisfied with his life of idleness, and was beginning to lose his respect for the Ouseleys. 'Lady Ouseley' he wrote 'is made for anything but to do the honours of an embassy & as a result does not cheer us up much ... her only concern is for her husband and child ... [and he too] does little to cheer us because he is too tied up with his family to think of making life agreeable for those who are not part of it' – which showed scant concern for Lady Ouseley's state of mind after the loss of a baby (and her miscarriage) and lack of gratitude to Sir Gore for giving him sole use of a small house next to his stables. Here James was no longer 'persecuted by the spitting, coughs & other noises made by my friends' and could enjoy the small garden with its 'jasmin, roses & hollyhocks ... [and] a trellis supporting a vine to cast a pleasant shade, and two or three Lombardy poplars.' But he was lonely and, echoing what, unknown to him, David had written only a year earlier (chapter 11), he told his mother:

> Although I have become used over a long time to living just with myself, & passing my time without anyone else's help, yet something is missing, I need someone to whom I can pour out my heart, and it is certainly not to a Persian beard or a pair of Turkish moustaches that one can do that ... If ever the good Lord is gracious enough to send me back safe and sound to you I can promise you that one of my first tasks will be to look actively for a wife who, having a modest fortune with good sense and virtue, would have all that I need & make me as happy as possible.[2]

The next news, however, was of the French retreat from Moscow, and James stayed where he was, bored with taking tea every day with Lady Ouseley and enduring court dinners. At least, however, he had recovered his interest in recording everything he saw. He spent much time making drawings of local dress, even managing, 'by getting sly peeps at them through cracks in the wall', to make sketches of what Persian women wore beneath the all enveloping robes they wore when in public[3], and, despite his declaration to David that he never wished to write about Persia again, he now began to put together another travel book. For a while there was anxiety lest the French should succeed after all in Russia, and they might all have to leave Persia in a hurry. This prospect, however, evaporated in mid-March when news was received of Bonaparte's complete defeat and withdrawal from Russia. This had the effect, not only of removing the Shah's fear of invasion, but of removing as well, in his view, the need for an accommodation with the Russians. So he went happily off as usual to his summer camp at Sultaniyya. Sir Gore, however, was determined to get him to make peace with the Russians, and he therefore decided to move his embassy to Hamadan to be near enough to make another attempt at mediation when he judged the atmosphere right. They set off from Tehran on 26 May. James was once again ill, it seems from jaundice, although he blamed it on being forced by Sir Gore to eat English-style food, instead of adapting to the Persian diet. Lady Ouseley was pregnant again, therefore the journey was desperately slow, and mostly at night. For James, in his state, it was a great burden to have to get up in the middle of the night, ride five or six hours on a mule, and then take a purge and eat only some rice and water: he felt 'deprived of energy, without strength, in a filthy temper, deprived of letters from home, in fact more miserable than an exile in Siberia.'[4] They reached Hamadan on 11 June, but Sir Gore thought the accommodation there quite inadequate and, after a few days, decided to go on to Tabriz. James was now lent a litter and allowed to set off on his own as night fell so that he could travel faster and reach the next stopping place in time to get a decent rest, but he found this 'a sorry conveyance … for the two mules that bore me were too weak to move quick, and the machine itself was everywhere falling to pieces.'[5]

On the way from Hamadan to Tabriz Sir Gore received news from Georgia which he felt might persuade the shah to agree again to peace talks with the Russians, and he decided he should make a detour to see him at once (and give him no opportunity to avoid a meeting). As he put it in a despatch to the Foreign Office, he felt that there was 'a very perverse trait in the Persian character which renders them insensible of and ungrateful for all favours conferred upon them; for, being the most selfish egotists in the world, they judge every one by themselves, and invariably impute some latent ignoble or even inimical motive to actions and propositions the most candid and ostensibly kind & disinterested.'[6] He therefore ignored the usual protocol of seeking permission to approach, arriving at the shah's tent 'with the trumpets of his bodyguard sounding, & the royal standard displayed.' Both the vizier and the shah were furious at this breach of etiquette, and there were at first some angry exchanges. Suddenly, however, the shah laughed and became friendly. James was with Sir Gore and commented that 'one of the greatest refinements of Persian subtlety is the power they have of rousing or suppressing their anger just as may best suit the exigency of the moment.'[7] And Sir Gore's tactics paid the excellent dividend of persuading the shah to give him full authority to negotiate a year's truce with the Russians, as a prelude to an attempt to bring about a full peace treaty. Sir Gore now arranged to move to Ujan, near the frontier, to be ready for such negotiations.

With this success they continued to Tabriz – arriving on 7 July. There they found a Frenchman, Captain Gaspard Drouville, who was making trouble and prejudicing Prince Abbas Mirza against reaching an accommodation with the Russians. Sir Gore determined to get rid of him and put James to the task; but, given the man's curious history, this was not easy. He had deserted to the British forces in Spain – according to his own story after killing one of his fellow officers. He had then been packed off to Constantinople, where it had been hoped he could be found some harmless occupation; but Stratford Canning, rather sensibly, had decided that he would only be a nuisance or worse there, and had sent him on to Persia, where Sir Gore had attached him to the British military mission in the hope that this would keep him in order. James first tried writing formally to him, but Drouville, believing he had the protection of Prince Abbas Mirza, ignored this. Sir Gore remonstrated with the prince, and insisted that Drouville was under British orders and must obey them. The prince gave way, and Drouville was summoned by James to his room for, as he explained to his mother, 'a good wigging':

> He had been behaving very badly, fighting, drawing his sword and pistols on everyone … everyone feared him as a wild beast … Knowing the kind of man he was … and expecting to find him in a towering rage, I had made a few precautionary arrangements, such as having my Stasso [whom he had persuaded to join him as his servant after the death of Hollingsworth] nearby and placing a loaded pistol near my chair. In due course my man arrived. Picture a man six and a half feet in height, with a great aquiline nose, moustaches up to his eyes, a wild look in his eyes, great pointed hat, huge sabre, & boots that could be heard half a league off, and you have an idea of this Captain Drouville – indeed, the portrait of Captain Rolando by Gil Blas. I invited him to sit, but instead of a tiger I found someone gentler than a lamb. He burst into tears, he accused himself of every sort of stupidity, he swore that he was ready to do whatever was required of him … until Mr Magistrate was so moved that he assured him that he would receive no more than justice demanded.[8]

What then happened is not recorded, but presumably Drouville left quietly and gave no more trouble.

Meanwhile, Sir Gore had been trying unsuccessfully – in correspondence with General Rtischiff – to get agreement on the terms of an armistice. It had become clear that these terms could not be settled without another meeting of plenipotentiaries from both sides; so it was arranged that Rtischiff for the Russians and Mirza Abul Hasan Khan for the Persians would meet at Gulistan. The former's ADC, a major, arrived at Tabriz with a detachment of Cossacks to conduct the latter to the meeting; but it was then found that there were still some important points to be settled before this could take place, so Sir Gore, James and the ADC took themselves off to Ujan to see the shah. This time it was Sir Gore who was unwell and had to travel in a litter; but they made the journey in one night nevertheless. James described the camp they found there in his journal:

> The palace of the King ... consists of a *Divan Khaneh* or hall of audience that is supported in front by two wooden gilded pillars & looks upon a garden scantily laid out in walks shaded by willows & poplars, & of an *Andarun* consisting of the harem for the women, besides baths & the other apartments common to a Persian establishment. It is also surrounded by a *Balakhaneh* or upper room, screened by curtains, whither the King retires to enjoy the breeze & the view of his camp ... The King, by an invention of self adulation scarcely to be exceeded by the divine honours exacted by Alexander, ordered every tent to be pitched with its entrance immediately facing the palace, & by thus obliging every one to face his abode as they came forth, he literally enjoyed the fullness of his otherwise empty title, the *Kebleh Alum* [cynosure of the world]. He became as it were the nave of a great wheel & by this means & happy invention in the science of engineering he so completely hemmed in his troops that had an enemy appeared it was impossible for any one to get at him unless he first set fire to the tents in his passage or made his way good by cutting thro' the complicated labyrinth of the ropes, pegs & poles ... Such was the intermixture of men & cattle, tents & baggage, baths & cook shops, soldier & citizen, master & servant, spears & muskets, great guns & swivels that the whole looked one immense jungle of canvas & rope, & like a great mass of clotted hair, not to be unravelled but by expertness & perseverance ... The King ... always carries his women & wives with him upon his marches, but not always in such great numbers. His travelling Harem is composed of a few of the favorites, the remainder who having exhausted their arts of pleasing or who have been convicted of old age are left at Teheran ... He is constantly however adding to his stock & on this occasion received a young beauty from the hands of his own son Abbas Mirza, & married her according to one of the accommodating forms of the Musulmans for ninety nine years. The total number of souls collected together at this camp was computed at 80 or 90 thousand, of which forty thousand were fighting: the remainder were composed of camp followers.[9]

Sir Gore and James were given tents in the middle of this 'Bartholomew Fair. On one side people beating drums, on the other firing guns, here camels growling, there horses neighing, everywhere shouting and hammering.'[10] Whether all this impressed the Russian ADC or amused him we know not; but he must certainly have been bemused by the shah's behaviour towards him.

After many arguments with the shah, and further exchanges of messages with Rtischiff, Sir Gore eventually succeeded in establishing a basis on which negotiations for an armistice could proceed; but there was one final point of protocol to be decided. How near could the Russian major be allowed to approach the shah for his formal leave-taking? Sir Gore, conscious that the Russians were Britain's allies, did not want to be party to any attempt to keep him in an inferior position, and insisted on his standing at his side. The shah insisted that the Russian could not approach nearer than the garden, which was not acceptable to Sir Gore. Deadlock seemed certain, when the shah suddenly suggested a compromise: he would sit on the raised 'shelf' at the back of his audience hall so that both would at least be below him. 'Thither he betook himself' wrote James

> with the air of a wild animal being kept at a distance so that it would do no harm. The ambassador, the vizier, the major & I entered by the door to the garden some quarter of a mile from the King's palace and began to approach, making our bows at the prescribed intervals. We took off our shoes half way to the palace and proceeded on our red stockinged feet to the audience chamber where we found His Majesty on his 'shelf'. He paid some compliments to the Russian and the rest of us and then declared that he had shown this degree of condescension only out of friendship for the ambassador, and that never again would he allow a Russian to approach so near him.'[11]

Honour having thus been satisfied, Abul Hasan and the ADC departed for Gulistan, while Sir Gore and James returned to Tabriz.

Lady Ouseley was delivered of a son late in August and, once again, had difficulty in procuring a suitable wet-nurse. After interviewing 'at least twenty fat Armenians' the choice fell on 'a young Mahomedan who was said to have less fleas and more gentleness than all the others'; but arguments continued for some time over the food she was to be allowed, finally settled only by the intervention of the mission doctor.[12] This nurse, to James's amusement, soon began to give herself airs:

> Formerly happy if allowed to ride on an ass, now my princess insists on travelling in a box pannier born by a mule. She has a poor runt of a husband who follows her round, eating scraps from her table. The husband is afraid the ambassador will fall in love with his wife and forbids her to paint her face ... Her curiosity knows no bounds, & as she believes herself to be of the highest importance there is no conversation, no sounding of a bell, no trumpet call which she does not think concerns her or her husband. She

assures him he will become at least a vizier & he, the animal, gives himself altogether comical airs of protector. Molière could have made good use of two such originals.[13]

But so well did the child flourish under the care of this nurse that they were able to leave Tabriz on 21 October for Tehran. Soon after their arrival there on 23 November, Abul Hasan turned up in triumph bearing the armistice agreement he had concluded at Gulistan.

Sir Gore threw a party to celebrate this success in the new brick-built residence he had had constructed, an impressive building by Persian standards; entered between four tall Doric columns at the top of a flight of wide shallow steps, with 'five good English-style' reception rooms on the ground floor, two of which had heating stoves much admired by the Persians. 'The doors and windows' wrote James

> have been made by an Englishman, & instead of miserable Persian fastenings we have installed pretty English ones which, however, have the inconvenience that only the English know how to operate them, for the Persians cannot fathom them ... It outshines all the other buildings of Teheran except the Grand Mosque ... [and] among the surrounding mud houses it stands out like a great lord surrounded by scamps and fishwives.

James had plans for making a garden in the front courtyard when he came into possession of this splendid 'English Palace', but wondered if it would be worth the effort. 'Perhaps' he wrote

> after everything is finished the king will die, there will be a revolution, people will be at each other's throats like wolves & he who possesses the throne will perhaps take himself off to the other end of his kingdom, & there will be the house, the doors, the windows, the fastenings, the staircase & all the beautiful things deserted, to be good for nothing except a caravanserai or granary.[14]

As for Abul Hasan, James had feared that 'for all his troubles the poor devil won't become rich. He will be thrust into the smoke but will smell the meat only from afar. Yet when he returns from his embassy he runs the risk of losing his head on suspicion of having enriched himself along the way.'[15] He was not wrong. Abul Hasan had spent some £1000 of his own money on presents for the Russians, receiving in exchange a diamond ring, a dagger and a cloak worth, perhaps, £500. On his return the shah appropriated these to his own use in exchange for one of his own, used cloaks. 'It must, however, be acknowledged' wrote James ironically 'that the honour of wearing something which has touched the sacred person of the King is beyond belief, & the more the garment is covered with the King's sweat & spittle the greater the honour.'[16] But Abul Hasan was now to be sent to Petersburg as ambassador, to negotiate a definitive peace treaty, a distinction which seemed to him to compensate for everything.

The next few months were uneventful as far as politics went, but involved James in some unusual activities, such as when, with the mission doctor himself too ill to help, he had to do what he could for a sick Persian servant of whom he was fond. Unfortunately, he had to tell David, he

> died under my inspection (for I was both doctor and mourner for the occasion) ... in spite of me & my James's Powders & my chicken broths. I fancy the fellows about here suppose I am going to turn musulman, for I have now got three or four mollahs hard at work burning candles & chaunting the Koran for him, thus either pushing him up the steep that leads to Paradise or allaying the infernal heat that may be singeing him in the smoking region of *Jehanum* ... Having got fellows to cry, tear their jackets & make the *dad* and *bidad* I trust the poor fellow has been laid in his grave much to his comfort, according to the strictest letter of his law, and to the forms required by the laws of society.[17]

James, despite his dislike of Persia and the Persians, could not but be kind and generous to them in misfortune.

It was also now that James found material which he later used to good effect in chapters XIX-XXI of *The Adventures of Hajji Baba*. It was in a letter to his mother that he first described the Persian reactions to western medicine when one of the newly born royal babies seemed to be dying and the shah, in desperation, called in Dr Campbell, 'who is full of character and the best fellow in the world', with miraculous results within three days:

> There was the reputation of English medicine raised high, there was Dr Campbell elevated to the heights & the Persian doctors rejected like ignoramuses ... every one wanted to see this famous doctor being compared to Plato, Aristotle & Hippocrates, all the court wanted their pulse felt by this miracle of medicine, & ill or not every one wanted one of his cures. The king makes a list of all his ills, real or imaginary ... all his old coughs, his old rheumatisms, fevers from the past century, even the colics of his ancestors, all are reviewed and discussed. The doctor, after considering everything carefully, returns with pills of his own making suitable for strengthening the royal constitution. But His Majesty, not wanting to be the first to try these drugs, calls to him all the gentlemen of the court and gives to each a number of the pills with orders to swallow them. Now the medecine begins its work. One is siezed with vomiting and spews like a dog. Another feels gripped by colic and groans like the damned. A third begins to sweat, a fourth feels pain in his heart, each is affected in a different way according to his temperament or the state of his stomach. After these experiences His Majesty

knows what to do, and there is every reason to believe that Dr Campbell's pills have all passed through the bodies of *Messieurs les Experimentalistes*, or else are hidden away in some cupboard.

But such events of course soon set the local medical profession up in arms, and when the mission doctors started with success to persuade mothers to have their babies vaccinated against smallpox

> the local doctors, seeing only an end to one of their sources of income & the loss of their reputation in this gift from heaven, began to spread all kinds of false rumours about it. They said that in receiving the vaccine in their blood the child risked becoming a cow and that they changed part of their nature for that of horned beasts.[18]

Although nothing had yet come from London authorising his departure, Sir Gore decided in April 1814 – on the advice of Dr Campbell – to wait no longer, and he and his family set off to travel home overland via Russia. This time, the weather being cool, they travelled by day, which at least meant that James, who had to escort them out of Persia, could compensate for the slowness by making occasional forays into the countryside to hunt game. But apart from giving him further material for his second travel book, it was a journey with little merit. There was some excitement getting across the river at Abbasabad, where the winter floods had destroyed the bridge of boats. A British military engineer had been sent forward to try to repair it, but he had to content himself with constructing a raft – a flat bottomed boat of forty feet by twelve with a mast at each end to which were fastened ropes to be pulled by men on each bank. A crowd of peasants and troops had been assembled to help, and the European members of the party soon managed a safe crossing; but, on a later trip, one of the masts gave way 'and the people who ought to have veered away the rope, having hauled the tighter, the boat was upset' leaving horses, mules and Persians floundering in the stream, fortunately without loss of life.[19] There was a meeting with 'two ignorant mollahs' who showed them what they claimed was the grave of Noah's mother, and even 'an Armenian priest with more wine than wisdom in his head who conducted us to what he called the tomb of Noah' himself; while the Armenian patriarch, no less, showed them, at the Three Churches, what he claimed was the head of the spear which had pierced Christ's side. James was clearly no admirer of the Armenians, and found such incidents ridiculous; but he had some words of approval for the patriarch himself, who 'exhibited a fine rosy face that wore all the marks of good living, and there was a frankness and benignity of expression about it which did the vile nation of which he is the chief great honour.'[20]

At Erivan James was told about the Georgian girl taken prisoner, who had been rescued by her young lover in a daring exploit, a tale which he turned into the story of Yûsûf related in chapter **XXXVII** of the *Adventures of Hajji Baba*. It is here that we find the first hard evidence that he was now thinking of the possibility of writing a novel set in Persia, for he noted in his journal that it 'would form a very good foundation for a romance' – unlike the 'stupid entertainment' given by the local ruler at which 'we sat upon the ground with our backs against the wall & our legs tucked up under us, doing nothing but staring at the old daubs of paintings that were executed on the walls and waiting anxiously for the dinner which when it came only proved a succession of coarse & greasy dishes that required all our appetite to swallow.'[21] The memory of this, however, was soon overlaid by the splendid dinner given by the commandant of the first Russian military post in Georgia:

> The first dish which appeared on the table was a great piece of pork – there were all the anglo-persians in ecstasy – we recognised a civilized country and our barbarians were soon forgot – each fell on the pork with all his strength and there we were all well filled with the animal which was to be forbidden for five more years. The feast finished with several rounds of punch which were two thirds pure rum, after which everyone mounted horses and there were the civilized Europeans galloping all over the place with loose reins, guided only by the influence of punch. But, my dear mother, do not think your son was one of these: no, he was as sober as a judge and I call upon Canning [Stratford's brother who had joined them as chaplain some time before and who was returning with Sir Gore] as my witness that I was an example of sobriety to all the others.[22]

Here, on 22 June 1814, James left the Ouseleys to return to Persia, happy in his new responsibilities as head of mission.

CHAPTER FIFTEEN

James 1814–1816

'Although full five years in Persia,
yet I never left a place with less regret.'

While at Erivan Sir Gore had received news that the Foreign Office were sending Henry Ellis* out with James's credentials, and instructions to re-negotiate parts of the treaty concluded in March 1812. James, therefore, decided to remain at Abaran, on the Persian side of the frontier, to await both Ellis and the return of the tents and servants being taken as far as Tiflis by the Ouseleys. He was not sorry, he told his mother, to see the last of the Ouseleys: 'She is always weeping, unhappy, full of prejudices, always thinking of herself and hers before others, as good & virtuous as you wish, but that is not enough.' As for Sir Gore, 'although he has a good nature & several good qualities, he doesn't succeed much in making real friends,' Moreover, 'he literally did every thing himself – he made a treaty, and he made music – he composed a despatch and he checked the kitchen accounts – he spent a hundred thousand pounds and counted broken dishes – he gave handsome presents and was mean to his servants.' But he now felt 'a completely different person with always something to do. I have a thousand tasks to attend to and my time passes in the fastest and most agreeable way possible.'[1] He felt the lack of a clerk for copying his letters and despatches (he had sent to India for one) but the remaining doctor, Sharpe (Campbell having gone with Sir Gore) helped out: a large man with a yellow complexion who was wedded to his profession and talked of nothing but pills, but 'the best child in the world' and a good companion.

A month passed happily. James and Sharpe fished daily for the plentiful trout in the river. There was a picnic excursion into the

---

* Henry Ellis, 1777–1855, was later a commissioner of the India Board of Control, made a privy councillor 1832, a special envoy to Brazil 1842 and became Sir Henry with KCB in 1848.

mountains with the Persian garrison commander, a visit to the Armenian patriarch at Echmiadzin and a formal visit on James by the governor of the province, Hosain Khan,

> an old man with a face to strike terror. He has eyes the colour of pale lead which protrude from their sockets and which he loves to roll like one of those monsters the Chinese make so well. He has only a single long tooth projecting below his moustache and glistening through his beard. He possesses all the vices of the world. He drinks wine in abundance. He is cruel and a great thief. But he is also very accomplished. He can sever the head from an ox with one blow from his sword and kill a donkey at two hundred paces with one shot.[2]

The servants and tents returned from Tiflis on 21 July. James decided to wait no longer for Ellis, but to set off for Tabriz. However, at his first stop, near Erivan, he learned that Ellis was only a few days' travel away, so he decided to await him there, on

> an eminence ... with a splendid view of that awful object Mt Arrarat constantly before me, laughing at the unfortunate inhabitants of the town & plain who are grilling at 110° whilst I am comparatively cool at 95° . However ... in addition to the fear of being bitten by the tarantulas that here are as numerous as common spiders, I have to dread the plague which not three miles off is destroying the inhabitants of the neighbouring village.[3]

James now had a considerable retinue to look after and keep in order. In addition to Stasso he had 30 servants, comprising a Goanese treasurer, a chief cook and two assistants, an *Arz Beggi* (a sort of all purpose master of ceremonies), a chief tent man and his ten assistants, three grooms, two footmen, a *shatir*, two water-carriers, five ostlers and a laundryman. To bring order 'among the numerous ragamuffins over whom I at present immediately preside' he told David 'I have ordered the manufacture of an instrument of great persuasion called a *feluk*, which I have exhibited *in terroram* in a conspicuous place before my tent' – i.e., the contraption used to restrain those to whom the *bastinado* was to be administered, beating the soles of the feet, a standard Persian punishment. Whether he ever ordered its use, and if so whether he watched over its application with hard-hearted pleasure, is not known; but his action in producing this threat – and in doing so displaying at least the appearance of being as uncivilized as he thought the Persians – reveals an unexpected facet of his character, one which emerges nowhere else from surviving contemporary papers. It may have been, however, no more than the action of one who was feeling insecure. Despite all his expressions in his letters home of delight in at last being given responsibility, he was anxious. Writing to his mother when Ellis had reached him, he admitted that this had 'lifted a terrible burden from my shoulders – I no longer flounder in the dark and now know what to do.'[4] For all his bravado, James was neither comfortable in a position of authority, nor a natural diplomat – and this became manifest some years later when he was sent on a special mission to Mexico.

Ellis turned up on 12 August, ill with fever and ague, so they remained where they were for the remainder of the month until he had recovered. The main instruction brought by Ellis was to explain to the Persians that they were not going to get the size of financial subsidy they were expecting; and one of the accompanying despatches greatly annoyed the new minister plenipotentiary as he prepared to do battle with the Persians over this. It was addressed to Sir Gore – on the assumption he would still be there when it was received – and it instructed him to reduce the expenses of the Mission before he left to a level compatible with the lower rank, which would be James's, and to send away all the British troops except for an honorary escort for the Mission.[5] Since James would have to carry out exactly the same functions as Sir Gore, at least until he could get agreement to a revised treaty, he took the not unreasonable view that the expenses could not be reduced until he had achieved this – and he firmly told the Foreign Office so.[6]

Once back in Tehran it did not take James and Ellis long to get agreement to a revised treaty, despite the shah's reluctance. But, when giving his ratification on 25 November, the shah did so only on condition that Ellis would immediately return to England with a personal appeal from him for the continuance of a generous subsidy. To this James agreed, at the same time using the opportunity to try to hasten his own departure. Ellis was also to take back a strong recommendation that it would be quite sufficient now for responsibility for relations with Persia to revert to the East India Company, and for the mission to be headed by nothing higher than a chargé d'affaires. As James later explained to David, he felt that

> the old King one of these fine days may take it into his head to slip his wind, which will throw this country into such a state of fermentation that I may be confined to this cursed town [Tehran] for years, without being able to get away, without receiving any news from Europe, and what's more with every chance of getting my head broke into the bargain. On that score alone it is nonsense having resident Ministers here … Our Ministers should

never be resident here except upon emergencies, when the superior riches of our Government would always give them a preponderating influence over those of other states come when they will. It is only necessary to reflect that our treaties are only valid during the life of the King, to judge of what little real value they are. The successor to this throne may be Lord knows who ... The appointment of A[bbas] M[irza] to be the successor to this throne is pretty nearly of as much use as appointing me.[7]

Ellis left on the 30th with Henry Willock, the commander of the mission's military guard, whom James strongly recommended to succeed him as chargé (a post he did indeed get).

James wrote ecstatically to David, at the new prospect of his release within a year, warmly commending Ellis to him:

I would rather that my interests lie in his hands than those of any other man I know. He is a fellow well worth being acquainted with, for altho' he has rather too great a turn to dissipation, yet he is such a fine, open, honorable hearted fellow that I feel myself more attached to him than to any man that I have known for so short a space of time. He has brilliant talents, and particularly a great turn in public speaking which when he comes to face a Minister will tell wonderfully in his favor.[8]

Despite this eulogy, however, it seems that they may not always have seen eye to eye. In a letter to David, James revealed that most of the despatches carried by Ellis were in fact written by him:

I did not dispute the task for reasons best explained when we meet. Suffice it to say, that had I not made many great sacrifices of my own inclinations to secure the publick good, it is likely that all our business had gone to the dogs, that Ellis and I had quarrelled, and that instead of his being on his way, all radiant with success, we should both have been here, hammer and tongs, and nothing terminated. As it is, thanks to my unremitting moderation (hum!) all is well – all finished – all contented with us – we contented with each other, & the government I trust contented with the whole.[9]

James, in other words, left on his own would have been so obstinate in sticking to the smallest details of his instructions that he would have yielded to the shah's first wish to send his own emissary to London to negotiate a treaty which he was disinclined to agree to on the terms put forward. Ellis, however, must have persuaded James to be more flexible. This lack of flexibility in diplomatic negotiation was very noticeable in James, possibly the result of his inbuilt suspicion of all foreigners, but perhaps too from a fear of getting into trouble for not following his instructions precisely. Ten years later it showed again, when he was negotiating a treaty with the Mexicans, and then as now he yielded to the persuasions of his junior to depart from the strict letter of his instructions. But somehow he was able to convince his superiors that he possessed all the qualities required of a diplomat. Sir Gore wrote a glowing recommendation before leaving Persia, in which he referred to James as one 'who to long experience, zeal and talents unites a conciliatory disposition and who merited and possessed my entire confidence on all political subjects during the 4 or 5 years he has acted with me.'[10] And the Foreign Office, unaware of the degree to which Ellis had been responsible for the success at this time in Persia, told him in June 1815 'your conduct at the Court of Persia especially in the late intricate and difficult negotiation with which you were entrusted, in conjunction with Mr Ellis, has met with the full approbation of His Royal Highness [the Prince Regent]'.[11] At least, however, James deserves credit for being so honest with his brother.

There is little in James's surviving letters to show how he occupied his time after he had sent Ellis home with the revised treaty. He could find nothing to write to the Foreign Office about: 'It is best to write nothing than nonsense, therefore they shall have nothing' he told David at the end of December:

> the most it can afford will be about one letter per annum, unless these Ministers like to be entertained with histories of decapitations, eye scoopings & toe titillations. I could also write a chapter upon Turkomans & Khorassanees, but 'twould puzzle the geographers in Downing Street to find out such barbarians.

The feeling of anti-climax was accentuated by the loss of the companionship of Ellis and Willock, and the loneliness made worse by learning that both Jack and David were about to get married. His main interest now was to get Willock sent out as 'agent, consul, chargé d'affaires, louse catcher, flea catcher or any thing you like at this Court, provided you get me away.' He felt he was 'getting stricken in years, crabbed, sulky, ill natured', and to cap it all he had to spend Christmas 1814 'reduced to arm chairs, crutches, night caps & fleecy hosiery' suffering from what Dr Sharpe told him was gout. He was reluctant to accept this diagnosis because 'from what I know of my parents & their papas & mamas, gout, not even among their cats or dogs, ever made its appearance'; and he asked David 'not to let the story get abroad among the fair sex at home, for fear I might go whistle for a wife amongst them.'[12] It probably was gout, for he suffered from it at intervals for the rest of his life. He was also concerned lest 'something might be said & remarked to my disadvantage', because

Ellis had been given the Persian Order of the Lion and Sun, but he had not. Although he professed to David that he was not upset for himself – 'Get me out of Persia, & deuce take all the Orders & Grand Cordons that were invented'[13] – when he did get it later it rankled for years that he was not allowed to accept it, because permission was only granted for foreign Orders 'in cases of distinguished service rendered in the field of battle'[14] (a rule by no means adhered to when it came to recipients of rank and title).

James, however, was not idle, even if he was disinclined to write despatches to the Foreign Office. 'I am daily getting fresh information upon every thing that relates to this & neighbouring states', he told David in March 1815. 'and I think I shall have enough to play the devil amongst the big quartos if ever I authorize again.'[15] This, of course, led to the publication of his second travel book in 1818, but he was also busy observing and recording much that would subsequently provide material for his novels. For instance, in this letter to his mother describing an audience with the shah:

> These visits are always more or less the same. We dress up in our red uniforms, our great pointed hats, our red stockings, our green high-heeled slippers, & in this outfit we go through dirty streets, smelly bazaars where we struggle through an immense crowd of sheepskin hats and bearded chins, & arrive eventually at the Asylum of the Universe, the gate of the King of Kings. We are taken to the grand vizier whom we find sitting in a dirty little room where we smoke a pipe. He leaves & soon we are summoned before his majesty. The grand vizier is ready to receive us: we enter a garden at the end of which the king is seated on the ground in a room on huge cushions. We make several baroque reverences in the local style & having removed our slippers some way off we continue unshod until we arrive before the august presence of the sovereign; more reverences & there we are stood against the wall like so many statues … [the shah today] appeared completely astonished when I gave him a description of our wars in Europe & explained that in the last few years there have been 2 million killed. Here a battle is a veritable masquerade. One prances about a bit, lance in hand, one emits terrible shouts, one fires a lot in the air, one makes a din from the other world; suddenly fear takes hold on one side or the other & then it is every one for himself [cf vol I chapter VII of *Zohrab the Hostage*]. A few unfortunates not fast enough on their feet are caught, their heads are cut off and taken before the general or the king who gives so much per head – and that's the end of it. As soon as it is finished, if the victory is to the king now come the congratulations and praise. Poets get to work, histories are written, pictures are painted & soon his majesty is immortalised higher than an Alexander or Bacchus [cf chapter VII of *Hajji Baba*]. Although all this is pitiful, it is amusing once or twice; but to have to listen to such stupidities for five years is enough to make one die of boredom.[16]

In May 1815 the shah moved his court to Sava, near Astarabad, the
seat of the Qajar dynasty (to which he belonged). James also wanted to
get out of the summer heat in Tehran, but saw no reason why he
should be near the shah. Using the excuse that the expense of following
him could not be justified, he moved the mission to Damavand, not far
from Tehran. Here, on a hillock at the foot of the mountains, he built
himself a small bungalow with 'a wide view over all the arid mountains
and most of the uncultivated plain, and Teheran' and with 'my servants,
goats, mules etc camped around me [lived] like Jupiter on Olympus.'[17]

This bungalow was the cause of a diplomatic 'incident'. He had got
permission, as he thought, from the vizier, both to stay behind when
the shah moved and to build it. He employed his own masons for the
work, but had asked for a Persian officer to be on duty to protect it.
He had been told this was unnecessary. In what appears to have been
an early exercise of planning controls, it was inspected on 26 May
and, next day, men arrived with orders to pull it down. James
understood this was on the orders of the governor of Tehran, and
protested to the vizier, suggesting also that it could hardly have
happened without the shah's specific approval. He complained that he
had 'been treated with no more consideration than one of the lowest'
of the shah's subjects, and that 'the sacred character & privileges of
my office, held so inviolable even by the most uncivilized nations has
been disregarded ... [that] the honour & dignity of my Sovereign has
been wantonly insulted.' Someone was sent to him with an apology,
which drew a further note from James complaining that 'a notoriously
innocent person' should have been sent to answer for the offence, and
he demanded immediate satisfaction. This produced a reply from the
vizier that neither the shah nor the Governor knew anything about the
incident because he, the vizier, had not had the courage to tell them.
Eventually the Governor, in the presence of the vizier, made an apology
in person, and a message came from the shah that although he knew
nothing of the matter, he was sorry for what had happened and had
ordered the bungalow to be rebuilt. James accepted the apologies for
himself but warned the vizier that he could not regard the matter as
closed until his government too accepted them. And in reporting to
the Foreign Office (from whom there is now no record of a reply) he
took the opportunity to add it to his arguments for downgrading the
post to chargé d'affaires:

> It is not to be concealed that Persia derives a great share of her present
> consequence from her connection with Great Britain, an avowal which her
> pride prevents her from making: by being deprived for a time of the presence
> of a Minister, she would learn to estimate more fully the value of that

connection ... Such a step it is to be hoped would in great measure temper those feelings of selfishness and cupidity by which these people generally proportionate their demonstrations of respect to others, and would teach them to establish that respect upon a less interested foundation.[18]

Who was in fact responsible for this incident, and why, remains a mystery. Judging by the tone of his letters to David it is possible that James, now that he was *elchi* (representative of his country), was behaving with excessive arrogance towards the Persians, and someone may have decided to teach him a lesson. There was in James a regrettable (but in those days – and even much later – by no means uncommon) tendency to display somewhat contemptuous superiority towards all other nations and races. Possibly he had given offence at the Persian New Year, when he had made clear that he was not going to conform to custom and dress up in the special clothes normally presented on the occasion. He had refused 'the musty, sweaty old cloathes worn by five thousand foul Mirzas that used to be sent to us' (as he put it in a letter to David) and to join in 'the masquerade on that day, for nothing could be more degratory to the representative character than to be the *elchi* figged out in gilded cloathes like a chimney sweeper on May Day, the laugh & ridicule of the bazaar.'[19]

The business of the bungalow behind him, James seems to have enjoyed his summer at Damavand. In his journal he wrote that he would:

never reflect upon the quiet life we passed there without particular feelings of delight ... The horses of the mission & those of the troops were picketed in a most picturesque spot about two hundred yards off under some spreading walnut trees, whilst all the servants attached to them took up quarters in the open air near them ... We scarcely ever passed a morning without taking a long ride, accompanied either with grey hounds or with fowling pieces, and occupied at least an hour in the day in the inspection of all the details of the stable.

But he continued to be irritated by the way the Persians treated him. He was given a *mehmandar*, but refused the first offered, Kerim Khan, because he knew him to have pretensions. He asked for someone less prominent, even though Kerim Khan offered 'never to speak but when spoken to & accept only a small present.' He was given Mahommed Reza Bey, 'one of the greatest bigots & sycophants' but who had recently been humbled over some incident. 'He addressed me as if he was talking to a prince' James recorded 'and wore the whole Koran as a talisman, half on each arm in silver cases ... he carried his humility so far that it became quite insupportable.'[20]

There was one interruption in this peaceful three months. The shah sent an invitation to visit him in his camp at Sava, which James accepted as a good opportunity to see a new part of Persia. The shah sent the governor of Damavand to escort him thither, Aga Khan – one of his chamberlains, a young man who, 'although bigotted to an excess and avowedly inimical to every religion but his own, yet he never permitted his feelings to get the better of his politeness. He constantly brought on discussions upon religious points, and although our arguments were carried on without reserve, yet he never lost his temper.'[21] They left Damavand on 22 July, and covered the 188 miles to the shah's camp in six days. From here James made an excursion to see Astarabad, against the wishes of the Grand Vizier, who was worried that he might be kidnapped by Turcomans and 'if the *elchi* were stolen his ransom could not be effected under 5000 tomauns (about £3500) which I should be obliged to pay'[22]; but the shah gave his permission. It was on this trip that James saw the scenery and features which later formed the backdrop to much of his novel *Zohrab the Hostage*.

While he was at Sava James received letters from home with the wonderful news of the victory over Bonaparte at Waterloo, and that he was going to be allowed to leave as soon as Willock (who was on his way) reached him. Willock joined him at Damavand on 17 September, bringing not only the official letter of recall, but also, to his great relief, the British ratification of the treaty he and Ellis had concluded. Together they moved almost at once to Tehran to await the return of the shah. James, having heard that the shah was not pleased that he was to be replaced by a mere chargé d'affaires, decided to mollify him by having the whole mission, not just himself, parade as part of the *isteqbal* greeting him. Early in the morning

> we were summoned by the Prime Minister in person, who was so anxious that we should be at our posts [on the road leading into the city] at the earliest moment, that he came almost unattended to us ... We were all in our smartest uniforms and on our most lively horses. The bodyguard in their handsome Indian dresses created a great clang, and what with the many servants & attendants attached to the mission I flattered myself we made a very brilliant show ... The old vizier at our head, apparently all the time in great trepidation lest we should be too late, put out his horse at the full trot, and at this rate we dashed through the great crowd of horse & foot passengers who had already thronged the road. When we had travelled about two miles from the town we were placed at our post ... where we dismounted

from our horses, smoaked & seated ourselves on the ground until His Majesty should appear. In the mean time the track of his route was distinguishable over the mountains & along the plain by a long line of dust created by his procession. His baggage & equipages were continually passing ... As they approached the order of the procession became more distinct. His more immediate arrival was marked by the drums & trumpets ... then long rows of shattars [sic], the shah totally insulated a speck on the plain, behind him the princes his sons with their suites ... As the King drew near, Mirza Sheffi [sic] marshalled us in a line about a hundred yards from the roadside, & when His Majesty beckoned to us to proceed we marched forwards in hasty strides, which the old vizier was anxious we should increase into a trot, it being the etiquette on these occasions ... The King ... ordered us to mount our horses & then requested me to ride near him ...He had the condescension to talk with me very familiarly & his remarks & manner are ever those of a highly polished man. He seemed also anxious to give us a public mark of his attentions for as we rode along at two different intervals he was presented with bowls filled with sugar candy, of which he first took a piece himself, & then ordered that it should be given to me & distributed to the gentlemen of the mission & the attendants ... and whilst we could not refrain from smiling at the strange custom that embarrassed our hands with large pieces of sugar candy on horseback, there was scarcely a Persian around us that would not willingly have given his beard for a similar distinction ... Among the crowd I perceived the whole of the Armenians headed by their clergy bearing crosses, painted banners, the gospel, long candles, who all commenced to chant psalms as the Shah drew near, & their zeal was only surpassed by those of the Jews, who equally had collected themselves into a body, conducted by their Rabbis who erected on high a carved representation in wood of the Tabernacle & made the most outrageous cries of devotion, accompanied by the most extravagant gestures of humiliation, determined that they at least should not pass unnoticed by the monarch.[23]

James made use of some of this as background in his novel *Zohrab the Hostage* and next day, when he and Willock handed over the ratification and the letter of recall, the shah continued to show his pleasure at the compliment he had been paid by this display of respect:

The King being aware that this ratification fixed the relations between the two countries, he resolved to make the solemnity more remarkable by receiving me in a new building in which he had never yet seated himself ... In our way we were met by ... two of the King's sons, who were on foot surrounded by their attendants, some of whom in the most peremptory manner ordered us to get off our horses. Considering the public object of my visit to the King I resisted them with some warmth & pushed forward attended by the whole escort in spite of every obstacle ... Mr Willock carried the ratification & I the letter ... [after the former had been delivered] I still

had my letter of recall to deliver, which being perceived by His Majesty he
was pleased to call me to him & as I knelt down to deliver it he did not bid
me place it on the carpet before him as on other occasions, but took it at
once into his own hand from mine.[24]

This was a signal mark of favour, but it must have riled the princes,
who had been so rudely treated shortly before.

James had now had his moment of grandeur and all he wanted was
to shake the dust of Persia from off his feet. He left Tehran on 6
October 1815. The shah had been 'pleased to express his sorrow at my
departure, but I must own that I never felt so much happiness as on
the day that I made my exit from the gates of Teheran ... In Persia
there is nothing to attach the heart – the people are hollow hearted,
the country is dreary, and the life we led was almost a life of banish-
ment.'[25] He repeated these sentiments in his second travel book, and it
is perhaps not surprising that when, in 1822, George Canning proposed
sending him back as minister, the Persians let it be known that he
would not be welcome, as parts of this had caused offence. Moreover,
that was by no means the only critical passage in James' writings on
Persia. Perhaps, if that posting had gone ahead (and although James
was not keen, he would have accepted it for the money) he would not
have risked publishing *The Adventures of Hajji Baba* when he did.

James was accompanied as far as Tabriz, which he reached on the
26th, by Willock and others. There he handed over to Prince Abbas
Mirza a gift from the prince regent – a gold snuff box set in diamonds
with a picture of the prince regent on the lid. After joining in a
hunting expedition at the invitation of Abbas Mirza, James continued
his journey on 1 November, accompanied only by a *mehmandar*, two
Turkish *tatars*, two servants, and his valet Stasso. A week later he 'came
quite unawares upon the venerable chief of the Armenian church who
received me in the most friendly manner and gave me his own
apartment to live in ... and ... entertained me at dinner, on a table set
out in the European manner and well furnished with wine.'[26] He
crossed into Turkey over the Arpachai on 10 November – 'the water
was over the top of my boots and it was with difficulty that I could
keep my horse's head above water.'[27] He had to cross high mountains
in bitter cold, and passed a night in an Armenian dyer's house in Kars
– which gave him background he subsequently used in his novel *Ayesha
Maid of Kars*. Later, struggling through the snow, they reached a village
in which he was

lodged as usual in a large stable in one corner of which was a place railed off for the purpose of habitation, and which in the company of four or five buffaloes and as many cows I found disagreeably warm. My bed was spread upon some planks, the ends of which rested upon heaps of dried grass, and after I had been asleep I was awoke on a sudden by the falling of it. An honest buffalo had been feeding upon the grass under the head of my bed, which at length had diminished so much in quantity that the planks fell by a natural consequence.[28]

At Erzerum, which he reached on 15 November, he called on the pasha, 'originally a Pehlivan or prize-fighter'[29] – and clearly the model for the pasha of Kars in *Ayesha* – and wrote to David:

full of joy, full of gratitude, full of feelings of thankfulness to the Almighty for all the manifold blessings conferred upon me, and particularly so for this one of restoring me again to the clasp of civilized beings. Not that I can exactly call the grim looking Turks of this place such, but that I trust in twenty days more to be amongst those who may [be] entitled to that appellation ... I have been particular in enquiring of Stasso what you did when on this jaunt, where you eat[sic], where you slept ... I felt no little pleasure in lying on the same spot, eating out of the same platter, and perhaps digging my spurs into the same unfortunate steed that you did. Notwithstanding that I am now seated in a Turkish room as dark as any cell in Newgate, yet I feel a sort of newness of mind, an inward light that seems to promise me an abundance of future happiness ... Although full five years in Persia, yet I never left a place with less regret than it.'[30]

He reached Constantinople on 7 December, where he found his father

in good spirits, with an undiminished appetite, and grown stouter and even fatter than before ... Old Time has been hard at work on him, during the six years which have elapsed since we last met, and has furrowed two or three strong wrinkles down his cheeks in addition to those which before existed. The greatest deficiency is the loss of several of his front teeth, which impedes the free articulation of his words. His hair is quite grey, and he is much incommoded by deafness. But he has preserved all his agility. His travels up and down stairs are performed with the same celerity and clatter as usual.[31]

Isaac was then four months into his 65th year, and had only two more years to live.

Tired of overland travelling, and in any case hearing of very severe winter conditions to the north, James decided to go by sea from Smyrna. But he could not find a ship to take him there and, eventually, he had to go overland. His disappointment, on reaching Smyrna at the end of February, at finding that he had just missed the chance of passage in HMS Phoenix to Malta was uncharitably (but understandably) removed when he heard a few days later that she had been shipwrecked.

He then had to spend nearly a month in Smyrna, but was

> not sorry to have reaped a store of reflection from having once again surveyed the localities where I first commenced my career in life ... I saw Sidiköy again with many tender feelings at heart [and found many old people in the village still alive] who recollect all our names and talk of us all as if we were still little boys ... The Van Lenneps have repaired & beautified the old house, but not so much as to destroy the remembrance of times past. I saw those old pictures of father & mother painted on copper ... There was also your [Jack's] picture & mine, you with a little bird on your finger & I with a cherry in my hand. The little oil paintings of the Turkish costumes remain in the hall, and the old clock in the corner with the tall green wooden chairs all round. Lady Radstock's & mother's drawings in chalks ornament the walls of the great parlour, along with the engraved views of the principal country seats in England.

But Smyrna itself he thought 'much altered for the worse as to society – the rising generation have no education, and the declining generation have a narrowness of intellect that is not to be equalled ... [yet] the emigrations to Malta [eight years earlier] have done a great deal of good ... The houses are more elegantly furnished, the ladies dress better & the men shave at least every other day.' He made no mention in his letters of the Wilkinsons, but perhaps his nostalgia was at least partly coloured by the recollection of his passing love for Maria. It was this, perhaps, as much as anything, that caused him to tell David: 'I long as much to get away as I did before to reach it, and with the exception of one or two friends do not care if I never see it or any thing that belongs to it again.'[32]

James found a ship sailing to Trieste on 30 March, and was landed there on 20 April. He was then incarcerated in quarantine, his only view 'a dead wall & some melancholy looking people like me lolling out of a window opposite. By twisting my neck round a corner I can see the sea & the tops of some ships' masts, and by getting on top of a little wall through some wooden bars I can just discover the summit of a mountain & a few peasants' houses.'[33] He was not prepared to put up with this if he could help it, and knowing 'that a great personage gets out of the lazaretto much sooner than a little one' he sent 'a pithy note' to the governor to explain his rank and status. The Governor sent a representative, 'a little dapper man clad in black, sword by his side, hat under his arm, who assured me that save transgressing the law of the land the Governor was ready to do anything I liked.' This led to somewhat better living conditions than those enjoyed by others of lesser rank, but it did not shorten his enforced stay, of which he simply had to make the best he could. He was amused one day when the Hapsburg Emperor, on a state visit to Trieste during which he was taken to see the lazaretto, had James pointed out to him when he 'poked his nose into my corner of it, and ... made me two bows whilst I was looking down at him from my window.' On the day of the Emperor's departure, James was allowed out onto the sea-shore to view the illuminations in his honour: 'The whole coast for about two miles was illumined by paper lanterns, but alas before they were all completely lighted there came a violent gale & rain which sent every thing into the air.'[34]

James had arrived at the quarantine station 'with a long list of occupations which I positively intended to go through with – drawings to finish, journals to bring up, books to study, essays to write', but he achieved little in his 'happy unsettledness of mind', and as he came within a week of release (on 20 May) he became almost apprehensive about his return home: 'I have been so long living by myself that I can scarcely tell what sort of an animal I am become – others must judge for me – but I believe I am nearly as merry as ever, and am certain that I am nearly three times as fat.'[35] But his apprehensions evaporated when he reached Vienna early in June. He was delighted to find Gordon on the staff of the embassy there, and was taken to meet Prince Clery* 'where I found grand people, but of a perfect goodness and politeness. I was thoroughly questioned and gazed upon wide-eyed, for a man coming from Persia is almost as rare as an elephant here.' He also renewed acquaintance with the renowned German Orientalist Joseph Hammer,† who was getting married and invited him to the wedding feast. 'It is pleasant living here' he told his mother: 'the people are so kind and the necessities of life cheap. You could live here comfortably for £800 a year, and I think that would be preferable to eating crusts in London for £1000.'[36] But he resisted the temptation to spend a long time there himself, moving on after a week to visit his brother Jack, who was now minister in Dresden, and then to Paris, where David was now consul general, via Vevey in Switzerland to check on his father's property.

Back in London in September he found 'old mother quite beautiful'

---

* There is no doubt that what James wrote in this letter was "Clery"; but there is no trace of a prince by that name or Cléry. It is possible that James was referring to Karl Joseph, Prince de Clery-Aldringen, a dilettante miniaturist (1777–1831) who was living in Vienna at that time.

† Joseph Hammer, 1774–1856, later Baron von Hammer-Purgstall, an Austrian honour.

and agreed to keep Stasso, who was 'improving in English every day & knows quite enough of it to misunderstand every body', for a few months more. He spent several days with Lord and Lady Arden at their country seat, where 'I got more intimately acquainted with Lady A than I had been before, & I must own a nearer inspection has not improved my opinion of her. She is an original with some good & some disagreeable qualities in her character' And he had his first taste for many years of the charms of English girls. He

> did not quite get in love ... altho' it run rather hard with me, as there was a certain sylph like body there on a visit ... whose person was everything a mortal could wish for. I had not time to probe into the mind, which I am inclined to believe is a great deal richer than her purse, a circumstance which I fear must oblige me to dash the fair object from my mind ... If that d—d money was not in the way I should be married before Xmas.'[37]

Money, indeed, now became one of his main preoccupations. He collected £1400 from the Foreign Office for his expenses on his journey home, justifying the claim – which he acknowledged to be high for his rank – on the grounds that he had travelled more than 4000 miles the 'most part of which was in uncivilized countries where I was obliged to hire guards for my safety and in many places to make presents to pachas and agas of the districts through which I passed.'[38] He was also awarded £500 for the property he had had to leave behind for the use of the mission in Persia. But his pension of only £800 a year did not seem to him enough to live on in the style he wanted. He tried to get one higher than his rank entitled him to, on the ground of having been head of a mission for a year; but 'Ld Castlereagh' he told David in October, 'thinks the times too hard to grant extraordinary pensions and therefore I must set down content with my £800.'[39]

CHAPTER SIXTEEN

James 1817–1849

'We are all, great and small,
under the direction of God's providence.'

Although it was it was to be several years before James began to write fiction, the idea of earning a living with his pen was already in his mind on his return from Persia at the end of August 1816; but after an exile (as he saw it) lasting six years, he declared that his first priority was to enjoy Christian civilization and find a wife. He could not but envy his brothers. In 1810 he had found Jack 'in the elegant employment of searching for a wife, Caleb like, amongst the great fortunes of the fashionable market.'[1] The search had taken some time, but he had finally married in December 1814 and was now minister plenipotentiary at Dresden. David had also married, in August 1815, and was now consul-general in Paris. James had never really taken to diplomacy, and was certainly not looking for a further appointment overseas. He was relieved when a proposal to send him to Brazil instead of giving him a pension came to nothing. He wanted leisure to see his friends and to sketch, about which he was 'perfectly mad.'[2] All the same, £800 was a slender resource for such a life, and when he heard that the post of secretary of Embassy in Spain could be his, taking the place of Charles Vaughan, he was tempted and thought he might accept if it were formally offered him. But was it

> worth the seeking – are not £800 p a in England writing books, getting wives, gulping gulps, etc, etc, better than £1200 p a among the Hidalgos with their bigotry and mustachios? I own I'm for the former plan, and perhaps with a little writing I may get a snug little envoyship of my own.'[3]

He was not, however, prepared to take active steps to secure another appointment overseas. Spain was not offered. Nor was a vacancy at Florence, which he also let it be known he would accept. And this reluctance to be tied again to government service adversely affected his search for a wife. He told David in November that although he had

'lots of desirable persons in the worldly acceptance of the word in
view ... I fear where I love I cannot marry, where I marry I cannot
love.'

He had run it close, however, for he explained that:

> One fair creature with a pair of eyes more expressive than cupid ipse has
> succeeded in making a dead shot – I am like Paddy, killed dead. She has
> every requisite for marriage but ready cash, which could I get a good
> envoyship I would most readily dispense with – and as she has a great deal
> in expectation after the death of a score of old aunts and uncles, perhaps
> even in a worldly point of view I should not be doing amiss.'[4]

But he soon had to explain that this had 'entirely blown over, and
indeed in a long evaporation of sighs, something like the putting out
of a large fire that had blazed up suddenly.'[5]

Despite these disappointments, for the next two years James managed
on his pension – and the proceeds from his travelbook – to lead his life
of leisure; visiting friends, attending balls, spending weeks at spas such
as Bath and Cheltenham, making a trip to Scotland by sea. And his
finances were improved when his second travel book was published in
1818. Once again, this was in the hands of Robert Inglis, although
James found him 'rather slow in reading manuscripts.'[6] As the author,
James had difficulty in deciding what shape to give this book: 'After
having wavered between narrative & dissertation until I had almost
determined to write no book at all' he wrote in January 1817 that he
'determined to leave this weighty point to the decision of Inglis, whose
opinion I look upon to be one of the best I could get on such a
subject.' His own view was: 'If a country is imperfectly known –
narrative – If a good deal has been said about it – then dissertation
or clarification.' He was tempted to follow 'the easiest way & certainly
the most amusing' by simply revising and correcting the journal kept
during his travels and publishing that, for

> compressing all under heads, which also leads to eternal reading & notes,
> really makes a book under such circumstances the undertaking of a whole
> life. For my part I am so tired of the scenes I have described, and the subjects
> from being so constantly under my own eyes have so little interest in them
> for me, that I should certainly prefer to see all that I have to say neatly &
> trimly classed under heads.

In fact, when he started on it his aim had been

> illustrations of scripture texts by modern manners ... [leaving] out trifling
> details of days marches, entertainments, processions, isteqbals etc, & only
> inserting such circumstances as would come in aid of my principal object.
> But in doing this, how much other informaton would be lost! Manners that

exist, without a corresponding subject in antiquity to illustrate — geography, topography, antique remains, modern towns etc, on all of which I have much to say, & what I trust would be found new.[7]

Fortunately he was persuaded to keep the much he had to say, and, although his knowledge and interpretation of antiquities was somewhat amateur, the book was well received precisely because it shed discerning light on a country and people of which there was still great ignorance in the west (it was also more readable than his first effort). Some of the credit is due to Inglis, who persuaded James to cut out much (but not all) of the laboured scriptural comparison he was so keen on. This remained an obsession, and near the end of his life he tried, but failed, to persuade John Murray to bring out a special edition of the Bible incorporating the comprehensive notes he had by then inscribed in his own copy of Bagster's Treasury Bible.

The success of this second travel book was overshadowed, however, by the unexpected death – at Constantinople – of his father on 17 August 1817, five days after his 67th birthday. This was almost certainly the result of cancer of the stomach, news of which had taken some time to reach London.* It was all the more poignant because he and his wife Clara had been physically separated for thirteen years, and the sons had been on the point of putting together a plan by which he would have been able to afford to retire and they could have resumed their life together. James appealed to the government for a pension for Clara, but was unsuccessful. Meanwhile they were also trying to help ease the financial problems of their sister Maria, who had rushed into marriage with the Reverend Francis Vyvyan Arundell on 17 October 1816, even though he had debts of over £3000.† James, as the only brother without his own family responsibilities, generously bore most of the burden, even borrowing money to do so. Nevertheless, when he agreed, at the end of 1818, to act as *mehmandar* to Abul Hasan on his second diplomatic mission to England, he refused payment for his services, deciding that it would give him 'something to do, some good dinners, and increase my claims for better employment'[8] and doubtless

---

* Isaac's death was certainly not the result of the plague, as stated in *The Dictionary of National Biography*. A long report by his medical attendant at Constantinople has been studied by two doctors who agree that the cause of death was almost certainly cancer of the stomach.

† Francis Vyvyan Jago Arundell, 1780–1846, antiquarian who attached more importance to his distant descent from one of the Arundells of Cornwall, one of whom had been a Marshal of England in the 13th century, than to disposing sensibly of his estates and paying off his debts.

believing it would leave him free to perform the duties in his own way without interference from the Foreign Office.

It is not clear how much time James spent with Abul Hasan in 1819-20. He met him on his arrival from France at Dover in April 1819, and saw him off from there again a year later. He was involved in several business meetings between the envoy and Castlereagh, and must have accompanied him on many formal engagements. But George Willock (Henry's brother) was now the personal aide who attended to Abul Hasan's domestic arrangements, and it was he who escorted him to Scotland at the end of October 1819. James, however, joined Abul Hasan when he went on from there to stay a few days with Castlereagh's father in Ireland; and previous to this he had accompanied him on visits to Oxford, Blenheim and Stowe. He had reported to David in September that 'a Mission is decidedly to be sent to Persia ... The Persian asked for me – My Lord [Castlereagh] made no objection, but required a delay before coming to a resolution.'[9] Perhaps James's need for more income was sufficient to set aside all his earlier determination never to return to that country, for he seems to have been ready to accept such an appointment. And Abul Hasan must have approved, for Castlereagh, when writing to him on 4 April 1820, thanked him for his commendation of James.[10] The government, however, had already decided a month earlier (and had so informed Abul Hasan) not to send a Minister Plenipotentiary to Persia at this time, but to leave Henry Willock there as chargé d'affaires.[11]

James was probably relieved at this decision not to send him back to Persia. He had found his time with Abul Hasan in 1809–10 stimulating, pleased then with all the consequent attention paid to him by distinguished people. But on this occasion he found Abul Hasan rather a trial. In an undated letter (but obviously written early in 1820) his mother had told David that there had been 'a cooling off' in the friendship between the two, but 'happily your brother's character is such that he can well ride above all the caprices and angers of the Persian who becomes daily more agitated at his failure to get replies [from the British government]. James is wise to keep away from him to escape these episodes of rage.' James also found his duties with Abul Hasan boring. 'Time hangs heavy on hand here' he told David: 'Were it not for the club,* where we have occasional dinners & smoking

---

* This must have been the *Friday Club*, instituted in 1803 by a literary group, to which Walter Scott belonged. James's name is not included in the list of members cited by John Lockhart in his *Memoirs of the Life of Sir Walter Scott*, and there is no evidence that James met Scott; but in letters he said that Scott 'sometimes attended'.

committees, I should absolutely see no one except the Eternal Beard – There (the club) is delightful, & likely to be the source of great conviviality – It is extra^{dy} what a sort of fraternal feeling one gets from all the Munchhausens* of the age.'[12] It is probable that it was at this time, with the renewed contact with Abul Hasan and the stimulus of this 'club', that the vague ideas which had been swimming in and out of James's mind over several years crystallised into a plan to write what eventually emerged as *The Adventures of Hajji Baba of Ispahan*. And no doubt it was with this in mind that he was anxious to get sight of the Persian's own journals. As he was seeing the envoy off to France he wrote to David in Paris that Abul Hasan 'is writing for me a short account of his stay in England – he is to send it to me from Paris – pray excite him to write it daily & be careful that he does not leave you without giving this up to you – I shall translate it.'[13] He also wanted to see the journal kept by Abul Hasan during his earlier stay in London (an edited translation of which is in Mrs Cloake's book already cited), for he referred to this also:

His great journal, which is now a large work, he talks of leaving at Paris to be published & translated there – because he says there are things in it concerning folk in England which he says that he is sure nobody in England will translate – do talk him out of this, & tell him the truth, that if no Englishman would dare to publish it, a fortiori no Frenchman w^d – & persuade him to send the great journal to me (which he is half inclined to do) and I will faithfully translate it.[14]

It seems that there was also some official concern over these journals. George Willock – who was still accompanying the Mirza in Paris – received a 'private and confidential' letter from Josef Planta (permanent secretary at the Foreign Office) of which there is now no trace, but which may have been instructions to him, in consultation with David, to try to prevent publication in France. Willock replied on 17 April 1820:

At present vigilance only is required and as long as I see the dreaded book on the table of the Secretary I feel in some measure at ease ... As yet I cannot see any preparations for the translation of the work and indeed unless it is abridged, to make a copy of it would be a labour of some time. The original only exists and which I believe is not altogether finished. When in London a small abridgement was commenced in the shape of a letter which was to have been given to Mr Morier. It consists only of a few pages. This is what I suspect may be published. However it is still incomplete ... His

---

* A reference to Karl Friedrich Hieronymous, Freiherr von Münchhausen (1720–97), the German raconteur who inspired Rudolph Erich Raspe to write his *Adventures of Baron Münchhausen* which was first published in English in 1793.

Excellency expressed his intention of delivering [to his French interpreter] the above mentioned letter. I combatted the matter as warmly as I could, grounding my opposition on my friendship towards himself and on the bad impression such a proceeding would make on the minds of the English in general. Since which I have not heard anything further on the subject.[15]

It is interesting that when the German Prince Pückler-Muskau – during his tour of England in 1826-28 – stayed at Hatfield House he met Sir Gore Ouseley, who told him that 'the late Persian Ambassador' on his return home had 'proved himself no wise discret but compromised several English ladies of rank in a shameful manner.'[16] Perhaps he had been making remarks about the shameless (to a Persian) way the ladies had flirted with him in London, and the authorities were worried that his journal would repeat these in a scandalous way. As is now known, it did not; but it must have been a disappointment to James not to have had sight of it.

James, however, now had other things on his mind. Where, when or how he met Harriet, daughter of William Fulke Greville, is not known; but he married her on 17 June 1820. An earlier wedding date had been planned, for on 25 April he had written to David:

> My dear girl is I am sorry to say very unwell & has been ordered to change the air for a fortnight or three weeks as the only chance of health. She has got a lodging at Paddington, at a place called Maida Vale, where she goes today – so our marriage must be put off for that time. I am *bien* with her father, who is an odd but a good gentleman.[17]

Harriet was well connected, and her father was wealthy. Her paternal grandfather had married the daughter of the 3rd Duke of Portland, and one of Harriet's brothers, Algernon, was aide-de-camp (and later private secretary) to Wellington in Paris – indeed he must have been known to James's brother David, which may have been how he and Harriet met. Her cousin, Charles Cavendish Fulke Greville, was clerk to the privy council, and later famous as a political diarist. An aunt (who died in 1818) was Frances Anne Greville, wife of John, 1st baron Crewe. But if James had been counting on all this to bring him the extra income he wanted, he was disappointed. For it is clear that Harriet can have brought little money with her in 1820. By early 1821 James had begun to find

> that I have many habits to get rid of & new ones to acquire. None gives me more trouble than the minute investigation of shillings and pence, which

when a batchelor I was wont to despise ... what a different creature the man is who is settled, & one who has to think to work his way in the world!'[18]

Her father was, in fact, a disagreeable old miser. Her cousin Charles visited him at his home in Dover in June 1833, when he was 'past 80, a cripple from a fall he had a few years ago.' He had not seen his uncle for 17 or 18 years, and wanted to persuade him to make up his quarrel with his son Algernon. He 'totally failed to soften the obdurate heart or bend the stubborness of the old wretch' whose 'only object and delight' was amassing wealth:

> When he touched on his son Algernon or Morier ... he flew out, and it is clear that with regard to them he has a tissue of complaints against them, upon grounds so frivolous that there is no replying to them – old stories raked and hashed up, and trifling circumstances perverted and exaggerated into undue importance ... A stronger case of pure unmixed avarice than this can rarely have existed ... '[19]

How James had offended the man he had been 'bien' with in 1820 is not known, but his father-in-law – in his Will drawn up less than a year before he died in 1837 – specifically excluded Harriet, James and their children from any benefit at all.

James may at first have assumed that Harriet would bring him money, but it is clear that he found in her qualities which were more important, and that, despite many later trials caused by her ill-health, he loved her with real devotion and loyalty. No pictorial likeness of her has been found,* and only one surviving family letter includes any reference to her appearance and character. James's mother had this to say of her in a letter to David:

> She pleases me with her affectionate ways: without being either beautiful or pretty she has, in my opinion, more than that in her very agreeable and animated physiognomy, humourous black eyes and at the same time a softness of expression in her movements which marks a sensitive heart. If appearances do not deceive it seems to me that this is just the woman to suit James's character.

And after writing, in another letter, about her 'difficult and disageeable' father, who was giving them no financial help and whose only wish seemed to be to get his daughter out of his house so that he could enjoy the 'solitary life of a misanthrope with his train of servants and carriages' she said it was 'fortunate that Miss Greville is devoid of any taste for vanities, whether in jewellery, fashion or fancy carriages.'[20]

---

* Her portrait was painted by William Charles Ross in 1824 and exhibited at The Royal Academy in 1827, but its subsequent history is not known.

The fourth Lord Holland, who met them in Italy in 1830, thought she was 'a clever woman, but painfully shy and silent in mixed company' – incidentally also finding James's conversation 'sensible and totally unaffected, but neither in wit nor eloquence [does he] make one judge him capable of having written that delightful book Hadji [sic] Baba.'[21]

James and Harriet were married at St George's Hanover Square, and began their honeymoon in the inn at the foot of Box Hill before going on to Brighton. They then went to Tunbridge Wells and took 'lodgings for two months in Mount Sion where with all reverence for so holy a name we enjoy as much of earthly bliss as plain mortals can expect.'[22] At the end of September they were in Wales staying with a cousin of Harriet's, Mrs Cunliffe (Lord Crewe's only daughter) whose husband gave James lessons in oil painting. In November they were staying with Lord Crewe himself, at his seat in Cheshire, which James thought 'affords one of the best specimens of old English hospitality ... The fare is sumptuous & shooting plentiful.' He was persuaded to hunt with a pack of harriers but 'for my pains had such a tumble on my noddle that will serve me for a long time to come. I was mounted on a mare not equal to my weight.'[23] Some time early in 1821 they settled in London, and it was probably then that James began his novel writing, for he told David that he had 'many plans for the future in the writing way' as a means of improving their finances.[24] Harriet gave birth to a son on 9 March. 'The creature was not in the world an hour' James told David 'before I had already made a plan for its education.'[25] But Harriet had had a bad time of it, and the baby died three weeks later – which is no doubt why they then moved, for a few months, to a rented house near her father on the outskirts of Boulogne. Another son, Greville, was born on 10 September 1822 (and survived). It is probable that James had let it be known at the Foreign Office that he was again looking for employment, for it was at about this time that George Canning thought of sending him back to Persia as Minister – the government having eventually decided to defer to Persian wishes and upgrade British representation there from chargé d'affaires. It is not clear if James knew about this, which would have presented him with a difficult choice, given that he almost certainly would have thought it unwise to take his wife and baby with him, yet badly needed the money. However, the Persians let it be known that he would not be welcome, some of what he had written in his second travel book having caused offence.

James must, by now, have been working hard on *The Adventures of Hajji Baba of Ispahan*. The first two manuscript volumes were sent to

John Murray on 29 May 1823, and the whole book had appeared in print by the end of the year. Early in January 1824 James was already able to write to David: 'I long to receive all you have to say about Hajji [sic] … I am happy to say that the book takes hugely & that I have not committed a foolish act in publishing it.'[26] His name did not appear on the title page, but he seems to have taken little trouble to conceal his authorship, for he was soon receiving direct compliments, and he was publicly identified as the author in the *Eclectic Review* of 21 April. Opinions in reviews of this picaresque novel, although mostly very favourable, were mixed. This was partly because it followed only four years after a somewhat similar novel, *Anastasius* by Thomas Hope, to which it was at first taken by some to be a sequel, and which some reviewers thought superior in art and sentiment. But the public took to it, and the whole of the first edition of 1250 copies was sold out within a few months. For James the greatest triumph was hearing from David in Paris, at the end of March 1824, that no less a person than Washington Irving* had 'spoken of it with enthusiasm, declaring his conviction that it could not fail of becoming an English classic'[27] – which it did: it has been re-issued in England many times, most recently in paperback in 1989, and translated into several languages (including Hausa, a language of northern Nigeria, in 1971), whereas *Anastasius* has long since vanished.

Despite its success, James did not, at first, make much money from the novel. According to the records in the archives of John Murray, his half share of the profits from the first edition was only £196-7-6d. Nevertheless he thought it was

> a blessing to an idle man like me to have such a recourse as this said authorising, and I do not grudge the years which I spent among Hajji countrymen, seeing they now repay me with such profit. I am very much encouraged to go on by every body, and indeed have great thoughts of so doing, altho' I feel that the difficulties will be considerably greater now than at first starting. The great evil to avoid will be personality; for if I do not even intend to designate any one in my description, there will not be wanting those who will be clever enough to discover a meaning that does not exist.[28]

He had hoped that John Murray would allow him a bigger share of the profits if it went to a second edition, but this was not to be. Although 1500 more copies were printed the same year, by 1827 only 946 had been sold, from which he got a mere £121-9-6d. It was translated into both French and German in 1824, but by December

---

* Washington Irving, 1783–1859, the 'first American man of letters', was travelling in Europe at this time and in 1824 was working in drama and opera in Paris.

1834, when James took possession of 95 unsold copies, he had received from John Murray only just over £400.

The critical success of Hajji Baba, added to the earlier success of his two travel books, was no doubt the reason why James received (and accepted) an invitation to be one of the first 506 members of The Athenaeum, the new London club founded early in 1824 (in which he later also served on the committee). But he was obviously feeling the financial pinch, for in the summer of that year he accepted appointment as a special commissioner to Mexico to continue negotiations which had already begun for the establishment of formal diplomatic relations with this former Spanish colony (which had declared its independence in 1821). It seems that he at first assumed he would take Harriet and the child with him, but on advice he changed his mind. When he left from Spithead, on 3 August, he did so alone, leaving them in Cheltenham. In May 1825, after difficult negotiations, he was able to set off home again with a treaty in his pocket and believing his job done; but Canning did not like parts of the treaty and sent him back in October to reopen the negotiations.* He finally returned to England for good on 6 June 1826; but at least his two years' separation from his family brought financial rewards. During his period of duty in Mexico he had been allowed to keep his Persian pension as well as his salary as Commissioner, and after his return his pension was increased to £1100. (Even then, however, he tried to get more. He was unsuccessful, which caused him to write to David: 'So much for justice! So much for a reward for services!'[29]) Early in 1827 it seems that he was offered further employment on diplomatic business abroad, but where is unclear. All he told his mother was that he had declined being sent 'to countries which are quite unknown to me'[30] where he would have to have gone again without his wife, who was pregnant (but suffered a miscarriage later).

James had the writer's instinct for always noticing and storing characters and incidents that would find their places in future books. His surviving letters provide no clues to his actual writing methods and programmes; but the works themselves show how his retentive memory provided innumerable building blocks which he included in later

---

* The full story of James's service in Mexico is related in the author's book *Missions to Mexico* (London 1992) – which was written without full access to the Morier papers and consequently contains some errors relating to James here corrected.

structures. It was not until 1837, for example, that he published his novel *Abel Allnutt*. This was mainly about English ways and manners; but the central theme was the effect of unwise investment in Mexican bonds, and he even had Abel's brother in Mexico involved in an incident based on a real one (the murder of a shoemaker) which he himself had not witnessed, but which had been the subject of an official despatch from his predecessor in Mexico.[31] (In this novel he also plagiarised a scene from Fanny Burney's *Evelina*, introduced another which obviously owed something to his brother Jack's experience with the Tripolitanian privateers in 1798 (chapter 2), and another clearly inspired by the sinking of the ship carrying Elgin's marbles back to England over 30 years earlier.) His next work after returning from Mexico, however, was *The Adventures of Hajji Baba of Ispahan in England*, a sequel to his first novel, in which James made extensive use of his experiences with Abul Hasan in London in 1809-10. He sent the almost complete manuscript to John Murray in January 1828, explaining that 'there will [be] about 20 or 30 pages more, mainly an introduction of about 20 pages.'[32] The first edition of 2500 copies had virtually all been sold by February 1835 when a second edition was brought out, followed by another in 1837. This time James had sold the copyright to John Murray for £420, and Murray made only £248-13 11d from the first edition; but James might have done better in the long run had he kept to royalties.

The success of *The Adventures of Hajji Baba of Ispahan* came as much from the insight it gave on Persian manners, customs and character as upon the wit with which it was written. The device of presenting this information through the mouth of an entertaining Persian rogue gave it a verisimilitude which was convincing, and James's ability to reproduce authentic sounding Persian dialogue in English added to this. He also, of course, was drawing heavily on his own experiences in Persia, using incidents and scenes which he had himself witnessed. Indeed, so authentic did he manage to make this tale that, when it was later translated into their own language, Persians found it almost impossible to believe that it had not been written by one of them. *The Adventures of Hajji Baba of Ispahan in England* was not quite so successful on this level, and it has not, like its predecessor, remained a classic still read at the end of the 20th century – although it ought to have. In this James was trying to convey the feelings of Persians about the English, portraying English manners and character as seen through Persian eyes, and at the same time giving rein to some of his own satirical views on them. The result was funny but, perhaps because it was attempting to hit two targets at once, it did not have quite as sharp a cutting edge as its predecessor – and his cousin Granville Waldegrave (now second baron Radstock) said he 'would not give 15/- for it.'[33] It may also have been affected by being written at a time when James's sense of humour must have been under some strain. In the autumn of 1827 he was suffering from a particularly bad attack of gout. 'Poor James' wrote his mother 'cannot rid himself of his gout, his feet, his hands, the knee, each in turn keep him prisoner ... he has been in no mood to laugh.'[34] To make matters worse his wife (still recovering from her miscarriage) and son were in Brighton, so he was on his own. This induced his mother, who considered that his 'dear half is not exactly made for easing his sufferings',[35] to add that it 'would be better to be a bachelor than be in his state.' At least, however, he had his mother to provide some comfort: 'James comes every day to see me, she wrote in March 1828 '& is delighted to find lunch ready, which proves that his appetite has not deserted him.'[36]

This novel marked the end of James's friendship with Abul Hasan. Perhaps it would have died in any case at such a distance, although it seems that he was corresponding with him occasionally – it is clear, for example, that he wrote to him during his few months in England back from Mexico in 1825. But his somewhat cruel, though witty, caricature of Abul Hasan in *Hajji Baba in England* must have been too much for the latter. The trouble began in fact with the first Hajji Baba book, at the end of which James introduced Mirza Farouz, the Persian ambassador to England to whom Hajji Baba was to be secretary. Despite James's protestation that he did 'not even intend to designate any one' in his descriptions of characters in his novels, he did not have enough imagination to invent completely new ones. It is not surprising that Abul Hasan, when he saw this book (which evidence suggests must have been by May 1826), took exception to his portrayal as Mirza Farouz. In his introduction to *Hajji Baba in England*, James quoted a letter he claimed to have received 'from one high in office' in Persia in which the writer voiced his objections not only to this caricature but to the way some Persian characteristics were portrayed. There is argument about whether this letter was genuine or an invention; but there is strong evidence that Abul Hasan was indeed upset by what James had written in his first Hajji Baba book.* He had become Persia's first foreign minister, and he must certainly have seen the sequel soon after it was published, for in 1830 Prince Abbas Mirza was trying to find a European to translate it into Persian. Reporting this to David,

---

* This is the subject of an article by the author in *Iran* volume XXXIII (1995), pp. 103–6, the journal of the British Institute of Persian Studies.

Henry Willock suggested that 'although he [Abbas Mirza] might secretly acknowledge the faithfulness of the picture, yet too many unseemly features are impressed on the canvas to render it pleasing or gratifying to national vanity'[37] (and in the end no translation was made until 1907). Abul Hasan would surely have been even more hurt by the way he was caricatured in this, and there is no evidence that he ever again communicated with James – of whom he had written so warmly in a letter, probably to Viscount Melville, on arrival in France after his 1819–20 visit to England:

> First I must thank for your kindness last time and this time and always now I wish give you one little more trouble and you make me happy your lordship know what morier done for me he is my oldest english friend what can do for him his youngest brother is captain I beg you make him post I hope not refuse your old friend.[38]

Abul Hasan must have felt that James's caricature was small reward for such attempts to help him.

Although James thought his pension of £1100 a year insufficient reward for his services, it did at least mean that he no longer had to make a 'minute investigation of shillings and pence', and he and Harriet (and their boy) now began to travel a lot, partly because of Harriet's poor health. Their London home at this time was in Brook Street, but they spent several of the winter months of 1828/29 with the Cunliffes, Lord Crewe and other friends. They then moved from Brook Street to 22 Charles Street, Berkeley Square, but they spent the next two years on the continent, not returning to London until the summer of 1831. Rather surprisingly, given his strong protestantism, James was presented to Pope Pius VIII in Rome in December 1829

> in company of many other gentlemen. The good old gentleman was frightened by the appearance of such a body (for we were 9 in number) of stout gentlemen, and the difficulty he had in pronouncing some of our names made some of the youngest titter quite indecorously. Marquis Northampton* was a puzzler – he bungled over his George Warrender, but when he came to Major General Sir Ruffane Donkin† he made it so like 'Rough Donkey' that the comical effect was irresistable. He is a tall man, but with age hobbles and squints.[39]

James continued writing during this time abroad, and it is interesting that he was doing so with a female readership in mind. In October

---

* Spencer Joshua Alwyn Compton, 1790–1851, second marquess of Northampton.
† Lieutenant-General Sir Rufane Shaw Donkin KCB, 1773–1841, founder of Port Elizabeth and later surveyor-general of the ordnance.

1831 he sent John Murray the manuscript of *Zohrab the Hostage*, accompanied by

> the best opinion which I have yet had of it. It is that of Miss Burney, sister of Mad. d'Arblay [Fanny Burney] to whom at Florence I lent it to read. She received it by portion at a time & this was one of her notes asking for a continuation. She is an author herself and likely to know the tastes of her sex & as they will form the greater part of my readers I think her approbation valuable. I am, I own, sanguine about its success, and I hope you will make one of your best offers.[40]

Whether John Murray was swayed by this, or simply by his own judgement, he published it next year (but there is no record now of what financial terms were agreed).

The reviewer of *Zohrab the Hostage* in *Fraser's Magazine* agreed with what John Lockhart wrote in the December issue of *The Quarterly Review* – that it was 'the best novel that has appeared for several years past; indeed, out of sight superior to all the rest of the recent brood.'[41] *Fraser's* added that 'novels of this stamp and character are valuable additions to literature.'[42] Not all reviews, however, were as favourable. Now one might agree with the *Athenaeum* reviewer that *Zohrab* could be 'tedious' to read, at least in parts. But the Rev Sydney Smith read it 'with the greatest pleasure' and was so delighted with it that he 'could not help writing a letter of congratulation and collaudation to Morier, the author, who, by the bye, is an excellent man.'[43] It is, on the whole, a 'rattling good yarn' with a romantic interest, which could probably be adapted without much difficulty as an exciting Persian 'western' for the cinema. It was published in Persian in 1946 and again in 1951. It is full of strong characterization based on actual historical events and people; and it is tempting to speculate that W S Gilbert may have based certain characteristics of Pooh Ba and Katisha in *The Mikado* on the James' characters Shir Khan Beg and Zulman.

The characterization of the hero and heroine in *Zohrab the Hostage* is somewhat shallow, but it was certainly a better book than James's next, *Ayesha, the Maid of Kars* – originally entitled *Osmond, or the Traveller in the East*.[44] In February 1834 he had settled the terms for publication (now unknown) with John Murray, and the final pages of the manuscript reached Murray on 24 May. The June issue of the *Quarterly Review* carried a favourable review by John Lockhart, and other reviewers praised it; but it is not surprising that, despite going to two editions in 1834, being translated the same year into French, and into Swedish and German in 1836, as well as being reissued in 1846 and 1877, it has not survived as an example of fine literature. It is a weak story, an absurdly fanciful tale of the kind that might have suited a

Rudolph Valentino film. The scene is set in Turkey, close to the border with Persia. The hero, Lord Osmond (who was partly based on James's brother David, whose letters written while travelling between Constantinople and Persia in 1809–10 clearly provided him with some of the background), falls in love with a beautiful Muslim girl and, after many improbable adventures, rescues her from the clutches of an evil schemer and discovers her to be the daughter of a noble English family who was stolen when a baby in Athens – and of course they marry. But it also has some scenes of realistic violent action, which are well described, as well as a scene in which Osmond tries to convince his Muslim captors of the superiority of Christianity over Islam, which must have owed much to James having heard the missionary Henry Martyn (1781–1812) arguing with mullahs in Persia. It is easy to see how it had a degree of success at the time – and it has the distinction of having been, according to the Oxford English Dictionary, the source of the introduction into the English language of the word 'bosh', a Turkish word meaning 'empty' or 'useless'.

Zohrab and *Ayesha* were good in their own ways, but James never again rose to the heights of his Hajji Baba novels. Indeed, he seems to have sunk to a shaming low immediately after *Ayesha* – although there is room for a scintilla of doubt whether he was in fact the author of two stories published by Richard Bentley (a firm later absorbed into Macmillan). *The Man of Honour* and *The Reclaimed* were anonymously published in the summer of 1834. In the Bentley Papers in the British Library there is a memorandum of agreement between James and Bentley dated 13 January 1834, which James entered into 'on behalf of the author' of these two stories.[45] However, the fact that the archives of Richard Bentley & Son index them under the Morier name is a strong, though not conclusive, indication that James did write them, bad as they are. The first is about a roué who eventually dies in a duel, the second is an improbable confession of vices, including murder, made by a young man to an innocent young girl. Both were slated in the <u>Athenaeum</u>,[46] and the *Gentleman's Magazine* even thought the author of the first was a woman.[47] If they were indeed written by James it was fortunate that this was not publicly revealed during his life, and one can only assume that he was 'pot boiling' to earn some money while working on his next novel, *Abel Allnutt*.

Abel Allnut, which was published in 1837, has not survived as a classic of English literature. But it was thought at the time, by some, to be not seriously below the standard set in the Hajji Baba books. It contains some shrewd observations on the pretensions of the English middle classes trying to emulate fashionable society. It also pokes clever (though

somewhat laboured) fun at pretentious antiquarians in the person of
Sir Pergrine Oldbourn, who is convinced that he has proved Persepolis
to be the Temple of Solomon. His portrayal of the almost unbelievably
innocent Allnutt family, who lose their all by investing in Mexican
bonds, is thin compared with what Jane Austen, for instance, would
have made of them; but at the time it was thought well of by, for
example, the *Athenaeum* – 'We love the Allnutt family … [and their]
well imagined characters'[48] – and the *Examiner* which thought James
had 'very narrowly escaped writing a very admirable book.'[49] Some
would have it that James had almost equalled the quality of Oliver
Goldsmith's *The Vicar of Wakefield*; but there were others who thought
the novel fell off badly in the final chapters, and it does rather smack
of an attempt to use up a rag-bag of disparate ideas stored up over
the years. But at least he made a decent sum from it, selling the
copyright to Bentley for £750,[50] although he himself probably thought
he had been 'done'. Some years later, advising his brother David on
how to deal with publishers, he described Bentley 'as sharp a fellow at
a bargain as ever I saw & I have always thought he got the best of the
bargain.' But he went on to say that perhaps he was being 'unfair to
him considering what risks publishers do run'[51] – a generous sentiment
that may not be all that common among authors.

By now James seems to have become a compulsive writer, but his
inspiration was waning. Perhaps this was the result of what was
becoming a dull life. His two-year continental tour in 1829-31 had
been undertaken, at least in part, as a search for better health for
Harriet. In this it was unsuccessful, and once they had returned to
London their social life seems to have become restricted. James even
resigned from The Athenaeum in 1832, although they were still living
in London. His mother's death in March 1834 affected him deeply –
'Dear blessed mother. Surely there was never on earth a purer being'[52]
he wrote after the funeral to David who could not get to it from
Switzerland – where he was by now Minister. But although he took his
son Greville on a trip up the Rhine in July of that year, it is evident
that he felt he had to devote himself to looking after Harriet, who
suffered continually from ailments of an unspecified nature. They spent
a few months in Paris in 1835, where they were received 'with the
greatest civility' by the ambassador, Lord Granville; but James's heart
was no longer in such contacts. He had told David a year earlier that
he never now mixed in public matters and did 'not seek them. I hear
nothing more than I read in the newspapers.'[53] There was a similar
note of resignation in his letter from Paris in which he also quoted an
old family friend there as saying: 'My desires are few and even for

those the desire is very slight', commenting that this was 'a happy mood to go out of the world with.'[54] The visit had not been a success, for towards the end Harriet had suffered 'a violent attack' and then four months of influenza back in London. Writing to David's wife in September 1836, from temporary lodgings at Richmond, Surrey, she said she had been 'in shock for 7 months' after this and in constant pain.

It would have been surprising if, in such circumstances, James's writing had not suffered. But he kept at it. In 1836 he was persuaded to contribute to the newly founded *Bentley's Miscellany*, of which the young Charles Dickens was editor. In addition to a slight two-page anecdote about Naples, presumably based on some incident during his travels in 1830, and a short story, *Two of a Trade*, about an argument between a Persian and an English barber in England, he published, as a series, ten short chapters of an unfinished work called *Remains of Hajji Baba*. These purported to be extracts from Hajji Baba's journal kept during a visit to England shortly after the passing of the Reform Act in 1832. Hajji has been sent, on his own, by the Shah, who had heard with horror of this dangerous development, and wanted to offer the King of England asylum should he be overthrown. But he also wanted to see what commercial advantage could now be won from a country which had shown so little concern for Persia's welfare. James, once again using the device of Hajji Baba as a cipher for his own views on English society, produced flashes of his old humour – as indeed he had done in *Two of a Trade* – and perhaps, if he had ever finished this tale, it might have turned out to be a success; but much of the dialogue was laboured, and Hajji Baba's own observations did not have the true Persian wit and colour so brilliantly expressed in the original novel.

Much the same could be said of James's final novel, *Martin Toutrond, a Frenchman in London 1831*, published shortly before his death in 1849. He may have been writing it as early as 1835/6, while he and Harriet were in Paris, for it is believed that he wrote it in French and then translated it into English. Here James was trying to portray English ways through French eyes, and once again the weakness is that the Frenchman's dialogue is not realistic enough. But as a satirical caricature of both French and English political and social attitudes it had an even greater success than *Abel Allnutt*, going to three editions. Between the two, James produced three other works with Levantine backgrounds; *An Oriental Tale* in 1839, *The Mirza* in 1841 and *Misselmah, a Persian Tale* in 1847. The first and last were printed privately, for sale in aid of charities, and were but pale shadows of what he had shown himself capable of. *An Oriental Tale* (which he said had been suggested on reading Lieutenant Burne's's Travels in Bokhara)* described the adventures of a rather stupid English traveller captured by Turcomans, who was subjected to many humiliations before he succeeded in restoring to health a girl beloved by the chief, who then put him in a privileged position as a doctor, a reward he repaid by successfully escaping with the girl. It was little more than a mish-mash of incidents from *Hajji Baba* and *Ayesha*. *Misselmah* was based on an anecdote related by Chardin nearly two hundred years earlier. In it James again introduced romance, this time involving a beautiful Georgian girl (Misselmah) and her rescue by her betrothed, Ferhad, from the Persian general who had captured her. *The Mirza* (which earned James some £400)[55] was a more serious work which had some merit, being a series of tales somewhat in the style of *The Arabian Nights* (allegedly related to James by the court poet in Persia) It did not, however, succeed in capturing the public's attention. In 1833 some of his Mexican memories had been used by James in *Pepita, a Mexican Story*, published in *The Keepsake*. (They were also published in French, in a collection called *Le Salmigondis*.) And in 1839 and 1847 he was involved as editor in English translations of two German works, *The Banished* by M Hauff (an historical novel about Swabia) and a romance called *St Roche*.

The lowest point in James's output must have been *The Adventures of Tom Spicer who advertised for a Wife*, a preposterously bad piece of humorous verse which, mercifully for his public reputation, was not published but only printed for private circulation in 1840, for what purpose or occasion is not known. He may have used a real incident known to him involving Harrow schoolboys (his son went there). In these verses a group of such boys cruelly lured Tom Spicer, a simple butcher, to a meeting with one of them, dressed as a girl who had answered his advertisement for a wife. The last of his stanzas read:

> And thus Tom Spicer learnt a Truth
>   That's worth to be repeated;
> When all the laugh is on one side,
>   Real Truth is sure defeated.

This somewhat enigmatic moral perhaps confirms that James never thought humour should be used cruelly – and that, for instance, he never intended to hurt Abul Hasan.

With the exception of *The Mirza*, which was a near miss, James never succeeded in matching the masterpiece which was his first novel

---

* *Travels into Bokhara* by Lieutenant Alexander Burnes, London 1834.

– and which deserves better than the quite awful 1954 semi-musical film 'based on' it (so loosely as to be barely recognisable apart from the title). It is sad that in his latter years he should have produced so much banality. Dr Terry Grabar wrote in her PhD dissertation – submitted in 1962 at the University of Michigan – that

> Morier was a comic artist of talent, but when he attempted to create characters that he himself took seriously, he failed. The protagonists of *Zohrab*, *Ayesha* and of *Abel Allnutt* are pale and unconvincing, partly because the fineness of character that they are intended to exhibit is unbelievable in itself, and partly because Morier was unable to see into his characters with any depth. When he attempts to portray the more inward aspects of character, or to show any profundity of feeling or complexity of motivation or emotion, he is embarrassed and awkward. He cannot create a character that appeals deeply to our emotions.

At the same time, however, as Ava Inez Weinberger put it in her PhD dissertation – submitted in 1984 at the University of Toronto – James 'was an interested and sensitive observer of Persian society, a traveller whose accounts of the nuances of gesture and speech of the Persians he met and of the misunderstandings in the meeting of East and West distinguish his travel records' – and of course his Hajji Baba novels. He was indeed an excellent observer, and had a gift for writing dialogue based on a retentive memory of what he had himself heard; and he had a sharp, satirical sense of humour. But he had little real imagination or feel for romantic emotion.

Was James simply incapable of translating emotion into words which carried conviction? Or did he never himself feel the kind of romantic emotion he tried, with little success, to convey in his later novels? It is difficult to find an answer to these questions. While his brother David could write letters which revealed, even though often only indirectly, deep feelings, only one of those written by James which have survived displays any real depth of feeling, and that only briefly: it was the one written to David from Persia on 26 February 1809 in which he referred to 'a brother, a friend whom I sincerely and ardently love as I do my dearest & best of Davids.' He could feel genuine compassion for those in misfortune, and he had a genuine unselfishness; and perhaps he did have romantic feelings for Maria Wilkinson. But he comes across as one who had little need for the kind of romantic love which David obviously looked for, and which perhaps is a necessary precondition for strongly felt emotions. He seems to have been an optimist who had little need for reassurance. As a young man, even when things seemed not to be going right, he would often refer in his letters to believing with Candide that everything was for the best in this best of all possible worlds. The truth seems to be that James was, by nature, an observer rather than participant in life. This was the reason for his success as a satirist. Even his love for Harriet and their son Greville (whom he called his 'little Hajji') may have had little deeply emotional content, although there can be no doubt about his genuine affection for them both.

⊕

By the early 1840s James and Harriet had moved to 25 Marine Parade, Brighton, although they kept their London house at 22 Charles Street to which James occasionally returned, but which he let for three years in 1845. James and Greville managed to get away on their own, for some visits to friends, in the summer of 1842. But they had to return in a hurry when they heard that Harriet had again become ill and was 'near death's door'. She had recovered by November, but James must have decided then that he should never leave her again. Philosophically, he wrote to David that Brighton suited him:

> I find that habit does everything for the mind; from being here so long I make enjoyments for myself which I cannot find elsewhere. What so full of matter for thought as the sea! ... At Brighton one is out of the great vortex of [the] world & the world's dissipation & doings. I do thank God in my inmost heart that my station in life is humble & retiring. When one remarks the almost universal yearning for distinction & elevation which obtains in common life, I think it a great blessing to be able to sneak by in the crowd unheeded & unobserved.[56]

And a year later he could write to Angela Burdett-Coutts:* 'Our air is bark quinine and port wine all in one and makes anybody live whether they will or not.'[57] But in April 1845 he was again 'waging a desperate war against illness in the person of poor Harriet. She has had a constant sickness upon her for the last 8 months,'[58] and later that year he spent £35 on getting 'the great Locock'† down from London to Brighton, but without its making much difference – he merely prescribed rest and some unnamed medicine. James found her sickness 'a great trial to us both,'[59] but whatever it was it cannot have been life threatening, for she outlived James by nine years.

---

* Angela Georgina Burdett-Coutts, 1814–1906, the wealthy philanthropist daughter of Sir Francis Burdett and granddaughter of Thomas Coutts the banker. Created baroness 1871.

† Sir Charles Locock, Bt, 1799–1875, obstetric physician, first physician-accoucheur to Queen Victoria.

For James and Harriet life now became very reclusive. In January 1849 he wrote that Harriet was 'always a great invalid leading a quiet life, never going out of the house but to take the air, & consequently is not a member of what is called society. Occasionally she sees her friends at about 4 o'clock.'[60] Their great joy was regular visits from Greville (now employed at the Foreign Office and lodging in Mount Street) who 'comes to us every Saturday (if he can) to stay till Monday'; and they were seeing Jack and his family 'pretty often'. Even now, however, although he was no longer writing for publication, James did not lose his interest in what was going on around him, and remained as shrewdly observant of humanity as ever. In that same letter he wrote:

> We have got the Prince & Princess Metternich here, who walk about in the crowd like other folk & who are a daily example of the vicissitudes of life, for during his long reign of forty odd years in Austria he might well be called the personification of the whole government of Germany.* He is only now a little individual in a pea jacket & a hooked stick under his arm, an old swell & dear old Twaddle, without a grain of power, and I fear with fewer pence. We have also here the Princess Lieven who was Russian ambassadress here for above 20 years, & who was obliged to leave Paris in a hurry leaving all her goods behind.† In fact one has only to look out of [a] window & one sees a bit of vicissitude walking about. Such examples teach us great lessons & make us feel that we are all, great & small, under the direction of God's providence. This poor lady is afflicted with bad eyes & should she lose them I dread to think of her fate, for she does not appear to possess a mind equal to great resignation. However, we are told not to judge any one, so who can say what passes in her mind upon so serious a subject?

But he was taken suddenly ill in March 1849, dying after a few days, intestate, on the 19th. He was 66 years old. The death certificate gave the cause of death as 'cerebral congestion', but this seems to have been a development from a severe liver attack – and the effect of taking a cold bath to cure it, which caused him to lose consciousness for several hours.[61] From this he recovered briefly and 'his patience & gentleness & thankfulness for every little service done him [during the next few days] was quite touching.'[62] He died quietly in his sleep while

---

* Prince Clemens Lothar Wenzel Metternich, 1773–1859, became Austrian foreign minister in 1809 and took a leading part in the Cogress of Vienna, but fled to England on the fall of the Austrian government in 1848 following the French revolution of that year. He returned to the continent in 1851 and died in Vienna.
† Dorothea von Benkendorf, 1784–1857, was married to the Russian diplomatist Prince Lieven, 1774–1857. Her salon in Paris after 1837 had been a great centre of diplomatic life and gossip until they too had to flee the 1848 revolution.

his son Greville, exhausted by constant attention on him, had himself fallen asleep in a chair.

⊕

When James died he at least had the satisfaction of knowing that he had made a name for himself with his two travel books and the Hajji Baba tales. And he knew that even his next three novels had been well received. He had never been particularly ambitious in a career sense. Although he probably felt a quiet pleasure at having been for a period in charge of a diplomatic mission, he had never had a real 'yearning for distinction & elevation'. He certainly took pleasure in being accepted by the well-born, and enjoyed their company; but perhaps he had more of his father's Swiss egalitarian attitudes in his make-up than he realised, for he was not comfortable with the notion that birth and money were in themselves the passport to power. He wanted enough money for himself to be able to live comfortably without paid employment, but he never hankered after great riches. Indeed, he saw no reason why those with great wealth should not have it taken from them for the benefit of others. The existence of poverty disturbed him, and the possession of great wealth offended him. Writing to David from Venice in 1831 he had thought it essential that a graduated income tax should be introduced: 'Take nothing from the poor – a small percentage on hundreds – a large upon thousands – increase greatly upon fives & tens of thousands, and an immense fine upon your folk of £100,000 per annum.'[63] Hardly the views of the high Tory some have believed him to be! But whether such views would have survived marriage to the great heiress he at one time seemed to be seeking may be doubted. However, it would be unfair to suggest that his was the politics of envy. It was natural for one who had begun life as a mere Smyrna merchant to feel that wealth should be earned not inherited; and, in fact, he had never thought of money, other than enough for comfort, or fame, to be worth expending a lot of effort to obtain. James' mother once wrote to David, referring to his running into debt to help his sister: 'I have never known a better nature than his. He deserves to be rich because he finds no happiness in possessions which do not last.'[64] It was accident that took him into diplomacy, and he soon found it a hollow prize. It was an accident for which, however, we should be grateful: but for that, the world would never have known *Hajji Baba* – and the members of an exclusive rug-collecting group in the United States would not now be called The Hajji Baba Club (an interesting detail culled from Ava Inez Wienberger's PhD dissertation).

CHAPTER SEVENTEEN

Postscript

Although Harriet's father had excluded her from any right to benefit from his very considerable estate, when James died she had sufficient wealth of her own to renounce her right to his estate of some £14,000, letting it all go to their son Greville. When she herself died, in her 69th year – at 22 Charles Street, Berkeley Square in London – on 11 May 1858 (of 'Pneumonia 13 weeks Hemiplegia 1 week' as the doctor put it in the death certificate) she left an estate nearly as large. How this came about is unclear. Her uncle, Lord Crewe, who died in 1829, may have left her money; she also had some claim on a Greville Trust in Ireland. Her son Greville inherited some of his mother's estate outright, and some in the form of a life interest; but when he died, aged only 48 – at 43 Russell Square, Brighton – on 14 December 1870 of 'Paralysis Exhaustion', he left less than £1,000.

Little is known of Greville's life. He went to Harrow, like his uncle David, in September 1834, and joined the Foreign Office as a clerk in 1843. He was sent on a special mission to Buenos Aires in 1847, and was then attaché at Rio de Janeiro for a few months, returning to England in August 1848. He married a Susan Cox from Warminster on 27 July 1852, was promoted assistant clerk in 1857 and senior clerk in 1860, but he retired with a pension on 1 January 1868 at the surprisingly early age of 45. Possibly he was already ill. There is no mention of children in his Will, drawn up only two months before he died.

He must have been living very extravagantly, and the story amongst Morier descendants that he had 'gone to the bad' may not be misplaced. It is significant that his mother, in a Will drawn up two years before her death and four years after Greville's marriage, although leaving him all her household and personal effects, tied up the rest of her estate (consisting of shares and some £5,000 due to her from a family Trust in Ireland) in trust. Only the interest from this went to

Greville, with instructions that should he 'alien, charge or encumber' this in a way 'which would have the effect of giving the benefit ... to any other person', the trustees were to treat him as though dead and give the benefit to one of her Greville nephews. Either she disapproved of his wife, and suspected her of gold-digging, or she knew he was running up debts – or both. Possibly he had already given his wife a lot of money, and she may even have left him. But if Greville had fallen out with his mother and gone to the bad, his character must have changed radically since his father's death. At that time his uncle David reported, in a letter to his wife dated 20 March 1849, that 'nothing can be more considerate & right minded & affectionate than dear Greville.' Yet there is a small sign that he may have been giving trouble before then, for on 13 August 1848, James had written to David that 'Greville ... has improved immensely by his travels & is the same merry hearted creature he ever was.' In surviving letters there is no subsequent mention of him.

⊕

Jack, the eldest of the brothers, survived James by four years, dying three months before his 75th birthday – at his home at 20 Upper Harley Street, London – on 20 August 1853 of 'Paralysis nearly 20 years Exhaustion' – which explains why there were references in letters to his taking the air at Brighton in the 1830s and 1840s in a bath-chair. His diplomatic career after his return from Greece in 1807 had been moderately successful, but not particularly distinguished. After spending some time at Cambridge in private study, he was taken back into the diplomatic service and sent as chargé d'affaires to Washington in July 1810. He preferred not to remain there under the new Minister, Augustus John Foster, and, in 1811, was appointed one of the three commissioners being sent out to South America to try to help Spain come to an understanding with her colonies; but he never took up the post. He left New York in February 1812 for Jamaica, where he expected to be picked up by the other commissioners. In October he discovered that the venture had been aborted, and he got back to London in February 1813. He was then made under-secretary at the Foreign Office, going on a special mission to Norway for a few months in 1814. He was back to be married on 3 December of that year to Horatia Maria Frances Seymour, daughter of the late Vice Admiral Lord Hugh Seymour‸ In 1816 he went as Minister Plenipotentiary to Dresden. He retired from there, and the diplomatic service, at the end of 1824. He fathered five daughters. His second daughter, Horatia Isabella Harriet,

‸, who was the fifth son of the first marquess of Hertford by his wife Lady Anne Horatia Waldegrave, daughter of the Duchess of Gloucester by her first marriage to the second Earl Waldegrave married Algernon, brother of the 13th duke of Somerset, who succeeded as the 14th duke in 1891. Two others, Frances Horatia (the eldest) and Catherine Georgina (the fourth), married brothers; the Reverends Edward Harbottle and Francis Sylvester Grimston (sons of the first earl of Verulam, grandsons of the third viscount Grimston). Jack's wife survived him by only six days, dying of 'ulceration of the larynx and tubercles of the lungs' at their London home on 26 August 1853.

David's life, after getting home from Constantinople with Stratford Canning at the end of September 1812, was more eventful than Jack's. In August 1813 his old Harrow friend, now the fourth earl of Aberdeen, took him as his secretary to Metternich's peace conference with Bonaparte. They both had some exciting adventures following the allied headquarters about Europe and dodging the French armies after the war erupted again, and David witnessed the triumphal return of Louis XVIII to Paris on 3 May 1814. He had by then been taken onto Castlereagh's personal staff, and was with him during the negotiation of the first Treaty of Paris. While on leave in England that summer he won the hand of Anna, tenth and youngest child of Robert Burnett Jones (who had been Attorney General of Barbados) but he then had to accompany Castlereagh to the Congress of Vienna. He returned to London with him in February 1815 and, after Waterloo, went with him for the negotiation of the second Treaty of Paris. He was allowed home to marry Anna in London on 18 August of that year, and took her back to Paris with him. He had already been appointed consul-general and one of the commissioners for the settlement of claims by British subjects on the French government. His post as consul-general was abolished in April 1832 and, almost immediately, he was appointed Minister Plenipotentiary to the Swiss Confederated States. He retired from the diplomatic service in June 1847, after a disagreement with Palmerston (also a Harrow contemporary). He fathered four daughters (one of whom died in infancy and two of whom died of measles in Switzerland) and a son, Robert, whose own diplomatic career culminated in the post of ambassador at St Petersburg and a knighthood. David's fourth daughter, Henrica Mary, married Sheffield Neave (later a governor of the Bank of England) and was the great-grandmother of the late Airey Neave MP. His eldest daughter, Dorothea (Dora) died unmarried in 1891. Robert married Alice Peel, granddaughter of Sir Robert Peel. His only son died while a young man and his only daughter, Victoria, married Rosslyn Wemyss – great-grand nephew of Lord Elcho, the famous Jacobite of the '45//later Admiral of the Fleet Baron Wester Wemyss, whose daughter was Alice, the owner of the family papers on which this book has been based.

David's wife, who had suffered much ill health in Switzerland, died in 1855. David himself survived into his 94th year, dying – at 45 Montagu Square, London – on 13 July 1877 of 'pleuritis'. In retirement he had kept contact, mostly by letter, with many distinguished people who valued him as a friend. In general, however, he appears to have kept out of the limelight, apart from publishing two rather heavy religious pamphlets; *What has Religion to do with Politics?* in 1848, and *The Basis of Morality* in 1869. But, in 1857, he also published a novel, *Photo the Suliot: a Tale of Modern Greece* – which had obviously been simmering since his days in Greece with his brother Jack. The theme was the brave resistance of the Suliots against Ali Pasha's cruel suppression, Photo being the young son of this mountain community's chief. Descriptive passages and many personalities were clearly drawn from life and David's own experiences, and the historical context was carefully composed; but David had none of James's skill in presenting violence and dialogue realisically, and the work failed to capture a large readership. This is a pity, for the story of the Suliots is the stuff of heroic romanticism, and a good novel about them, based on the kind of personal knowledge gained by David, would have been a splendid memorial.

⊕

The fourth and youngest brother, William, has barely featured in this story, because the course of his life only rarely touched even the fringes of the others'. In fact it is difficult to extract material for a biography from such letters relating to him which have survived. He went to a day school in Finsbury Square, run by a Mr Kelly, and, when he was 9, to a boarding school in Ealing, run by a Dr Nicholas. At 11 he went to Harrow – where he was a contemporary of Byron – but had to leave in 1803 when his father got into debt and could not afford the fees. In November, aged 13, he joined the navy as a 1st class volunteer in HMS Illustrious. Over the next five years he rose to the rank of Lieutenant, serving in the Mediterranean and Adriatic, twice under command of his cousin Granville Waldegrave. He displayed dash and courage in one or two small engagements, for which he was rewarded by his uncle, Lord Radstock, with the gift of a sword. In 1813 he took part in the bombardment of Stonington – during the war which had broken out with the USA – and he commanded sloops in the North Sea between 1826 and 1828. Despite Abul Hasan's efforts on his behalf (chapter 16), he was not made Post Captain until January 1830, when he retired. During his retirement he published a *Memoir on the Countries about the Caspian and Aral Seas, illustrative of the late Russian expedition against Khiva* (1840), being a translation into English of the original by Lieutenant Karl Zimmerman of the Prussian army; and he was promoted to vice admiral in 1855 and admiral in 1862. He died on 29 July 1864. In 1841, at the fairly advanced age of 51, he had married the daughter of David Bevan (a wealthy banker), Frances (Fanny) Lee, by whom he had four children. His eldest daughter, Augusta Louisa, married her cousin, Frederick Lincoln Bevan, and was the grandmother of Bernard Bevan (who is mentioned in the preface to this book); ʌ [see below]

As already mentioned, the second daughter of Isaac and Clara Morier, Ann Mary (Maria), married the Reverend Vyvyan Arundell (on 17 October 1816). The two other daughters, Emilia Maria and Clara Elizabeth (Tolla) never married, the former dying on 11 December 1861, the latter on 3 December 1858.

⊕

The Morier/Van Lennep connection, which began with Isaac's marriage to Clara in Smyrna in 1778, brought unexpected distinction to the Morier name through their four sons. It is unlikely, however, that this distinction would have been achieved without the Van Lennep/Waldegrave connection begun by Clara's sister's marriage in 1785. It is appropriate, therefore, that through both Jack and William the Morier line later became directly linked to the Waldegrave, thus perpetuating the close affection between Clara Morier and her brother-in-law, William Waldegrave, which certainly on William's side was 'at least equal to [the love] that a brother ever felt for a sister'. The British male Morier line has died out, as has the male line of that particular Waldegrave branch. But Hajji Baba, a creation born of the intertwined adventures of one generation of Moriers, lives on.

ʌ and a nephew, Edwyn, married Mary Waldegrave, daughter of the fourth baron Radstock. His youngest daughter, Agneta, became the second wife, on 14 August 1918, of the Reverend Henry Giles Alington, father by his first marriage of the famous headmaster of Eton.

Sources

Most sources are contemporary unpublished letters included in the collection of Morier papers donated to Balliol College, Oxford by the late Alice Cunnack. unless indicated otherwise. Abbreviations used are:

JPM: John (Jack) Philip Morier
JJM: James Justinian Morier
DRM: David Richard Morier

Other sources include:

Add Ms: The Manuscript Collections in the British Library
Vaughan: The papers of Charles Vaughan in the Codrington Library, All Souls College, Oxford
Kentchurch: The Kentchurch collection in Hereford and Worcester County Record Office
FO or ADM: Foreign Office or Admiralty papers in the Public Record Office at Kew. The first number is the group reference, the second the piece number within that group, and the third (if any) the numbered folio within the piece

Quotations from James Morier's published travel books are indicated as Travel I and Travel II – referring respectively to *A Journey through Persia, Armenia and Asia Minor in the years 1808 and 1809* (London 1812) and *A Second Journey through Persia, Armenia and Asia Minor to Constantinople between the years 1810 and 1816* (London 1818)

Chapter 1   A close–knit family

1 Ray, Gordon (ed.), *The Letters and Private Papers of William Makepeace Thakeray* (London 1945) Vol II, p. 563, letter to Mrs Brookfield dated 13 July 1849
2 *Souvenirs du Lieutenant Général Comte Mathieu Dumas de 1770 à 1836* (Paris 1839), Vol I, pp. 320–21
3 JJM to cousin Granville Waldegrave 6/11/1804 (private collection)
4 JPM to mother 30/3/1794
5 JPM to mother 12/2/1788

6 JPM to mother 26/2/1788
7 JPM to father 5/5/1788
8 JPM to mother 11/6/1788
9 JPM to mother 12/7/1788
10 ibid, postscript by Mrs Jay
11 JPM to mother 17/12/1788

Chapter 2   Jack 1793–1798

1 JPM to mother 30/3/1794
2 ibid
3 JPM to mother 3/4/1794
4 ADM 51/1103 Part 3 – log of HMS *Romney*
5 JPM to father 30/6/1794
6 JPM to father 1/5/1795
7 JPM to mother 29/3/1796
8 JPM to father 28/4/1796
9 JPM to parents 18/5/1795
10 JPM to father 1/10/1795
11 JPM to father 16/5/1796
12 JPM to father 2/9/1795
13 JPM to father 29/12/1795
14 JPM to father 13/2/1797
15 JPM to parents 13/6/1798

Chapter 3   James 1799–1803

1 JJM to mother 5/4/1799
2 JJM to father 15/6/1799
3 JJM to father 30/1/1800
4 JJM to father 17/7/1799
5 JJM to parents 1/10/1799
6 JJM to father 30/1/1800
7 JJM to mother 4/4/1800
8 JJM to father 29/12/1800
9 JJM to father 29/11/1801
10 JJM to father 2/5/1801
11 JJM to father 16/8/1801
12 JJM to father 24/1/1802
13 JJM to father 15/9/1801
14 JJM to DRM 23/7/1802
15 JJM to father 6/12/1802
16 JJM to father 16/4/1803

Chapter 4 Jack 1798–1803

1 JPM to father 20/12/1800
2 JPM to father 12/9/1799
3 letter from Philip Hunt to his father, quoted by William St Clair in *Lord Elgin and the Marbles* (London 1967) p. 12
4 JPM to father 12/9/1799
5 ADM 51/1320 and 52/3285 – log of HMS *Phaeton*
6 JPM to parents 10 & 12/11 and 10/12/1799
7 JPM to father 10/12/1799
8 FO 78/24/143 Elgin No. 11 11/12/1799
9 JPM to father 10/12/1799
10 FO 78/24/229 Elgin to JPM 22/12/1799
11 FO 78/24/31 Elgin No. 5 8/12/1799
12 JPM to William Waldegrave 4/1/1800
13 JPM to father 10/12/1799
14 JPM to William Waldegrave 4/1/1800
15 JPM to mother 19/1/1800
16 JPM to parents 6/2/1800
17 Morier, J P, *Memoir of a Campaign with the Ottoman Army in Egypt* (London 1801) p. 21
18 JPM to mother 22/2/1800
19 Morier, J P, op cit, pp. 22–7
20 JPM to father 22/2/1800
21 JPM's captured journal, entry dated 14/3/1800
22 FO 78/29/146 JPM No. 11 5/4/1800
23 FO 78/29/158 JPM No. 12 12/4/1800
24 FO 78/29/224 JPM No. 14 27/4/1800
25 FO 78/29/345 JPM (in French) to Murat Bey 2/5/1800
26 JPM to parents 17/4/1800
27 JPM to parents 22/5/1800
28 JPM to Philip Hunt 25/5/1800
29 *Courier de Londres* (French émigré paper published in London) Vol. 48, No. 20, 5/9/1800
30 FO 78/30/10 Menou to Sidney Smith, enclosed with JPM despatch to Elgin 27/6/1800
31 *Courier de l'Egypte* No. 74, dated 27 Messidor (15/7/1800)
32 JPM to Elgin 27/6/1800 (private collection)
33 JPM to Elgin 5/7/1800 (private collection)
34 Köhler to Elgin 4/7/1800 (private collection)
35 FO 78/30/261 Elgin No. 104 30/11/1800
36 FO 78/30/3 Elgin No. 72 22/7/1800
37 FO 78/29/318 Elgin No. 64 9/7/1800
38 FO 78/30/112 Memo by JPM, enclosed with his No. 19 to Elgin 6/7/1800
39 Barrow, John, *The Life and Correspondence of Admiral Sir William Sidney Smith* (London 1848) Vol I , p.422, letter from Smith to Elgin 15/2/1801
40 FO 78/38/43 extract from Granville No. 13 to Elgin 8/9/1800 enclosed with Elgin to Hawkesbury 13/1/1803

41 *Courier de Londres* Vol 48, No. 20 5/9/1800
42 JPM to father 20/12/1800
43 Elgin to Abercromby 11/12/1800 (private collection)
44 JPM to parents 9/12/1800
45 JPM to father 11/12/1800
46 JPM to Philip Hunt 20/12/1800 (private collection)
47 JPM to father 2/1/1801
48 JPM to father 7/2/1801
49 FO 78/31/181 Abercromby to Elgin 21/1/1801
50 JPM to father 7/2/1801
51 FO 78/31/390 JPM to Elgin 19/4/1801
52 FO 78/32/36 Elgin No. 66 31/6/1802
53 JPM to mother 6/2/1801
54 JPM to mother undated, probably August or September 1801
55 FO 78/32/160 enclosed in letter JPM to Hammond 5/7/1801
56 JPM to mother 12/8/1802
57 Add Ms 33110 f 188: memo from Lord Radstock to Lord Pelham 21/11/1802
58 JPM to father 25/12/1802
59 FO 24/2/16

Chapter 5 James 1803–1806

1 JJM to father 29/12/1803
2 JJM to DRM 12/3/1804
3 JJM to DRM 23/3/1804
4 JJM to DRM 12/3/1804
5 JJM to father 14/5/1804
6 JJM to cousin Granville Waldegrave 6/11/1804 (private collection)
7 JJM to his sisters 16/3/1805
8 Isaac Morier to his wife 15/2/1805 (private collection)
9 JJM to mother 10/5/1805
10 JJM to mother 25/6/1805

Chapter 6 Jack and David 1804–1806

1 Lord Radstock to Lord Hobart 26/10/1801
2 FO 78/44/3 FO No. 1 to JPM 13/1/1804
3 DRM to parents 2/2/1804
4 DRM to father 3/2/1804
5 DRM to parents 12/2/1804
6 DRM to father 9/3/1804
7 DRM to mother 12/4/1804
8 DRM to his sisters 13/4/1804
9 DRM to mother 28/4/1804
10 FO 78/44/24 JPM No. 1 24/4/1804

11 FO 78/44/37 JPM to FO 17/5/1804
12 ibid
13 JPM/DRM to Lord Radstock 28/4/1804
14 Plomer, William, *The Diamond of Jannina* (London 1970) p. 82, quoting Baron Frédéric–François–Guillaume Vaudoncourt (1772–1845)
15 FO 78/44/79 JPM No. 9 30/6/1804
16 FO 78/44/84 JPM No. 10 30/6/1804
17 FO 78/44/94 JPM No. 11 31/7/1804
18 DRM to Lord Radstock 23/7/1804
19 DRM to mother 16/7/1804
20 JPM to mother, undated but probably 21/10/1804
21 FO 78/44/144, unnumbered JPM to FO 29/10/1804
22 DRM to mother 19/11/1804
23 DRM to Lord Radstock 26/10/1804
24 DRM to mother 20/12/1804
25 DRM to mother 27/12/1804
26 DRM to Lord Radstock 28/12/1804
27 DRM to mother 27/12/1804
28 DRM to his sisters 27/12/1804
29 DRM to Lord Radstock 28/12/1804
30 FO 78/44/122, unnumbered FO to JPM 19/10/1804
31 FO 78/47/3 JPM No. 1 5/1/1805
32 FO 78/47/28 Leake to JPM 19/1/1805
33 FO 78/47/60 JPM No. 8 26/2/1805
34 FO 78/44/28 JPM No. 2 5/5/1804
35 FO 78/47/60 JPM No. 8 26/2/1805
36 DRM to Lord Radstock 29/3/1805
37 FO 78/47/93 JPM No. 9 8/4/1805
38 FO 78/47/148 JPM No. 12 19/4/1805
39 FO 78/47/181 JPM to Arbuthnot 20/6/1805
40 DRM to mother 27/6/1805
41 FO 78/53/3 JPM to Ali Pasha 25/10/1805
42 DRM to his sister Emily 9/7/1805
43 DRM to mother 18/7/1805
44 JPM to Lord Radstock 29/7/1805
45 FO 78/47/212 JPM No. 21 17/10/1805
46 DRM to mother 23/10/1805
47 DRM to mother 28/11/1805
48 DRM to mother 30/12/1805
49 DRM to mother 14/1/1806
50 DRM to JJM 3/2/1806
51 DRM to mother 12/2/1806
52 DRM to JJM 21/2/1806
53 JPM to Lord Radstock 4/6/1806

Chapter 7 James and Harford Jones 1806–1807

1 DRM to mother 20/12/1804
2 JJM to mother 15/2/1805
3 DRM to mother 5/11/1805
4 DRM to mother 12/2/1806
5 JJM to mother 10/10/1806

Chapter 8 James 1807–1809

1 DRM to JPM 22/1/1807
2 JJM to mother 11/9/1807
3 JJM to his cousin Granville Waldegrave 11/9/1807
4 JJM to mother 11/9/1807
5 JJM to mother 10/9/1807
6 JJM to Granville Waldegrave 11/9/1807
7 JJM to mother 19/8/1807
8 JJM to mother 19/8/1808
9 Vaughan A/36/2: JJM to Charles Vaughan 6/9/1808
10 ibid
11 JJM to mother 10/9/1808
12 JJM to mother 10/12/1808
13 Travel I, p. 12
14 ibid, p. 13
15 ibid, p. 14
16 ibid, p. 20
17 ibid, p. 23
18 ibid, p. 29
19 JJM to DRM 16/11/1808
20 ibid
21 JJM to mother 2/11/1808
22 Travel I, p. 65
23 JJM to DRM 16/11/1808
24 quoted in JJM to mother 11/1/1809
25 JJM to mother 10/12/1808
26 JJM to DRM 16/11/1808
27 Travel I, pp. 69–70
28 Jones Brydges, Sir Harford, *An account of the transactions of His Majesty's Mission to the Court of Persia in the years 1807–11* (London 1834) Vol. I , p. 71
29 Travel I , p. 47
30 ibid, p. 109
31 ibid, pp. 115–6
32 JJM to mother 8/1/1809
33 FO 60/2/3 Harford Jones No. 1 11/1/1809
34 JJM to mother 8/1/1809
35 Travel I, pp. 120–1

36 ibid, p. 149
37 ibid, pp. 188–91
38 ibid, pp. 193–4
39 FO 60/2/54 Minute by JJM 9/4/1809, enclosed with Harford Jones No. 6 12/4/1809
40 Travel I, pp. 219–20
41 JJM to DRM 26/2/1809

Chapter 9 David 1807–1809

1 JJM to his brother William 5/1/1808, with postscript by Emily
2 DRM to JPM 22/1/1807
3 FO 78/56/1 FO No. 1 to Paget May 1807
4 DRM to his brother William 26/5/1807
5 DRM to mother 30/5/1807
6 DRM to JJM 29/5/1807
7 DRM to JJM 31/5/1807
8 DRM to JJM 1/6/1807
9 ibid
10 DRM to mother 5/6/1807
11 DRM to mother 6/7/1807
12 DRM to mother 29/7/1807
13 DRM to his sister Emily 28/9/1807
14 Paget, The Rt Hon Sir Augustus B (ed.), *The Paget Papers* (London 1896) Vol II, p. 335
15 DRM to mother 4/8/1807
16 DRM to his sister Emily 28/9/1807
17 DRM to mother 28/9/1807
18 DRM to JPM 2/11/1807
19 FO 78/58/42 DRM to FO 4/11/1807
20 DRM to JPM 2/11/1807
21 DRM to mother 15/11/1807
22 DRM to Bartholomew Frere 3/3/1808
23 DRM to mother 3/6/1808
24 DRM to his sister Emily 15/3/1809
25 DRM to mother 17/5/1808
26 DRM to mother 9/8/1808
27 DRM to JPM 10/9/1808
28 DRM to mother 7/10/1808
29 ibid
30 Lane–Poole, Stanley, *The Life of The Right Honourable Stratford Canning* (London 1888) Vol I, p. 86
31 DRM to JPM 3/10/1808
32 Adair, Sir Robert, *The Negotiations for the Peace of the Dardanelles in 1808–9* (London 1845) Vol I, pp. 32–3
33 DRM to JPM 3/10/1808

34 DRM to mother 6/2/1809
35 DRM to JPM 19/2/1809
36 ibid

Chapter 10 James 1809–1810

1 JJM to DRM 16/6/1809
2 Travel I, p. 285
3 JJM to DRM 16/6/1809
4 Travel I,   pp. 324–5
5 ibid, p. 333
6 ibid, p. 356
7 ibid, p. 362
8 DRM to mother 2/8/1809
9 ibid
10 Travel I, pp. 365–6
11 JJM to DRM 1/9/1809
12 Travel I, p. 367
13 JJM to DRM 6/9/1809
14 Margaret Morris Cloake (ed.), *A Persian at the Court of King George* (Mirza Abul Hasan's journal) (London 1988) p24
15 ibid, p. 25
16 Kentchurch: JJM to Harford Jones 2/3/1810
17 Travel II, p. 402
18 Kentchurch: JJM to Harford Jones 27/1/1810
19 Kentchurch: JJM to Harford Jones 12/12/1810
20 *The Courier* 21/12/1809
21 *The Morning Post* 21/12/1809
22 Cloake, op cit, p. 60
23 Blake, Mrs Warrenne, *An Irish Beauty of the Regency* (London 1911) p. 160
24 Kentchurch: JJM to Harford Jones 11/3/1810
25 Cloake, op cit, p. 273
26 Kentchurch: undated letter to Harford Jones
27 Kentchurch: JJM to Harford Jones 11/3/1810
28 Cloake, op cit, entry for 14/12/1809 (omitted from published version)
29 ibid, entry for 15/12/1809
30 Cloake, op cit, p. 136
31 ibid entry for 11/6/1810 (omitted from published version)
32 Cloake, op cit, pp. 151, 214, 294
33 ibid, p. 194
34 Kentchurch: undated letter to Harford Jones
35 Kentchurch: JJM to Harford Jones 11/3/1810
36 JJM to DRM 9/5/1811
37 William Morier to DRM 6/9/1812
38 Kentchurch: JJM to Harford Jones 11/3/1810
39 Kentchurch: JJM to Harford Jones 13/4/1810

Chapter 11   David 1809–1812

1   DRM to JPM 3/1/1809
2   DRM to mother 3/1/1809
3   DRM to JJM 30/3/1809
4   DRM to JPM 23/4/1809
5   DRM to JPM 4/8/1809
6   DRM to Lord Radstock 28/7/1809
7   Add Ms 43231 f10: DRM to Aberdeen 5/8/1809
8   DRM to mother 11/11/1809
9   DRM to his sister Emily 13/12/1809
10 ibid
11 DRM to father 23/10/1809
12 ibid
13 ibid
14 Kentchurch: DRM to Harford Jones 13/8/1809
15 DRM to mother 12/12/1809
16 DRM to Stratford Canning 23/3/1810
17 DRM to JPM 25/3/1810
18 Adair to DRM 10/6/1810
19 DRM to his sister Emily 28/9/1810
20 ibid
21 Lane–Poole, op cit, Vol I , p. 69
22 ibid, p. 89
23 ibid, p. 73
24 DRM to mother 26/8/1810
25 DRM to mother 6/8/1810
26 DRM to mother 31/8/1811
27 DRM to mother 26/8/1810
28 ibid
29 DRM to Lord Radstock 30/4/1811
30 DRM to mother 1/1/1811
31 DRM to mother 26/8/1810
32 DRM to mother 23/2/1811
33 DRM to mother 8/5/1811
34 DRM to mother 26/8/1810
35 DRM to mother 31/8/1811
36 DRM to his sister Emily 28/9/1810
37 DRM to mother 18/6/1811
38 DRM to his sister Emily 28/9/1810
39 DRM to mother 28/9/1810
40 Bruce, Ian (ed.), *The Nun of Lebanon* (London 1951) p. 115
41 ibid, p. 123
42 DRM to mother 1/5/1812
43 DRM to Bartholomew Frere 3/12/1812

Chapter 12 James and Harford Jones 1810–1811

1 Kentchurch: JJM to Harford Jones 2/3/1810
2 Kentchurch: JJM to Harford Jones 3/1/1810
3 JJM to his brother William 25/5/1810
4 Add Ms 33839: JJM journal entry for 18/7/1810
5 JJM to mother 9/9/1810
6 FO 60/5/67 Letter from Captain Heathcote 1/9/1811
7 Add Ms 33839: JJM journal entry for 16/9/1810
8 ibid, 20/11/1810 (and Travel II, p. 10)
9 ibid, 12/1/1811
10 Travel II, p. 16
11 Add Ms 33839: JJM journal entry for 12/1/1811
12 JJM to mother 20/1/1811
13 Kentchurch: JJM to Harford Jones 2/3/1810
14 Kentchurch: JJM to Harford Jones 11/3/1810
15 Kentchurch: JJM to Harford Jones 2/3/1810
16 Cloake, op cit, p. 229 and unpublished entry for 28/6/1810
17 Kentchurch: JJM to Harford Jones 20/3/1810
18 Jones Brydges, op cit, Vol I, p. 229
19 Harford Jones to DRM 31/10/1810
20 Harford Jones to DRM 13/11/1810
21 Kentchurch: JJM to Harford Jones 13/1/1810
22 Add Ms 43209 f9: letter from Gordon to brother dated 28/1/1811
23 Kentchurch: JJM to Harford Jones 2/3/1811
24 Kentchurch: JJM to Harford Jones 6/3/1811
25 Sir Gore Ouseley, journal entry for 25/3/1811
26 Kentchurch: JJM to Harford Jones 25/3/1811
27 JJM to Harford Jones April 1811
28 JJM to DRM 8/5/1811
29 Kentchurch: DRM to Harford Jones
30 JJM to mother 1/5/1812
31 JJM to DRM 20/6/1812
32 DRM to mother 10/12/1808

Chapter 13 James 1811–1812

1 Ouseley, Sir William, *Travels in Various Countries of the East; more particularly Persia* (London 1819) Vol I, p. 227
2 JJM to Harford Jones 2/4/1811
3 JJM to mother 20/4/1811
4 Sir Gore Ouseley journal entry for 1/4/1811
5 FO 60/6/64 Gore Ouseley to The Secret Committee of the Court of the East India Directors 28/6/1811
6 JJM to DRM 1/6/1811
7 FO 60/6/27 Gore Ouseley No. 5 18/4/1811

8 JJM to mother 20/4/1811
9 JJM to DRM 9/5/1811
10 Add Ms 33840: JJM journal entry for 8/6/1811
11 ibid entry for 29/4/1811
12 JJM to DRM 1/6/1811
13 JJM to DRM 9/5/1811
14 Travel II, p. 124
15 JJM to mother 13/8/1811
16 Travel II, p. 130
17 Sir Gore Ouseley journal entry for 29/7/1811
18 JJM to mother 13/8/1811
19 JJM to George Moore 23/8/1811
20 JJM to mother 13/8/1811
21 FO 60/6/13 Gore Ouseley No. 3 21/4/1811
22 JJM to his sisters 21/11/1811
23 JJM to mother 23/11/1811
24 Travel II, p. 184
25 ibid, pp. 185–7
26 ibid, p. 188
27 JJM to mother 23/11/1811
28 Add Ms 43209 f54: letter from Gordon to brother dated 28/2/1812
29 ibid f66: letter dated 1/5/1812
30 JJM to mother 26/6/1812
31 JJM to mother 1/5/1812
32 JJM to his sister Emily 30/6/1812
33 Travel II, pp. 197–8
34 JJM to DRM 10/6/1812
35 JJM to mother 13/6/1812
36 ibid
37 Add Ms 33842: JJM journal entry for 19/6/1812
38 ibid
39 JJM to DRM 6/8/1812
40 JJM to DRM 12/10/1812
41 ibid
42 JJM to mother 24/11/1812
43 Add Ms 33842: JJM journal entry for 31/10/1812
44 JJM to DRM 29/11/1812

Chapter 14 James 1813–1814

1 FO 60/8/3 Gore Ouseley No. 1 16/1/1813
2 JJM to mother 14/12/1812
3 JJM to his cousin Harriet Waldegrave 15/3/1813
4 JJM to mother 28/6/1813
5 Add Ms 33843: JJM journal undated entry
6 FO 60/8/29 Gore Ouseley No. 9 10/7/1813

7   Add Ms 33843: JJM journal undated entry
8   JJM to mother 14/7/1813
9   Add Ms 33843: JJM journal undated entry
10 JJM to mother 27/9/1813
11 ibid
12 ibid
13 JJM to mother 1/11/1813
14 JJM to mother 14/12/1813
15 JJM to mother 3/9/1813
16 JJM to mother 14/12/1813
17 JJM to DRM 9/12/1813
18 JJM to mother 16/2/1814
19 Travel II, pp. 310–11
20 Add Ms 33843: JJM journal undated entry
21 ibid
22 JJM to mother 27/6/1814

Chapter 15 James 1814–1816

1   JJM to mother 27/6/1814
2   ibid
3   JJM to DRM 30/7/1814
4   JJM to mother 20/8/1814
5   FO 60/9/19 FO No. 4 28/4/1814
6   FO 60/9/97
7   JJM to DRM 10/3/1815
8   JJM to DRM 26/11/1814
9   JJM to DRM 23/12/1814
10 FO 60/9/51 Gore Ouseley No. 4 4/5/1814
11 FO 60 10/43 FO to JJM No. 3 30/6/1815
12 JJM to DRM 10/3/1815
13 ibid
14 FO 60/10/39 FO to JJM No. 1 30/6/1815
15 JJM to DRM 10/3/1815
16 JJM to mother 17/3/1815
17 JJM to mother 23/5/1815
18 FO 60/10/85 JJM No. 9 13/6/1815
19 JJM to DRM 10/3/1815
20 Add Ms 33844: JJM journal entry for 18/6/1815
21 Travel II, p. 359
22 ibid, p. 372
23 Add Ms 33844: JJM journal undated entry
24 ibid
25 ibid
26 Travel II, pp. 394–5
27 ibid, p. 396

28 ibid, p. 399
29 ibid
30 JJM to DRM 16/11/1815
31 JJM to DRM 11/12/1815
32 JJM to DRM 21/3/1816 and to JPM 25/4/1816
33 JJM to JPM 25/4/1816
34 JJM to DRM 6/5/1816
35 JJM to DRM 14/5/1816
36 JJM to mother 9/6/1816
37 JJM to DRM 23/9/1816
38 FO 60/10/108 JJM to FO 28/10/1816
39 JJM to DRM 22/10/1816

Chapter 16 James 1817–1849

1 Kentchurch: JJM to Harford Jones 2/3/1810
2 JJM to DRM 23/9/1816
3 JJM to DRM 22/10/1816
4 JJM to DRM 26/11/1816
5 JJM to DRM 3/1/1817
6 JJM to DRM 18/3/1817
7 JJM to DRM 2/1/1817
8 JJM to DRM 12/2/1818
9 JJM to DRM 10/9/1819
10 FO 60/19/39
11 FO 60/16/59 Memorandum of meeting between Castlereagh and Abul Hasan 3/3/1820
12 JJM to DRM 10/9/1819
13 JJM to DRM 3/4/1820
14 ibid
15 George Willock to Josef Planta 17/11/1820 (copy)
16 E M Butler (ed.), *A Regency Visitor* (Letters of Prince Pückler–Muskau, London 1957) letter dated 13/12/1827
17 JJM to DRM 25/4/1820
18 JJM to DRM 28/2/1821
19 Strachey, Lytton and Fulford, Roger (ed.), *The Greville Memoirs 1814–1860* (London 1938) Vol II, pp. 375–7 diary entry for 3/6/1833
20 Mother to DRM 27/1820
21 Ilchester, Earl of (ed.), *The Journal of the Hon Henry Edward Fox* (London 1923) p. 371, entry for 26/3/1830
22 JJM to DRM 13/7/1820
23 JJM to DRM 26/11/1820
24 JJM to DRM 28/2/1821
25 JJM to DRM 12/3/1821
26 JJM to DRM 9/1/1824
27 DRM to JJM 28/3/1824 (John Murray archives)

28 JJM to DRM 8/4/1824

29 JJM to DRM 4/8/1827

30 JJM to his mother, undated but probably 8/3/1827

31 FO 50/5/136 despatch from Mexico No. 41, dated 9/9/1824
     and McKenzie Johnston, Henry, *Missions to Mexico* (1922), p82

32 JJM to John Murray 23/1/1828 (John Murray archives)

33 Granville Waldegrave (Radstock) to William Morier 13/5/1828

34 Clara to William 21/10/1827

35 idem 23/9/1827

36 idem 24/3/1828

37 Henry Willock to DRM 30/1/1830

38 Add Ms 41768 f213

39 JJM to his mother 9/12/1829

40 JJM to John Murray 27/10/1831 (John Murray archives)

41 *Quarterly Review* vol. XLVIII (1832)

42 *Fraser's Magazine* vol .VI (1832)

43 Smith, Nowell C (ed.), *The Letters of Sydney Smith* (London 1953) Vol II, p. 570
letter dated 27/12/1832 to Sir George Philips

44 JJM to DRM 27/2/1834

45 Add Ms 46612 f62

46 *Athenæum* 23/8/1834

47 *Gentleman's Magazine* August 1834

48 *Athenaeum* 18/2/1837

49 *Examiner* 19/2/1837

50 Add Ms 46612 f 312

51 JJM to DRM 13/8/1848

52 JJM to DRM 24/3/1834

53 JJM to DRM 27/2/1834

54 JJM to DRM 17/12/1835

55 Add Ms 46613

56 JJM to DRM 10/11/1842

57 Quoted by Edna Healy in *Lady Unknown, the life of Angela Burdett–Coutts* (London
1978)

58 JJM to DRM 8/4/1845

59 JJM to DRM 10/7/1845

60 JJM to his sister Maria 28/1/1849

61 DRM to his wife 17/3/1849

62 DRM to JPM 19/3/1849

63 JJM to DRM 30/5/1831

64 Mother to DRM 14/3/1817

Outline Chronology

1750
August 11   Isaac Morier born in Switzerland
                   1755–83 American War of Independence

1758
April 11   marriage of David Van Lennep to Anne Marie Leytstar in Smyrna

1760
February 27   Clara Van Lennep born in Smyrna

1778
February 18   marriage of Isaac Morier to Clara Van Lennep in Smyrna
November 23   John Philip (Jack) Morier born in Smyrna

1782
August 15   James Justinian Morier born in Smyrna

1783
September 3   *end of American War of Independence at Treaty of Paris*

1784
January 8   David Richard Morier born in Smyrna

1787
June   Isaac Morier and family move to London

1788
January   Isaac returns to Smyrna

1789
July 14   *fall of the Bastille*
December   Isaac returns to London

1793
February   *outbreak of war between Britain and France*

1794
March   Jack goes to Smyrna
July 28   *execution of Robespierre in Paris*

1797
October 17   *Franco-Austrian Treaty of Campo Formio*

1798
March   Jack leaves Smyrna to return to London
July   *French invasion of Egypt*
August 2   *Battle of the Nile, Nelson destroys French fleet*   Battle
September   Turkey declares war on France

1799
May   *French defeat at Acre*
June   James arrives in Smyrna
November   Jack to Constantinople with Lord Elgin

1800
January 24   *Franco-Turkish Convention of El Arish*
January 31   Jack attached to Turkish army at El Arish
March 20   *French victory over Turks at Heliopolis*
                         Jack briefly a prisoner of the French
July   Jack back in Constantinople
December   Jack attached to British forces invading Egypt

1801
February   Jack back in Constantinople
March   Jack again to British forces
April   Jack back to Constantinople
June   *Final French defeat in Egypt*
July   Jack back in London
November   Jack back in Constantinople

1802
March 27   *Franco-British Peace of Amiens*

1803
January   Jack leaves Constantinople with Elgins
May   *resumption of Franco-British war*
April   James back in London
August   Jack back in London
December   James returns to Smyrna

1804

February	Jack and David to Greece
	Russia invades Persian Caucasian provinces

1805

April	Isaac to Constantinople as consul general
October 10	*Nelson's naval victory at Trafalgar*
December 2	*French victory at Austerlitz*

1806

January 23	*death of Pitt the Younger*
June	David returns to England
November	*war between Russia and Turkey*

1807

January	*Turkey becomes ally of France, British ambassador leaves Constantinople*
February	Isaac to Malta
March	Jack to Malta
May	*Persian Treaty of Finkenstein with France*
June	David joins Paget mission to restore relations with Turkey
July	*Franco-Russian Treaty of Tilsit*
August	Paget mission fails
October	James to Persia with Sir Harford Jones
November	David in Malta

1808

August	David joins Adair mission to Turkey
October	James reaches Persia

1809

January	*Adair concludes Peace of the Dardanelles with Turkey*
March	*Sir Harford Jones concludes provisional treaty with Persia*
May	James leaves Persia with Mirza Abul Hasan
August	David to Persia
November	James reaches England

1810

May	David returns to Constantinople
July	James to Persia with Sir Gore Ouseley

1811

February	*Regency in England*
March	James reaches Persia
November	James reaches Tehran

1812
March — *Sir Gore Ouseley's treaty with Persians*
May 11 — *assassination of British prime minister, Perceval*
May 28 — *Russo-Turkish war ended at Treaty of Bucharest*
June — *war between Britain and USA*
September — David back to England
October — *French retreat from Moscow*
publication of James's first travel book

1813
October — *armistice between Persia and Russia*

1814
April — *abdication of Bonaparte*
May — *First Treaty of Paris ends war with France*
June — James becomes chargé d'affaires in Persia
November — James concludes revised treaty with Persians
December 3 — marriage of Jack to Horatia Frances Seymour
December 24 — *end of British war with USA, Treaty of Ghent*

1815
March 20 — *start of Bonaparte's '100 days'*
June 18 — *final victory over Bonaparte at Waterloo*
August 8 — marriage of David to Anna Burnet Jones
October — James leaves Tehran for England
November 20 — *Second Treaty of Paris*

1816
September — James back in England

1817
August 8 — death of Isaac Morier in Constantinople

1818
publication of James's second travel book

1820
January 29 — *death of King George III*
June 17 — marriage of James to Harriet Fulke Greville

1824
publication of *The Adventures of Hajji Baba of Ispahan*
April 19 — *death of Byron*
October — James to Mexico

1826
June — James back from Mexico

1828

               publication of *The Adventures of Hajji Baba of Ispahan in England*

January 9   *Wellington becomes prime minister*

1830

June 26   *death of King George IV*

1832

               publication of *Zohrab the Hostage*
               Reform Act

1833

               publication of *Pepita, a Mexican Story*

1834

March 17   death of Clara Morier in London
               publication of *Ayesha, the Maid of Kars*
               publication anonymously of *The Man of Honour and The Reclaimed*

1836

               publication of *Two of a Trade and Remains of Hajji Baba*

1837

               publication of *Abel Allnutt*

June 20   *accession of Queen Victoria*

1839

               publication privately of *An Oriental Tale*

1840

               publication privately of *The Adventures of Tom Spicer*

1841

               publication of *The Mirza*

1847

               publication privately of *Misselmah*

1849

               publication of *Martin Toutrond*

March 19   death of James Morier in Brighton

1853

August 20   death of Jack Morier in London

October   *start of Crimean War to February* **1856**

1858
May 11   death of Harriet Morier in London

1877
July 13   death of David Morier in London

Select Bibliography

Adair, Sir Robert., *The Negotiations for the Peace of the Dardanelles in 1808–9*, London 1845.

Amini, Iradj, *Napoléon et la Perse*, Paris 1995.

Anderson, M.S., *The Eastern Question 1774–1823*, Macmillan 1996.

Barber, Noel, *The Lords of the Golden Horn*, Macmillan 1973.

Barrow, John, *The Life and Correspondence of Admiral Sir William Sidney Smith GCB*, London 1848.

Burgoyne, Lieut-Col Sir John, *A Short History of the Naval and Military Operations in Egypt from 1798–1802*, London 1885.

Checkland, Sydney G, *The Elgins 1788–1917*, Aberdeen University Press 1988.

Cunningham, Allan, *Anglo-Ottoman Encounters in the Age of Revolution – Collected Essays, Vol I* (ed. Edward Ingram), Frank Cass 1993

Cunningham, Allan, *Eastern Questions in the Nineteenth Century – Collected Essays, Vol II*, (ed. Edward Ingram), Frank Cass 1993

Davis, Ralph, *Aleppo and Devonshire Square* [the Levant Company], Macmillan 1967.

Drouville, Gaspard, *Voyage en Perse fait en 1812 et 1813*, Paris 1825.

Ehram, John, *The Younger Pitt*, London 1996.

Eton, W., *A Survey of the Turkish Empire*, London 1801.

Foss, Arthur, *Epirus*, Faber 1978.

Frangatis-Syrett, Elene, *The Commerce of Smyrna in the Eighteenth Century (1700–1820)*, Athens 1992.

Hamilton Grant, Lt Col Nisbet, *Letters of Mary Nisbet, Countess of Elgin*, John Murray 1926

Herold, J.C., *Bonaparte in Egypt*, Hamish Hamilton 1963

Hurewitz, J.C., *Diplomacy in the Near and Middle East*, (Vol I), New York 1956

Ingram, Edward, *Britain's Persian Connection 1798–1828*, Oxford University Press 1992.

James, William, *The Naval History of Great Britain from the Declaration of War by France in 1793 to the Accession of George IV*, (Vol IV), London 1837.

Kaye, John William, *The Life and Correspondence of Major-General Sir John Malcolm KCB* (Vol I), London 1856.

Lane-Poole, Stanley, *The Life of Stratford Canning*, London 1888.

Leigh Fermor, Patrick, *Roumeli*, John Murray 1966.

Leigh Fermor, Patrick, *Mani*, John Murray 1966.

MacFarlane, Charles, *Constantinople in 1828*, London 1829.

Macgill, T., *Travels in Turkey, Italy and Russia 1803–1806*, London 1808.

McKenzie Johnston, Henry, *Missions to Mexico: a Tale of British Diplomacy in the 1820s*, London 1992.

McNeill, *Memoir of the Rt. Hon. Sir John by his granddaughter*, John Murray 1910.

Malcolm, Major-General Sir John, *The History of Persia*, London 1829.

Miller, William, *The Ottoman Empire 1801–1913*, Cambridge University Press 1913.

Morier, J., *A Journey through Persia, Armenia and Asia Minor in the years 1808 and 1809*, London 1812.

Morier, J., *A Second Journey through Persia, Armenia and Asia Minor to Constantinople between the years 1810 and 1816*, London 1818.

Morier, J.P., *Memoir of a Campaign with the Ottoman Army in Egypt 1800*, London 1801.

Olivier, G.A., *Voyage dans l'Empire Othoman, l'Egypte et Perse*, Paris 1802.

Ouseley, William, *Travels in Various Countries of the East, more particularly Persia, 1810–12*, London 1819.

Paget, The Rt. Hon. Sir Augustus B. (ed), *The Paget Papers 1794–1807*, London 1896.

Plomer, William, *The Diamond of Jannina*, Cape 1970.

Pocock, Tom, *A Thirst for Glory: the Life of Admiral Sir Sidney Smith*, London 1996.

Puryear, Vernon J., *Napoleon and the Dardanelles*, University of California 1951.

St Clair, William, *Lord Elgin and the Marbles*, Oxford University Press 1967.

Sargent, The Reverend John, *A Memoir of the Reverend Henry Martyn*, London 1821.

Savory, R.M., 'British and French Diplomacy in Persia 1800–1810', *Iran*, Vol X, 1972, pp. 31–44.

Wagstaff, J.M., 'John Philip Morier's Account of the Mani, 1804,' pp. 273–286 of *Témoignages sur l'espace et la société: Voyageurs et expéditions scientifiques (XVe–XIX^{e}s.)*, Institut de Recherches Néohelléniques, F.N.R.S., Athens 1996.

Warr, Michael, *A Biography of Stratford Canning*, Oxford University Press 1989.

Wittman, William MD, *Travels in Turkey, Asia Minor, Syria and Egypt 1799–1801*, London 1803.

Wright, Denis, *The English amongst the Persians*, Heinemann 1977.

Wright, Denis, *The Persians amongst the English*, I.B.Tauris 1985.

Index

254